JONATHAN EDWARDS
ON KNOWING CHRIST

JONATHAN EDWARDS ON KNOWING CHRIST

THE BANNER OF TRUTH TRUST

THE BANNER OF TRUTH TRUST
3 Murrayfield Road, Edinburgh EH12 6EL
PO Box 621, Carlisle, Pennsylvania 17013, U.S.A.

*   *   *

The sermons in this volume are from the 1839
London edition of Edwards' Works.

First published by the Banner of Truth under the title *Select Works of Jonathan Edwards*
Volume 2 1958
Reprinted 1959
Reprinted as *Jonathan Edwards on Knowing Christ*, 1990

ISBN 0 85151 583 5

*   *   *

Printed and bound in Great Britain by Billing & Sons Ltd, Worcester.

Contents

CONTENTS

SELECT WORKS OF JONATHAN EDWARDS

Sermon I

CHRISTIAN KNOWLEDGE

HEBREWS V. 12

For when for the time ye ought to be teachers, ye have need that one teach you again which be the first principles of the oracles of God; and are become such as have need of milk, and not of strong meat.

THESE words are a complaint, which the apostle makes against the christian Hebrews, for their want of such proficiency in the knowledge of the doctrines and mysteries of religion, as might have been expected of them. The apostle complains, that they had not made that progress in their acquaintance with the things taught in the oracles of God, which they ought to have made. And he means to reprove them, not merely for their deficiency in *spiritual* and *experimental* knowledge of divine things, but for their deficiency in a *doctrinal* acquaintance with the principles of religion, and the truths of christian divinity; as is evident by the manner in which the apostle introduces this reproof. The occasion of his introducing it is this: In the next text but one preceding, he mentions Christ as being "Called of God an high priest after the order of Melchizedek." In the Old Testament, the oracles of God, Melchizedek was held forth as an eminent type of Christ; and the account we there have of him contains many gospel mysteries. These mysteries the apostle was willing to point out to the christian Hebrews; but he apprehended, that through their weakness in knowledge, they would not understand him; and therefore breaks off for the present from saying any thing about Melchizedek, thus (ver. 11.) "Of whom we have many things to say, and hard to be uttered; seeing ye are all dull of hearing;" *i.e.* there are many things concerning Melchizedek which contain wonderful gospel-mysteries, and which I would

9

take notice of to you, were it not that I am afraid, that through your dulness, and backwardness in understanding these things, you would only be puzzled and confounded by my discourse, and so receive no benefit; and that it would be too hard for you, as meat that is too strong.

Then come in the words of the text: "For when for the time ye ought to be teachers, ye have need that one teach you again which be the first principles of the oracles of God; and are become such as have need of milk, and not of strong meat." As much as to say, Indeed it might have been expected of you, that you should have known enough of the Holy Scriptures, to be able to understand and digest such mysteries: but it is not so with you. The apostle speaks of their proficiency in such knowledge as is conveyed by *human* teaching: as appears by that expression, "When for the time ye ought to be teachers;" which includes not only a practical and experimental, but also a *doctrinal, knowledge* of the truths and mysteries of religion.

Again, the apostle speaks of such knowledge, whereby Christians are enabled to understand those things in divinity which are more abstruse and difficult to be understood, and which require great skill in things of this nature. This is more fully expressed in the two next verses: "For every one that useth milk is unskilful in the word of righteousness; for he is a babe. But strong meat belongeth to them that are of full age, even those who, by reason of use, have their senses exercised to discern both good and evil." It is such knowledge, that proficiency in it shall carry persons beyond the first principles of religion. As here; "Ye have need that one teach you again which be the first principles of the oracles of God." Therefore the apostle, in the beginning of the next chapter, advises them " to leave the first principles of the doctrine of Christ, and to go on unto perfection."

We may observe that the fault of this defect appears, in that they had not made *proficiency* according to their time.—For the time, they ought to have been teachers. As they were Christians, their business was to learn and gain christian knowledge. They were scholars in the school of Christ; and if they had improved their time in learning, as they ought to have done, they might, by the time when the apostle wrote, have been fit to be teachers in this school. To whatever business any one is devoted, it may be expected that his perfection in it shall be answerable to the time he has had to learn and perfect himself.—Christians should not always remain babes, but should grow in christian knowledge; and leaving the food of babes, they should learn to digest strong meat.

DOCTRINE. Every Christian should make a business of endeavouring to grow in knowledge in divinity.—This is indeed esteemed the business of divines and ministers: it is commonly thought to be their work, by the study of the Scriptures, and other instructive books, to gain knowledge; and most seem to think that it may be left to them, as what belongeth not to others. But if the apostle had entertained this notion, he would never have blamed the christian Hebrews for not having acquired knowledge enough to be teachers. Or if he had thought, that this concerned Christians in general only as a thing by the by, and that their time should not in a considerable measure be taken up with this business; he never would have so much blamed them, that their proficiency in knowledge had not been answerable to the time which they had had to learn.

In handling this subject, I shall show—what is intended by divinity—what kind of *knowledge* in divinity is intended—*why* knowledge in divinity is *necessary*.

And why all Christians should make a business of endeavouring to *grow* in this knowledge. why knowledge in Divinity is necessary

SECT. I

What is intended by divinity, as the object of christian knowledge

VARIOUS definitions have been given of this subject by those who have treated on it. I shall not now stand to inquire which, according to the rules of art, is the most accurate definition; but shall so define or describe it, as I think has the greatest tendency to convey a proper notion of it.—It is that science or doctrine which comprehends all those truths and rules which concern the great business of religion.

There are various kinds of arts and sciences taught and learned in the schools, which are conversant about various objects; about the works of nature in general, as philosophy; or the visible heavens, as astronomy; or the sea, as navigation; or the earth, as geography; or the body of man, as physic and anatomy; or the soul of man, with regard to its natural powers and qualities, as logic and pneumatology; or about human government, as politics and jurisprudence. But one science, or kind of knowledge and doctrine, is above all the rest; as it treats concerning God and the great business of religion. Divinity is not learned, as other sciences, merely by the improvement of man's natural reason, but is taught by God himself in a book full of instruction, which he hath given us for that end. This is the rule which God hath given to the world to be their guide in searching after this kind of knowledge, and is a summary of all things of this nature needful for us to know. Upon this account divinity is rather called a doctrine, than an art or science.

Indeed there is what is called *natural religion*. There are many truths concerning God, and our duty to him, which are evident by the light of nature. But *christian divinity*, properly so called, is not evident by the light of nature; it depends on revelation. Such are our circumstances now in our fallen state, that nothing which it is needful for us to know concerning God, is manifest by the light of nature, in the manner in which it is necessary for us to know it. For the knowledge of no truth in divinity is of significance to us, any otherwise than as it some way or other belongs to the gospel-scheme, or as it relates to a Mediator. But the light of nature teaches us no truth in this matter. Therefore it cannot be said, that we come to the knowledge of any part of christian truth by the light of nature. It is only the word of God, contained in the Old and New Testament, which teaches us christian divinity.

This comprehends all that is taught in the Scriptures, and so all that we need know, or is to be known, concerning God and Jesus Christ, concerning our duty to God, and our happiness in God. Divinity is commonly defined, *the doctrine of living to God;* and by some who seem to be more accurate, *the doctrine of living to God by Christ.* It comprehends all christian doctrines as they are in Jesus, and all christian rules directing us in living to God by Christ. There is no one doctrine, no promise, no rule, but what some way or other relates to the christian and divine life, or our living to God by Christ. They all relate to this, in two respects, *viz.* as they tend to promote our living to God here in this world, in a life of faith and holiness, and also as they tend to bring us to a life of perfect holiness and happiness, in the full enjoyment of God hereafter.

SECT. II

What kind of knowledge in divinity, is intended in the doctrine

THERE are two kinds of knowledge of divine truth, *viz.* speculative and *practical*, or in other terms, *natural* and *spiritual*. The former remains only in the head. No other faculty but the understanding is concerned in it. It consists in having a natural or rational knowledge of the things of religion, or such a knowledge as is to be obtained by the natural exercise of our own faculties, without any special illumination of the Spirit of God. The latter rests not entirely in the head, or in the speculative ideas of things; but the heart is concerned in it: it principally consists in the sense of the heart. The mere intellect, without the will or the inclination, is not the seat of it. And it may not only be called seeing, but feeling or tasting. Thus there is a difference between having a right speculative notion of the doctrines contained in the word of God, and having a due sense of them in the heart. In the former consists the speculative or natural knowledge, in the latter consists the spiritual or practical knowledge of them.

Neither of these is intended in the doctrine exclusively of the other: but it is intended that we should seek the former *in order* to the latter. The latter, or the spiritual and practical, is of the greatest importance; for a speculative without a spiritual knowledge, is to no purpose, but to make our condemnation the greater. Yet a speculative knowledge is also of infinite importance in this respect, that without it we can have no spiritual or practical knowledge.

I have already shown, that the apostle speaks not only of a spiritual knowledge, but of such as can be acquired, and communicated from one to another. Yet it is not to be thought, that he means this exclusively of the other. But he would have the christian Hebrews seek the one, in order to the other. Therefore

the former is first and most *directly* intended; it is intended that
Christians should, by reading and other proper means, seek a
good *rational knowledge* of the things of divinity: while the
latter is more *indirectly* intended, since it is to be sought by the
other. But I proceed to

SECT. III

*The usefulness and necessity of the knowledge of divine
truths*

THERE is no other way by which any means of grace whatsoever can be of any benefit, but by knowledge. All teaching is in
vain, without learning. Therefore the preaching of the gospel
would be wholly to no purpose, if it conveyed no knowledge to
the mind. There is an order of men which Christ has appointed
on purpose to be teachers in his church. But they teach in vain,
if no knowledge in these things is gained by their teaching. It
is impossible that their teaching and preaching should be a mean
of grace, or of any good in the hearts of their hearers, any otherwise than by knowledge imparted to the understanding. Otherwise it would be of as much benefit to the auditory, if the minister
should preach in some unknown tongue. All the difference is,
that preaching in a known tongue conveys something to the
understanding, which preaching in an unknown tongue doth not.
On this account, such preaching must be unprofitable. In such
things men receive nothing, when they understand nothing; and
are not at all edified, unless some knowledge be conveyed; agreeable to the apostle's arguing, I Cor. xiv. 2-6.

No speech can be a mean of grace, but by conveying knowledge. Otherwise the speech is as much lost as if there had
been no man there, and if he that spoke, had spoken only into
the air; as it follows in the passage just quoted, ver. 6-10. God
deals with man as with a rational creature; and when faith is in
exercise, it is not about something he knows not what. Therefore
hearing is absolutely necessary to faith; because hearing is necessary to understanding, Rom. x. 14. "How shall they believe in
him of whom they have not heard?" In like manner, there can
be no love without knowledge. It is not according to the nature
of the human soul, to love an object which is entirely unknown.

The heart cannot be set upon an object of which there is no idea in the understanding. The reasons which induce the soul to love, must first be understood, before they can have a reasonable influence on the heart.

God hath given us the Bible, which is a book of instructions. But this book can be of no manner of profit to us, any otherwise than as it conveys some knowledge to the mind: it can profit us no more than if it were written in the Chinese or Tartarian language, of which we know not one word. So the sacraments of the gospel can have a proper effect no other way, than by conveying some knowledge. They represent certain things by visible signs. And what is the end of signs, but to convey some knowledge of the things signified? Such is the nature of man, that no object can come at the heart but through the door of the understanding: and there can be no spiritual knowledge of that of which there is not first a rational knowledge. It is impossible that any one should see the truth or excellency of any doctrine of the gospel, who knows not what that doctrine is. A man cannot see the wonderful excellency and love of Christ in doing such and such things for sinners, unless his understanding be first informed how those things were done. He cannot have a taste of the sweetness and excellency of divine truth, unless he first have a notion that there is such a thing.

Without knowledge in divinity, none would differ from the most ignorant and barbarous heathens. The heathens remain in gross darkness, because they are not instructed, and have not obtained the knowledge of divine truths.

If men have no knowledge of these things, the faculty of reason in them will be wholly in vain. The faculty of reason and understanding was given for *actual* understanding and knowledge. If a man have no actual knowledge, the faculty or capacity of knowing is of no use to him. And if he have actual knowledge, yet if he be destitute of the knowledge of those things which are the last end of his being, and for the sake of the knowledge of which he had more understanding given him than the beasts; then still his faculty of reason is in vain; he might as well have been a beast as a man. But divine subjects are the things, to know which we had the faculty of reason given us. They are the things which appertain to the end of our being, and to the great business for which we are made. Therefore a man cannot have his faculty of understanding to any good purpose, further than he hath knowledge of divine truth.

So that this kind of knowledge is absolutely necessary.—Other kinds of knowledge may be very useful. Some other sciences, such as astronomy, natural philosophy, and geography, may be very excellent in their kind. But the knowledge of this divine science is infinitely more useful and important than that of all other sciences whatever.

SECT. IV

Why all Christians should make a business of endeavouring to grow in the knowledge of divinity

CHRISTIANS ought not to content themselves with such degrees of knowledge of divinity as they have already obtained. It should not satisfy them, as they know as much as is absolutely necessary to salvation, but should seek to make progress.

This endeavour to make progress in such knowledge ought not to be attended to as a thing by the bye, but all Christians should make a *business* of it. They should look upon it as a part of their *daily* business, and no small part of it neither. It should be attended to as a considerable part of the work of their high calling.—For,

1. Our business should doubtless much consist in employing those faculties, by which we are distinguished from the beasts, about those things which are the main end of those faculties. The reason why we have faculties superior to those of the brutes given us, is, that we are indeed designed for a superior employment. That which the Creator intended should be our main employment, is something above what he intended the beast for, and therefore hath given us superior powers. Therefore, without doubt, it should be a considerable part of our business to improve those superior faculties. But the faculty by which we are chiefly distinguished from the brutes, is the faculty of understanding. It follows then, that we should make it our chief business to improve this faculty, and should by no means prosecute it as a business by the bye. For us to make the improvement of this faculty a business by the bye, is in effect for us to make the faculty of understanding itself a *by-faculty*, if I may

so speak, a faculty of less importance than others: whereas indeed it is the highest faculty we have.

But we cannot make a business of the improvement of our intellectual faculty, any otherwise than by making a business of improving ourselves in actual knowledge. So that those who make not this very much their business; but instead of improving their understanding to acquire knowledge, are chiefly devoted to their inferior power—to please their senses, and gratify their animal appetites—not only behave themselves in a manner not becoming Christians, but also act as if they had forgotten that they are men, and that God hath set them above the brutes, by giving them understanding.

God hath given to man some things in common with the brutes, as his outward senses, his bodily appetites, a capacity of bodily pleasure and pain, and other animal faculties: and some things he hath given him superior to the brutes, the chief of which is a faculty of understanding and reason. Now God never gave man these faculties to be subject to those which he hath in common with the brutes. This would be great confusion, and equivalent to making man to be a servant of the beasts. On the contrary, he has given those inferior powers to be employed in subserviency to man's understanding; and therefore it must be a great part of man's principal business to improve his understanding by acquiring knowledge. If so, then it will follow, that it should be a main part of his business to improve his understanding in acquiring *divine* knowledge, or the knowledge of the things of divinity: for the knowledge of these things is the principal end of this faculty. God gave man the faculty of understanding, chiefly, that he might understand divine things.

The wiser heathens were sensible that the main business of man was the improvement and exercise of his understanding. But they knew not the object about which the understanding should chiefly be employed. That science which many of them thought should chiefly employ the understanding, was philosophy; and accordingly they made it their chief business to study it. But we who enjoy the light of the gospel are more happy; we are not left, as to this particular, in the dark. God hath told us about what things we should chiefly employ our understandings, having given us a book full of divine instructions, holding forth many glorious objects about which all rational creatures should

B

chiefly employ their understandings. These instructions are accommodated to persons of all capacities and conditions, and proper to be studied, not only by men of learning, but by persons of every character, learned and unlearned, young and old, men and women. Therefore the acquisition of knowledge in these things should be a main business of all those who have the advantage of enjoying the Holy Scriptures.

2. The truths of divinity are of superlative excellency, and are worthy that all should make a business of endeavouring to grow in the knowledge of them. They are as much above those things which are treated of in other sciences, as heaven is above the earth. God himself, the eternal Three in one, is the chief object of this science; and next Jesus Christ, as God-man and Mediator, and the glorious work of redemption, the most glorious work that ever was wrought: then the great things of the heavenly world, the glorious and eternal inheritance purchased by Christ, and promised in the gospel; the work of the Holy Spirit of God on the hearts of men; our duty to God, and the way in which we ourselves may become like angels, and like God himself in our measure. All these are objects of this science.

Such things as these have been the main subject of the study of the holy patriarchs, prophets, and apostles, and the most excellent men that ever existed; and they are also the subject of study to the angels in heaven; 1 Pet. i. 10-12.—They are so excellent and worthy to be known, that the knowledge of them will richly pay for all the pains and labour of an earnest seeking of it. If there were a great treasure of gold and pearls accidentally found, and opened with such circumstances that all might have as much as they could gather; would not every one think it worth his while to make a business of gathering while it should last? But that treasure of divine knowledge, which is contained in the Scriptures, and is provided for every one to gather to himself as much of it as he can, is far more rich than any one of gold and pearls. How busy are all sorts of men, all over the world, in getting riches! But this knowledge is a far better kind of riches, than that after which they so diligently and laboriously pursue.

3. Divine truths not only concern ministers, but are of infinite importance to all Christians. It is not with the doctrine of divinity as it is with the doctrines of philosophy and other sciences. These last are generally speculative points, which are

of little concern in human life; and it very little alters the case
as to our temporal or spiritual interests, whether we know them
or not. Philosophers differ about them, some being of one
opinion, and others of another. And while they are engaged in
warm disputes about them, others may well leave them to dispute among themselves, without troubling their heads much
about them; it being of little concern to them, whether the one
or the other be in the right.—But it is not thus in matters of
divinity. The doctrines of this nearly concern every one. They
are about those things which relate to every man's eternal salvation and happiness. The common people cannot say, Let us leave
these matters to ministers and divines; let them dispute them out
among themselves as they can; they concern not us: for they are
of infinite importance to every man. Those doctrines which
relate to the essence, attributes, and subsistencies of God, concern
all; as it is of infinite importance to common people, as well as to
ministers, to know what kind of being God is. For he is a Being
who hath made us all, " in whom we live, and move, and have
our being;" who is the Lord of all; the Being to whom we are all
accountable; who is the last end of our being, and the only
fountain of our happiness.

The doctrines also which relate to Jesus Christ and his mediation, his incarnation, his life and death, his resurrection and
ascension, his sitting at the right hand of the Father, his satisfaction and intercession, infinitely concern common people as
well as divines. They stand in as much need of this Saviour, and
of an interest in his person and offices, and the things which he
hath done and suffered, as ministers and divines.—The same
may be said of the doctrines which relate to the manner of a
sinner's justification, or the way in which he becomes interested
in the mediation of Christ. They equally concern all; for all
stand in equal necessity of justification before God. That eternal
condemnation, to which we are all naturally exposed, is equally
dreadful. So with respect to those doctrines which relate to the
work of the Spirit of God on the heart, in the application of
redemption in our effectual calling and sanctification, all are
equally concerned in them. There is no doctrine of divinity
whatever, which doth not some way or other concern the eternal
interest of every Christian.

4. We may argue in favour of the same position, from the

great things which God hath done in order to give us instruction in these things. As to other sciences, he hath left us to ourselves, to the light of our own reason. But divine things being of infinitely greater importance to us, he hath not left us to an uncertain guide; but hath himself given us a revelation of the truth in these matters, and hath done very great things to convey and confirm it to us; raising up many prophets in different ages, immediately inspiring them with his Holy Spirit, and confirming their doctrine with innumerable miracles or wonderful works out of the established course of nature. Yea, he raised up a succession of prophets, which was upheld for several ages.

It was very much for this end that God separated the people of Israel, in so wonderful a manner, from all other people, and kept them separate; that to them he might commit the oracles of God, and that from them they might be communicated to the world. He hath also often sent angels to bring divine instructions to men; and hath often himself appeared in miraculous symbols or representations of his presence: and now in these last days hath sent his own Son into the world, to be his great prophet, to teach us divine truth. Heb. i. 1, etc. God hath given us a book of divine instructions, which contains the sum of divinity. Now, these things hath God done, not only for the instruction of ministers and men of learning; but for the instruction of all men, of all sorts, learned and unlearned, men, women, and children. And certainly if God doth such great things to *teach* us, we ought to do something to *learn*.

God giving instructions to men in these things, is not a business by the by; but what he hath undertaken and prosecuted in a course of great and wonderful dispensations, as an affair in which his heart hath been greatly engaged; which is sometimes in Scripture signified by the expression of God's rising early to teach us, and to send us prophets and teachers. Jer. vii. 25. "Since that day that your fathers came forth out of the land of Egypt, unto this day, I have even sent unto you all my servants the prophets, daily rising up early, and sending them." And ver. 13. "I spake unto you, rising up early, and speaking." This is a figurative speech, signifying, that God hath done this as a business of great importance, in which he took great care, and had his heart much engaged; because persons are wont to rise early to prosecute such business as they are earnestly engaged in.

—If God hath been so engaged in teaching, certainly we should not be negligent in learning; but should make growing in knowledge a great part of the business of our lives.

5. It may be argued from the abundance of the instructions which God hath given us, from the largeness of that book which God hath given to teach us divinity, and from the great variety that is therein contained. Much was taught by Moses of old, which we have transmitted down to us; after that, other books were from time to time added; much is taught us by David and Solomon; and many and excellent are the instructions communicated by the prophets: yet God did not think all this enough, but after this sent Christ and his apostles, by whom there is added a great and excellent treasure to that holy book, which is to be our rule in the study of this important subject.

This book was written for the use of all; all are directed to search the Scriptures, John v. 39. "Search the Scriptures, for in them ye think ye have eternal life; and they are they that testify of me;" and Isa. xxxiv. 16. "Seek ye out of the book of the Lord, and read." They that read and understand are pronounced blessed, Rev. i. 3. "Blessed is he that readeth, and they that understand the words of this prophecy." If this be true of that particular book of the *Revelation*, much more is it true of the Bible in general. Nor is it to be believed that God would have given instructions in such abundance, if he had intended that receiving instruction should be only a bye concern with us.

It is to be considered, that all those abundant instructions which are contained in the Scriptures were written that they might be understood: otherwise they are not instructions. That which is not given that the learner may understand it, is not given for the learner's instruction; unless we endeavour to grow in the knowledge of divinity, a very great part of those instructions will to us be in vain; for we can receive benefit by no more of the Scriptures than we understand. We have reason to bless God that he hath given us such various and plentiful instruction in his word; but we shall be hypocritical in so doing, if we after all content ourselves with but little of this instruction.

When God hath opened a very large treasure before us, for the supply of our wants, and we thank him that he hath given us so much; if at the same time we be willing to remain destitute of the greatest part of it, because we are too lazy to gather it, this will not show the sincerity of our thankfulness. We are now under much greater advantages to acquire knowledge in divinity, than the people of God were of old, because since that time the canon of Scripture is much increased. But if we be negligent of our advantages, we may be never the better for them, and may remain with as little knowledge as they.

6. However diligent we apply ourselves, there is room enough to increase our knowledge in divine truth. None have this excuse to make for not diligently applying themselves to gain knowledge in divinity, that they already know all; nor can they make this excuse, that they have no need diligently to apply themselves, in order to know all that is to be known. None can excuse themselves for want of business in which to employ themselves. There is room enough to employ ourselves for ever in this divine science, with the utmost application. Those who have applied themselves most closely, have studied the longest, and have made the greatest attainments in this knowledge, know but little of what is to be known. The subject is inexhaustible. That divine Being, who is the main subject of this science, is infinite, and there is no end to the glory of his perfections. His works at the same time are wonderful, and cannot be found out to perfection; especially the work of redemption, about which the science of divinity is chiefly conversant, is full of unsearchable wonders.

The word of God, which is given for our instruction in divinity, contains enough in it to employ us to the end of our lives, and then we shall leave enough uninvestigated to employ the heads of the ablest divines to the end of the world. The psalmist found an end to the things that are human; but he could never find an end to what is contained in the word of God : Psal. cxix. 96. " I have seen an end to all perfection; but thy command is exceeding broad." There is enough in this divine science to employ the understandings of saints and angels to all eternity.

7. It doubtless concerns every one to endeavour to excel in the knowledge of things which pertain to his profession, or principal calling. If it concerns men to excel in any thing, or in any wisdom or knowledge at all, it certainly concerns them to excel in the affairs of their main profession and work. But the calling and work of every Christian is to live to God. This is said to be his *high calling*, Phil. iii. 14. This is the business, and, if I may

so speak, the *trade* of a Christian, his main work, and indeed should be his only work. No business should be done by a Christian, but as it is some way or other a part of this. Therefore certainly the Christian should endeavour to be well acquainted with those things which belong to this work, that he may fulfil it, and be thoroughly furnished to it.

It becomes one who is called to be a soldier, to excel in the art of war. It becomes a mariner, to excel in the art of navigation. It becomes a physician, to excel in the knowledge of those things which pertain to the art of physic. So it becomes all such as profess to be Christians, and to devote themselves to the practice of Christianity, to endeavour to excel in the knowledge of divinity.

8. It may be argued hence, that God hath appointed an order of men for this end, to assist persons in gaining knowledge in these things. He hath appointed them to be teachers, 1 Cor. xii. 28. and God hath set some in the church; first apostles, secondarily prophets, thirdly teachers: Eph. iv. 11, 12. " He gave some apostles, some prophets, some evangelists, some pastors and teachers, for the perfecting of the saints, for the work of the ministry, for the edifying of the body of Christ." If God hath set them to be teachers, making that their business, then he hath made it their business to impart knowledge. But what kind of knowledge? not the knowledge of philosophy, or of human laws, or of mechanical arts, but of divinity.

If God have made it the business of some to be teachers, it will follow, that he hath made it the business of others to be learners; for teachers and learners are correlates, one of which was never intended to be without the other. God hath never made it the duty of some to take pains to teach those who are not obliged to take pains to learn. He hath not commanded ministers to spend themselves, in order to impart knowledge to those who are not obliged to apply themselves to receive it.

The name by which Christians are commonly called in the New Testament is *disciples*, the signification of which word is *scholars* or *learners*. All Christians are put into the school of Christ, where their business is to learn, or receive knowledge from Christ, their common master and teacher, and from those inferior teachers appointed by him to instruct in his name.

9. God hath in the Scriptures plainly revealed it to be his will,

that all Christians should diligently endeavour to excel in the knowledge of divine things. It is the revealed will of God, that Christians should not only have some knowledge of things of this nature, but that they should be *enriched with all knowledge*: 1 Cor. i. 4, 5. "I thank my God always on your behalf, for the grace of God that is given you by Jesus Christ, that in every thing ye are enriched by him, in all utterance, and in *all knowledge*." So the apostle earnestly prayed, that the christian Philippians might abound more and more, not only in love, but in christian *knowledge*; Phil. i. 9. "And this I pray, that your love may abound yet more and more in *knowledge, and in all judgment*." So the apostle Peter advises to "give all diligence to add to faith virtue, and to virtue *knowledge*," 2 Pet. i. 5, and the apostle Paul, in the next chapter to that wherein is the text, counsels the christian Hebrews, leaving the first principles of the doctrine of Christ, to go on to perfection. He would by no means have them always to rest only in those fundamental doctrines of repentance, and faith, and the resurrection from the dead, and the eternal judgment, in which they were instructed when baptized, at their first initiation in Christianity. (See Heb. vi., etc.)

SECT. V

An exhortation that all may diligently endeavour to gain christian knowledge

CONSIDER yourselves as scholars or disciples, put into the school of Christ; and therefore be diligent to make proficiency in christian knowledge. Content not yourselves with this, that you have been taught your catechism in your childhood, and that you know as much of the principles of religion as is necessary to salvation; else you will be guilty of what the apostle warns against, *viz.* going no further than laying the foundation of repentance from dead works, etc.

You are all called to be Christians, and this is your profession. Endeavour, therefore, to acquire knowledge in things which pertain to your profession. Let not your teachers have cause to complain, that while they spend and are spent, to impart knowledge to you, you take little pains to learn. It is a great encouragement to an instructor, to have such to teach as make a business of learning, bending their minds to it. This makes teaching a pleasure, when otherwise it will be a very heavy and burdensome task.

You all have by you a large treasure of divine knowledge, in that you have the Bible in your hands; therefore be not contented in possessing but little of this treasure. God hath spoken much to you in the Scriptures; labour to understand as much of what he saith as you can. God hath made you all reasonable creatures; therefore let not the noble faculty of reason or understanding lie neglected. Content not yourselves with having so much knowledge as is thrown in your way, and receive in some sense unavoidably by the frequent inculcation of divine truth in the preaching of the word, of which you are obliged to be hearers, or accidentally gain in conversation; but let it be very much your business to search for it, and that with the same diligence and labour with which men are wont to dig in mines of silver and gold.

Especially I would advise those who are young to employ themselves in this way. Men are never too old to learn; but the time of youth is especially the time for learning; it is peculiarly proper for gaining and storing up knowledge.—Further, to stir up all, both old and young, to this duty, let me entreat you to consider,

1. If you apply yourselves diligently to this work, you will not want employment, when you are at leisure from your common secular business. In this way, you may find something in which you may profitably employ yourselves. You will find something else to do, besides going about from house to house, spending one hour after another in unprofitable conversation, or, at best, to no other purpose but to amuse yourselves, to fill up and wear away your time. And it is to be feared that very much of the time spent in evening visits, is spent to a much worse purpose than that which I have now mentioned. Solomon tells us, Prov. x. 19. "That in the multitude of words, there wanteth not sin." And is not this verified in those who find little else to do but to go to one another's houses, and spend the time in such talk as comes next, or such as any one's present disposition happens to suggest?

Some diversion is doubtless lawful; but for Christians to spend so much of their time, so many long evenings, in no other conversation than that which tends to divert and amuse, if nothing worse, is a sinful way of spending time, and tends to poverty of soul at least, if not to outward poverty: Prov. xiv. 23. "In all labour there is profit; but the talk of the lips tendeth only to *penury*." Besides, when persons for so much of their time have nothing else to do, but to sit, and talk, and chat, there is great danger of falling into foolish and sinful conversation, venting their corrupt dispositions, in talking against others, expressing their jealousies and evil surmises concerning their neighbours; not considering what Christ hath said, Matt. xii. 36, "Of every idle word that men shall speak, shall they give account in the day of judgment."

If you would comply with what you have heard from this doctrine, you would find something else to employ your time besides contention, or talking about those public affairs which tend to contention. Young people might find something else to do, besides spending their time in vain company; something that would be much more profitable to themselves, as it would really turn to some good account; something, in doing which they would both be more out of the way of temptation, and be more in the way of duty, and of a divine blessing. And even aged people would have something to employ themselves in, after they are become incapable of bodily labour. Their time, as is now often the case, would not lie heavy upon their hands, as they would with both profit and pleasure be engaged in searching the Scriptures, and in comparing and meditating upon the various truths which they should find there.

2. This would be a *noble* way of spending your time.—The Holy Spirit gives the Bereans this epithet, because they diligently employed themselves in this business: Acts xvii. 11. "These were more *noble* than those of Thessalonica, in that they received the word with all readiness of mind, and searched the Scriptures daily, whether those things were so." Similar to this is very much the employment of heaven. The inhabitants of that world spend much of their time in searching into the great things of divinity, and endeavouring to acquire knowledge in them, as we are told of the angels, 1 Pet. i. 12. "Which things the angels desire to look into." This will be very agreeable to what you hope will be your business to all eternity, as you doubtless hope to join in the same employment with the angels of light. Solomon says, Prov. xxv. 2. "It is the honour of kings to

search out a matter;" and certainly, above all others, to search out divine matters. Now, if this be the honour even of kings, is it not much more your honour?

3. This is a pleasant way of improving time. Knowledge is pleasant and delightful to intelligent creatures, and above all, the knowledge of divine things; for in them are the most excellent truths, and the most beautiful and amiable objects held forth to view. However tedious the labour necessarily attending this business may be, yet the knowledge once obtained will richly requite the pains taken to obtain it. "When wisdom entereth the heart, knowledge is pleasant to the soul." Prov. ii. 10.

4. This knowledge is exceedingly *useful* in christian practice. Such as have much knowledge in divinity have great means and advantages for spiritual and saving knowledge; for no means of grace have a saving effect, otherwise than by the knowledge they impart. The more you have of a rational knowledge of divine things, the more opportunity will there be, when the Spirit shall be breathed into your heart, to see the excellency of these things, and to taste the sweetness of them. The heathens, who have no rational knowledge of the things of the gospel, have no opportunity to see the excellency of them; and therefore the more rational knowledge of these things you have, the more opportunity and advantage you have to see the divine excellency and glory of them.

Again, The more knowledge you have of divine things, the better will you know your duty; your knowledge will be of great use to direct you as to your duty in particular cases. You will also be the better furnished against the temptations of the devil. For the devil often takes advantage of persons' ignorance to ply them with temptations which otherwise would have no hold of them. By having much knowledge, you will be under greater advantages to conduct yourselves with prudence and discretion in your christian course, and so to live much more to the honour of God and religion. Many who mean well, and are full of a good spirit, yet for want of prudence, conduct themselves so as to wound religion. Many have a zeal of God, which doth more hurt than good, because it is not according to knowledge, Rom. x. 2. The reason why many good men behave no better in many instances, is not so much that they want grace, as that they want knowledge. Beside, an increase of knowledge would be a great help to profitable conversation. It would supply you with matter for conversation when you come together, or when you visit your neighbours: and so you would have less temptation to spend the time in such conversation as tends to your own and others' hurt.

5. Consider the advantages you are under to grow in the knowledge of divinity. We are under far greater advantages to gain much of this knowledge now, than God's people under the Old Testament, both because the canon of Scripture is so much enlarged since that time, and also because evangelical truths are now so much more plainly revealed. So that common men are now in some respects under advantages to know more, than the greatest prophets were then. Thus that saying of Christ is in a sense applicable to us, Luke x. 23, 24. "Blessed are the eyes which see the things which ye see. For I tell you, that many prophets and kings have desired to see those things which ye see, and have not seen them; and to hear those things which ye hear, and have not heard them." We are in some respects under far greater advantages for gaining knowledge, now in these latter ages of the church, than Christians were formerly; especially by reason of the art of printing, of which God hath given us the benefit, whereby Bibles and other books of divinity are exceedingly multiplied, and persons may now be furnished with helps for the obtaining of christian knowledge, at a much easier and cheaper rate than they formerly could.

6. We know not what opposition we may meet with in the religious principles which we hold. We know that there are many adversaries to the gospel and its truths. If therefore we embrace those truths, we must expect to be attacked by the said adversaries; and unless we be well informed concerning divine things, how shall we be able to defend ourselves? Beside, the apostle Paul enjoins it upon us, always to be ready to give an answer to every man who asketh us a reason of the hope that is in us. But this we cannot expect to do without considerable knowledge in divine things.

SECT. VI

Directions for the acquisition of christian knowledge

1. BE assiduous in reading the Holy Scriptures. This is the fountain whence all knowledge in divinity must be derived.

Therefore let not this treasure lie by you neglected. Every man of common understanding who can read, may, if he please, become well acquainted with the Scriptures. And what an excellent attainment would this be!

2. Content not yourselves with only a cursory reading, without regarding the sense. This is an ill way of reading, to which, however, many accustom themselves all their days. When you read, observe what you read. Observe how things come in. Take notice of the drift of the discourse, and compare one scripture with another. For the Scripture, by the harmony of its different parts, casts great light upon itself.—We are expressly directed by Christ, to *search* the Scriptures, which evidently intends something more than a mere cursory reading. And use means to find out the meaning of the Scripture. When you have it explained in the preaching of the word, take notice of it; and if at any time a scripture that you did not understand be cleared up to your satisfaction, mark it, lay it up, and if possible remember it.

3. Procure, and diligently use, other books which may help you to grow in this knowledge. There are many excellent books extant, which might greatly forward you in this knowledge, and afford you a very profitable and pleasant entertainment in your leisure hours. There is doubtless a great defect in many, that through a lothness to be at a little expense, they furnish themselves with no more helps of this nature. They have a few books indeed, which now and then on sabbath-days they read; but they have had them so long, and read them so often, that they are weary of them, and it is now become a dull story, a mere task to read them.

4. Improve conversation with others to this end. How much might persons promote each other's knowledge in divine things, if they would improve conversation as they might; if men that are ignorant were not ashamed to show their ignorance, and were willing to learn of others; if those that have knowledge would communicate it, without pride and ostentation; and if all were more disposed to enter on such conversation as would be for their mutual edification and instruction.

5. Seek not to grow in knowledge chiefly for the sake of applause, and to enable you to dispute with others; but seek it for the benefit of your souls, and in order to practice.—If applause be your end, you will not be so likely to be led to the

knowledge of the truth, but may justly, as often is the case of those who are proud of their knowledge, be led into error to your own perdition. This being your end, if you should obtain much rational knowledge, it would not be likely to be of any benefit to you, but would puff you up with pride: 1 Cor. viii. 1. "Knowledge puffeth up."

6. Seek to God, that he would direct you, and bless you, in this pursuit after knowledge. This is the apostle's direction, James i. 5. "If any man lack wisdom, let him ask it of God, who giveth to all liberally, and upbraideth not." God is the fountain of all divine knowledge: Prov. ii. 6. "The Lord giveth wisdom: out of his mouth cometh knowledge and understanding." Labour to be sensible of your own blindness and ignorance, and your need of the help of God, lest you be led into error, instead of true knowledge: 1 Cor. iii. 18. "If any man would be wise, let him become a fool, that he may be wise."

7. Practise according to what knowledge you have. This will be the way to know more. The psalmist warmly recommends this way of seeking knowledge in divine truth, from his own experience: Psal. cxix. 100. "I understand more than the ancients, because I keep thy precepts." Christ also recommends the same: John vii. 17. "If any man will do his will, he shall know of the doctrine, whether it be of God, or whether I speak of myself."

ADVERTISEMENT TO THE READER

It was with no small difficulty that the author's youth and modesty were prevailed on to let him appear a preacher in our public lecture, and afterwards to give us a copy of his discourse, at the desire of divers ministers and others who heard it. But as we quickly found him a workman that needs not to be ashamed before his brethren, our satisfaction was the greater to see him pitching upon so noble a subject, and treating it with so much strength and clearness, as the judicious reader will perceive in the following composure: a subject which secures to God his great design in the work of fallen man's redemption by the Lord Jesus Christ, which is evidently so laid out, as that the glory of the whole should return to him, the blessed ordainer, purchaser, and applier; a subject which enters deep into practical religion; without the belief of which, that must soon die in the hearts and lives of men.

For in proportion to the sense we have of our dependence on the sovereign God for all the good we want, will be our value for him, our trust in him, our fear to offend him, and our care to please him; as likewise our gratitude and love, our delight and praise, upon our sensible experience of his free benefits.

In short, it is the very soul of piety, to apprehend and own that all our springs are in him; the springs of our present grace and comfort, and of our future glory and blessedness; and that they all entirely flow through Christ, by the efficacious influence of the Holy Spirit. By these things saints live, and in all these things is the life of our spirits.

Such doctrines as these, which, by humbling the minds of men, prepare them for the exaltations of God, he has signally owned and prospered in the reformed world, and in our land especially, in the days of our forefathers; and we hope they will never grow unfashionable among us; for, we are well assured, if those which we call the doctrines of grace ever come to be contemned or disrelished, vital piety will proportionably languish and wear away; as these doctrines always sink in the esteem of men upon the decay of serious religion.

We cannot therefore but express our joy and thankfulness, that the great Head of the church is pleased still to raise up from among the children of his people, for the supply of his churches, those who assert and maintain these evangelical principles; and that our churches (notwithstanding all their degeneracies) have still a high value for such principles, and for those who publicly own and teach them.

And as we cannot but wish and pray that the college in the neighbouring colony (as well as our own) may be a fruitful mother of many such sons as the author, by the blessing of Heaven on the care of their present worthy rector; so we heartily rejoice in the special favour of Providence in bestowing such a rich gift on the happy church of Northampton, which has for so many lustres of years flourished under the influence of such pious doctrines, taught them in the excellent ministry of their late venerable pastor, whose gift and spirit, we hope, will long live and shine in this his grandson, to the end that they may abound yet more in all the lovely fruits of evangelical humility and thankfulness, to the glory of God.

To his blessing we commit them all, with this discourse, and every one that reads it; and are

Your servants in the gospel,

T. PRINCE.

W. COOPER.

Boston, August 17, 1731.

Sermon II *

GOD GLORIFIED IN MAN'S DEPENDENCE

1 Cor. i. 29, 30, 31

*That no flesh should glory in his presence. But of him are
ye in Christ Jesus, who of God is made unto us wisdom, and
righteousness, and sanctification, and redemption: that,
according as it is written, He that glorieth, let him glory in
the Lord.*

THOSE Christians to whom the apostle directed this epistle,
dwelt in a part of the world where human wisdom was in great
repute; as the apostle observes in the 22nd verse of this chapter,
"The Greeks seek after wisdom." Corinth was not far from
Athens, that had been for many ages the most famous seat of
philosophy and learning in the world. The apostle therefore
observes to them, how God by the gospel destroyed, and brought
to nought, their wisdom. The learned Grecians, and their great
philosophers, by all their wisdom did not know God, they were
not able to find out the truth in divine things. But, after they
had done their utmost to no effect, it pleased God at length to
reveal himself by the gospel, which they accounted foolishness.
He "chose the foolish things of the world to confound the wise,
and the weak things of the world to confound the things which
are mighty, and the base things of the world, and things that are
despised, yea, and things which are not, to bring to nought the
things that are." And the apostle informs them in the text why
he thus did, *That no flesh should glory in his presence,* etc.—In
which words may be observed,

    1. What God aims at in the disposition of things in the affair
of redemption, *viz.* that man should not glory in himself, but
alone in God; *That no flesh should glory in his presence,—that,*

* Preached on the Public Lecture in Boston, July 8, 1731; and published at the desire of several ministers and others in Boston who heard
it.—This was the first piece published by Mr. Edwards.

according as it is written, He that glorieth, let him glory in the Lord.

2. How this end is attained in the work of redemption, *viz.* by that absolute and immediate dependence which men have upon God in that work, for all their good. Inasmuch as,

First, All the good that they have is in and through Christ; He *is made unto us wisdom, righteousness, sanctification, and redemption.* All the good of the fallen and redeemed creature is concerned in these four things, and cannot be better distributed than into them; but Christ is each of them to us, and we have none of them any otherwise than in him. *He is made of God unto us wisdom:* in him are all the proper good and true excellency of the understanding. Wisdom was a thing that the Greeks admired; but Christ is the true light of the world; it is through him alone that true wisdom is imparted to the mind. It is in and by Christ that we have *righteousness:* it is by being in him that we are justified, have our sins pardoned, and are received as righteous into God's favour. It is by Christ that we have *sanctification:* we have in him true excellency of heart as well as of understanding; and he is made unto us inherent as well as imputed righteousness. It is by Christ that we have *redemption,* or the actual deliverance from all misery, and the bestowment of all happiness and glory. Thus we have all our good by Christ, who is God.

Secondly, Another instance wherein our dependence on God for all our good appears, is this, That it is God that has given us Christ, that we might have these benefits through him; he *of God is made unto us wisdom, righteousness,* etc.

Thirdly, It is of him that we are in Christ Jesus, and come to have an interest in him, and so do receive those blessings which he is made unto us. It is God that gives us faith whereby we close with Christ.

So that in this verse is shown our dependence on each person in the Trinity for all our good. We are dependent on Christ the Son of God, as he is our wisdom, righteousness, sanctification, and redemption. We are dependent on the Father, who has given us Christ, and made him to be these things to us. We are dependent on the Holy Ghost, for it is *of him that we are in Christ Jesus;* it is the Spirit of God that gives faith in him, whereby we receive him, and close with him.

DOCTRINE

" God is glorified in the work of redemption in this, that there appears in it so absolute and universal a dependence of the redeemed on him."—Here I propose to show, 1st, That there is an absolute and universal dependence of the redeemed on God for all their good. And, 2dly, That God hereby is exalted and glorified in the work of redemption.

I. There is an absolute and universal dependence of the redeemed on God. The nature and contrivance of our redemption is such, that the redeemed are in every thing directly, immediately, and entirely dependent on God: they are dependent on him for all, and are dependent on him every way.

The several ways wherein the dependence of one being may be upon another for its good, and wherein the redeemed of Jesus Christ depend on God for all their good, are these, viz. That they have all their good of him, and that they have all through him, and that they have all in him: That he is the *cause* and original whence all their good comes, therein it is *of* him; and that he is the *medium* by which it is obtained and conveyed, therein they have it *through* him; and that he is the *good itself* given and conveyed, therein it is *in* him. Now those that are redeemed by Jesus Christ do, in all these respects, very directly and entirely depend on God for their all.

First, The redeemed have all their good *of* God. God is the great *author* of it. He is the *first* cause of it; and not only so, but he is the *only* proper cause. It is of God that we have our Redeemer. It is God that has provided a Saviour for us. Jesus Christ is not only of God in his person, as he is the only-begotten Son of God, but he is from God, as we are concerned in him, and in his office of Mediator. He is the gift of God to us: God chose and anointed him, appointed him his work, and sent him into the world. And as it is God that *gives,* so it is God that *accepts* the Saviour. He gives the purchaser, and he affords the thing purchased.

It is of God that Christ becomes ours, that we are brought to him, and are united to him. It is of God that we receive faith to close with him, that we may have an interest in him. Eph. ii. 8.

"For by grace ye are saved, through faith; and that not of your-selves, it is the gift of God." It is of God that we actually re-ceive all the benefits that Christ has purchased. It is God that pardons and justifies, and delivers from going down to hell; and into his favour the redeemed are received, when they are justi-fied. So it is God that delivers from the dominion of sin, cleanses us from our filthiness, and changes us from our deformity. It is of God that the redeemed receive all their true excellency, wisdom, and holiness; and that two ways, *viz*. as the Holy Ghost by whom these things are immediately wrought is from God, proceeds from him, and is sent by him; and also as the Holy Ghost himself is God, by whose operation and indwelling the knowledge of God and divine things, a holy disposition and all grace, are conferred and upheld. And though means are made use of in conferring grace on men's souls, yet it is of God that we have these means of grace, and it is he that makes them effectual. It is of God that we have the Holy Scriptures; they are his word. It is of God that we have ordinances, and their efficacy depends on the immediate influence of his Spirit. The ministers of the gospel are sent of God, and all their sufficiency is of him.—2 Cor. iv. 7. "We have this treasure in earthen vessels, that the excel-lency of the power may be of God, and not of us." Their success depends entirely and absolutely on the immediate blessing and influence of God.

1. The redeemed have all from the *grace* of God. It was of mere grace that God gave us his only-begotten Son. The grace is great in proportion to the excellency of what is given. The gift was infinitely precious, because it was of a person infinitely worthy, a person of infinite glory; and also because it was of a person infinitely near and dear to God. The grace is great in proportion to the benefit we have given us in him. The benefit is doubly infinite, in that in him we have deliverance from an infinite, because an eternal, misery, and do also receive eternal joy and glory. The grace in bestowing this gift is great in pro-portion to our unworthiness to whom it is given; instead of de-serving such a gift, we merited infinitely ill of God's hands. The grace is great according to the manner of giving, or in proportion to the humiliation and expense of the method and means by which a way is made for our having the gift. He gave him to dwell amongst us; he gave him to us incarnate, or in our nature;

and in the like though sinless infirmities. He gave him to us in a low and afflicted state; and not only so, but as slain, that he might be a feast for our souls.

The grace of God in bestowing this gift is most free. It was what God was under no obligation to bestow. He might have rejected fallen man, as he did the fallen angels. It was what we never did any thing to merit; it was given while we were yet enemies, and before we had so much as repented. It was from the love of God who saw no excellency in us to attract it; and it was without expectation of ever being requited for it.—And it is from mere grace that the benefits of Christ are applied to such and such particular persons. Those that are called and sanctified are to attribute it alone to the good pleasure of God's goodness, by which they are distinguished. He is sovereign, and hath mercy on whom he will have mercy.

Man hath now a greater dependence on the grace of God than he had before the fall. He depends on the free goodness of God for much more than he did then. Then he depended on God's goodness for conferring the reward of perfect obedience; for God was not obliged to promise and bestow that reward. But now we are dependent on the grace of God for much more; we stand in need of grace, not only to bestow glory upon us, but to deliver us from hell and eternal wrath. Under the first covenant we depended on God's goodness to give us the reward of righteousness; and so we do now; but we stand in need of God's free and sovereign grace to give us that righteousness; to pardon our sin, and release us from the guilt and infinite demerit of it.

And as we are dependent on the goodness of God for more now than under the first covenant, so we are dependent on a much greater, more free and wonderful goodness. We are now more dependent on God's arbitrary and sovereign good pleasure. We were in our first estate dependent on God for holiness. We had our original righteousness from him; but then holiness was not bestowed in such a way of sovereign good pleasure as it is now. Man was created holy, for it became God to create holy all his reasonable creatures. It would have been a disparagement to the holiness of God's nature, if he had made an intelligent creature unholy. But now when fallen man is made holy, it is from mere and arbitrary grace; God may for ever deny holi-

ness to the fallen creature if he pleases, without any disparagement to any of his perfections.

And we are not only indeed more dependent on the grace of
God, but our dependence is much more conspicuous, because our
own insufficiency and helplessness in ourselves is much more
apparent in our fallen and undone state, than it was before we
were either sinful or miserable. We are more apparently dependent on God for holiness, because we are first sinful, and
utterly polluted, and afterward holy. So the production of the
effect is sensible, and its derivation from God more obvious. If
man was ever holy and always was so, it would not be so apparent, that he had not holiness necessarily, as an inseparable
qualification of human nature. So we are more apparently dependent on free grace for the favour of God, for we are first justly
the objects of his displeasure, and afterwards are received into
favour. We are more apparently dependent on God for happiness, being first miserable, and afterwards happy. It is more apparently free and without merit in us, because we are actually
without any kind of excellency to merit, if there could be any
such thing as merit in creature-excellency. And we are not only
without any true excellency, but are full of, and wholly defiled
with, that which is infinitely odious. All our good is more apparently from God, because we are first naked and wholly without any good, and afterwards enriched with all good.

2. We receive all from the *power* of God. Man's redemption
is often spoken of as a work of wonderful power as well as grace.
The great power of God appears in bringing a sinner from his
low state, from the depths of sin and misery, to such an exalted
state of holiness and happiness. Eph. i. 19. "And what is the
exceeding greatness of his power to us-ward who believe, according to the working of his mighty power."——

We are dependent on God's power through every step of our
redemption. We are dependent on the power of God to convert
us, and give faith in Jesus Christ, and the new nature. It is a
work of creation: "If any man be in Christ, he is a new creature," 2 Cor. v. 17. "We are created in Christ Jesus," Eph. ii. 10.
The fallen creature cannot attain to true holiness, but by being
created again. Eph. iv. 24. "And that ye put on the new man,
which after God is created in righteousness and true holiness."
It is a raising from the dead. Colos. ii. 12, 13. "Wherein also ye

are risen with him through the faith of the operation of God, who hath raised him from the dead." Yea, it is a more glorious work of power than mere creation, or raising a dead body to life, in that the effect attained is greater and more excellent. That holy and happy being, and spiritual life, which is produced in the work of conversion, is a far greater and more glorious effect, than mere being and life. And the state from whence the change is made—a death in sin, a total corruption of nature, and depth of misery—is far more remote from the state attained, than mere death or non-entity.

It is by God's power also that we are preserved in a state of grace. I Pet. i. 5. " Who are kept by the power of God through faith unto salvation." As grace is at first from God, so it is continually from him, and is maintained by him, as much as light in the atmosphere is all day long from the sun, as well as at first dawning, or sun-rising.—Men are dependent on the power of God for every exercise of grace, and for carrying on that work in the heart, for subduing sin and corruption, increasing holy principles, and enabling to bring forth fruit in good works. Man is dependent on divine power in bringing grace to its perfection, in making the soul completely amiable in Christ's glorious likeness, and filling of it with a satisfying joy and blessedness; and for the raising of the body to life, and to such a perfect state, that it shall be suitable for a habitation and organ for a soul so perfected and blessed. These are the most glorious effects of the power of God, that are seen in the series of God's acts with respect to the creatures.

Man was dependent on the power of God in his first estate, but he is more dependent on his power now; he needs God's power to do more things for him, and depends on a more wonderful exercise of his power. It was an effect of the power of God to make man holy at the first; but more remarkably so now, because there is a great deal of opposition and difficulty in the way. It is a more glorious effect of power to make that holy that was so depraved, and under the dominion of sin, than to confer holiness on that which before had nothing of the contrary. It is a more glorious work of power to rescue a soul out of the hands of the devil, and from the powers of darkness, and to bring it into a state of salvation, than to confer holiness where there was no prepossession or opposition. Luke xi. 21, 22. " When a strong man armed keepeth his palace, his goods are in peace; but when a stronger than he shall come upon him, and overcome him, he taketh from him all his armour, wherein he trusted, and divideth his spoils." So it is a more glorious work of power to uphold a soul in a state of grace and holiness, and to carry it on till it is brought to glory, when there is so much sin remaining in the heart resisting, and Satan with all his might opposing, than it would have been to have kept man from falling at first, when Satan had nothing in man.—Thus we have shown how the redeemed are dependent on God for all their good, as they have all of him.

Secondly, They are also dependent on God for all, as they have all *through* him. God is the medium of it, as well as the author and fountain of it. All we have, wisdom, the pardon of sin, deliverance from hell, acceptance into God's favour, grace and holiness, true comfort and happiness, eternal life and glory, is from God by a Mediator; and this Mediator is God; which Mediator we have an absolute dependence upon, as he through whom we receive all. So that here is another way wherein we have our dependence on God for all good. God not only gives us the Mediator, and accepts his mediation, and of his power and grace bestows the things purchased by the Mediator; but he the Mediator is God.

Our blessings are what we have by purchase; and the purchase is made of God, the blessings are purchased of him, and God gives the purchaser; and not only so, but God is the purchaser. Yea God is both the purchaser and the price; for Christ, who is God, purchased these blessings for us, by offering up himself as the price of our salvation. He purchased eternal life by the sacrifice of himself. Heb. vii. 27. "He offered up himself." And ix. 26. "He hath appeared to take away sin by the sacrifice of himself." Indeed it was the human nature that was offered; but it was the same person with the divine, and therefore was an infinite price.

As we thus have our good through God, we have a dependence on him in a respect that man in his first estate had not. Man was to have eternal life then through his own righteousness; so that he had partly a dependence upon what was in himself; for we have a dependence upon that through which we have our good, as well as that from which we have it; and though man's righteousness that he then depended on was indeed from God, yet it was his own, it was inherent in himself; so that his dependence was not so *immediately* on God. But now the righteousness that we are dependent on is not in ourselves, but in God. We are saved through the righteousness of Christ: He *is made unto us righteousness;* and therefore is prophesied of, Jer. xxiii. 6, under that name, "the Lord our righteousness." In that the righteousness we are justified by is the righteousness of Christ, it is the righteousness of God. 2 Cor. v. 21. "That we might be made the righteousness of God in him."—Thus in redemption we have not only all things of God, but by and through him, 1 Cor. viii. 6. "But to us there is but one God, the Father, of whom are all things, and we in him; and one Lord Jesus Christ, by whom are all things, and we by him."

Thirdly, The redeemed have all their good *in God.* We not only have it of him, and through him, but it consists in him; he is all our good.—The good of the redeemed is either objective or inherent. By their objective good, I mean that extrinsic object, in the possession and enjoyment of which they are happy. Their inherent good is that excellency or pleasure which is in the soul itself. With respect to both of which the redeemed have all their good in God, or which is the same thing, God himself is all their good.

1. The redeemed have all their *objective* good in God. God himself is the great good which they are brought to the possession and enjoyment of by redemption. He is the highest good, and the sum of all that good which Christ purchased. God is the inheritance of the saints; he is the portion of their souls. God is their wealth and treasure, their food, their life, their dwelling-place, their ornament and diadem, and their everlasting honour and glory. They have none in heaven but God; he is the great good which the redeemed are received to at death, and which they are to rise to at the end of the world. The Lord God is the light of the heavenly Jerusalem; and is the "river of the water of life" that runs, and "the tree of life that grows, in the midst of the paradise of God." The glorious excellencies and beauty of God will be what will for ever entertain the minds of the saints, and the love of God will be their everlasting feast. The redeemed will indeed enjoy other things; they will enjoy the angels, and will enjoy one another; but that which they shall

enjoy in the angels, or each other, or in any thing else whatsoever that will yield them delight and happiness, will be what shall be seen of God in them.

2. The redeemed have all their *inherent* good in God. Inherent good is twofold; it is either excellency or pleasure. These the redeemed not only derive from God, as caused by him, but have them in him. They have spiritual excellency and joy by a kind of participation of God. They are made excellent by a communication of God's excellency. God puts his own beauty, *i.e.* his beautiful likeness, upon their souls. They are made partakers of the divine nature, or moral image of God, 2 Pet. i. 4. They are holy by being made partakers of God's holiness. Heb. xii. 10. The saints are beautiful and blessed by a communication of God's holiness and joy, as the moon and planets are bright by the sun's light. The saint hath spiritual joy and pleasure by a kind of effusion of God on the soul. In these things the redeemed have communion with God; that is, they partake with him and of him.

The saints have both their spiritual excellency and blessedness by the gift of the Holy Ghost, and his dwelling in them. They are not only caused by the Holy Ghost, but are in him as their principle. The Holy Spirit becoming an inhabitant, is a vital principle in the soul. He, acting in, upon, and with the soul, becomes a fountain of true holiness and joy, as a spring is of water, by the exertion and diffusion of itself. John iv. 14. "But whosoever drinketh of the water that I shall give him, shall never thirst; but the water that I shall give him, shall be in him a well of water springing up into everlasting life." Compared with chap. vii. 38, 39. "He that believeth on me, as the Scripture hath said, out of his belly shall flow rivers of living water; but this spake he of the Spirit, which they that believe on him should receive." The sum of what Christ has purchased for us, is that spring of water spoken of in the former of those places, and those rivers of living water spoken of in the latter. And the sum of the blessings, which the redeemed shall receive in heaven, is that river of water of life that proceeds from the throne of God and the Lamb, Rev. xxii. 1. Which doubtless signifies the same with those rivers of living water, explained, John vii. 38, 39, which is elsewhere called the "river of God's pleasures." Herein consists the fulness of good, which the saints receive of Christ.

It is by partaking of the Holy Spirit, that they have communion with Christ in his fulness. God hath given the Spirit, not by measure unto him; and they do receive of his fulness, and grace for grace. This is the sum of the saints' inheritance; and therefore that little of the Holy Ghost which believers have in this world, is said to be the earnest of their inheritance, 2 Cor. i. 22. "Who hath also sealed us, and given us the earnest of the Spirit in our hearts." And chap. v. 5. "Now he that hath wrought us for the self-same thing, is God, who also hath given unto us the earnest of the Spirit." And Eph. i. 13, 14. "Ye were sealed with that holy Spirit of promise, which is the earnest of our inheritance, until the redemption of the purchased possession."

The Holy Spirit and good things are spoken of in Scripture as the same; as if the Spirit of God communicated to the soul, comprised all good things, Matt. vii. 11. "How much more shall your heavenly Father give good things to them that ask him?" In Luke it is, chap. xi. 13. "How much more shall your heavenly Father give the Holy Spirit to them that ask him?" This is the sum of the blessings that Christ died to procure, and the subject of gospel-promises. Gal. iii. 13, 14. "He was made a curse for us, that we might receive the promise of the Spirit through faith." The Spirit of God is the great promise of the Father, Luke xxiv. 49. "Behold, I send the promise of my Father upon you." The Spirit of God therefore is called "the Spirit of promise," Eph. i. 33. This promised thing Christ received, and had given into his hand, as soon as he had finished the work of our redemption, to bestow on all that he had redeemed; Acts ii. 13. "Therefore being by the right hand of God exalted, and having received of the Father the promise of the Holy Ghost, he hath shed forth this, which ye both see and hear." So that all the holiness and happiness of the redeemed is in God. It is in the communications, indwelling, and acting of the Spirit of God. Holiness and happiness is in the fruit, here and hereafter, because God dwells in them, and they in God.

Thus God has given us the Redeemer, and it is by him that our good is purchased. So God is the Redeemer and the price; and he also is the good purchased. So that all that we have is of God, and through him, and in him. Rom. xi. 36. "For of him, and through him, and to him, or in him, are all things." The same in the Greek that is here rendered *to him*, is rendered *in him*, 1 Cor. viii. 6.

II. God is glorified in the work of redemption by this means, viz. By there being so great and universal a dependence of the redeemed on him.

1. Man hath so much the greater occasion and obligation to notice and acknowledge God's perfections and all-sufficiency. The greater the creature's dependence is on God's perfections, and the greater concern he has with them, so much the greater occasion has he to take notice of them. So much the greater concern any one has with and dependence upon the power and grace of God, so much the greater occasion has he to take notice of that power and grace. So much the greater and more immediate dependence there is on the divine holiness, so much the greater occasion to take notice of and acknowledge that. So much the greater and more absolute dependence we have on the divine perfections, as belonging to the several persons of the Trinity, so much the greater occasion have we to observe and own the divine glory of each of them. That which we are most concerned with, is surely most in the way of our observation and notice; and this kind of concern with any thing, viz. dependence, does especially tend to command and oblige the attention and observation. Those things that we are not much dependent upon, it is easy to neglect; but we can scarce do any other than mind that which we have a great dependence on. By reason of our so great dependence on God, and his perfections, and in so many respects, he and his glory are the more directly set in our view, which way soever we turn our eyes.

We have the greater occasion to take notice of God's all-sufficiency, when all our sufficiency is thus every way of him. We have the more occasion to contemplate him as an infinite good, and as the fountain of all good. Such a dependence on God demonstrates his all-sufficiency. So much as the dependence of the creature is on God, so much the greater does the creature's emptiness in himself appear; and so much the greater the creature's emptiness, so much the greater must the fulness of the Being be who supplies him. Our having all *of* God, shows the fulness of his power and grace; our having all *through* him, shows the fulness of his merit and worthiness; and our having all *in* him, demonstrates his fulness of beauty, love, and happiness.

And the redeemed, by reason of the greatness of their dependence on God, have not only so much the greater occasion, but obligation to contemplate and acknowledge the glory and fulness of God. How unreasonable and ungrateful should we be, if we did not acknowledge that sufficiency and glory which we absolutely, immediately, and universally depend upon!

2. Hereby is demonstrated how great God's glory is considered comparatively, or as compared with the creature's.—By the creature being thus wholly and universally dependent on God, it appears that the creature is nothing, and that God is all. Hereby it appears that God is infinitely above us; that God's strength, and wisdom, and holiness, are infinitely greater than ours. However great and glorious the creature apprehends God to be, yet if he be not sensible of the difference between God and him, so as to see that God's glory is great, compared with his own, he will not be disposed to give God the glory due to his name. If the creature in any respects sets himself upon a level with God, or exalts himself to any competition with him, however he may apprehend that great honour and profound respect may belong to God from those that are at a greater distance, he will not be so sensible of its being due from him. So much the more men exalt themselves, so much the less will they surely be disposed to exalt God. It is certainly what God aims at in the disposition of things in redemption, (if we allow the Scriptures to be a revelation of God's mind,) that God should appear full, and man in himself empty, that God should appear all, and man nothing. It is God's declared design that others should not " glory in his presence;" which implies that it is his design to advance his own comparative glory. So much the more man " glories in God's presence," so much the less glory is ascribed to God.

3. By its being thus ordered, that the creature should have so absolute and universal a dependence on God, provision is made that God should have our whole souls, and should be the object of our undivided respect. If we had our dependence partly on God, and partly on something else, man's respect would be divided to those different things on which he had dependence. Thus it would be if we depended on God only for a part of our good, and on ourselves, or some other being, for another part: or if we had our good only from God, and through another that was not God, and in something else distinct from both, our

hearts would be divided between the good itself, and him from whom, and him through whom, we received it. But now there is no occasion for this, God being not only he from or of whom we have all good, but also through whom, and is that good itself, that we have from him and through him. So that whatsoever there is to attract our respect, the tendency is still directly towards God; all unites in him as the centre.

USE

1. We may here observe the marvellous wisdom of God, in the work of redemption. God hath made man's emptiness and misery, his low, lost, and ruined state, into which he sunk by the fall, an occasion of the greater advancement of his own glory, as in other ways, so particularly in this, that there is now much more universal and apparent dependence of man on God. Though God be pleased to lift man out of that dismal abyss of sin and woe into which he was fallen, and exceedingly to exalt him in excellency and honour, and to a high pitch of glory and blessedness, yet the creature hath nothing in any respect to glory of; all the glory evidently belongs to God, all is in a mere, and most absolute, and divine dependence on the Father, Son, and Holy Ghost. And each person of the Trinity is equally glorified in this work: there is an absolute dependence of the creature on every one for all: all is of the Father, all through the Son, and all in the Holy Ghost. Thus God appears in the work of redemption as all in all. It is fit that he who is, and there is none else, should be the Alpha and Omega, the first and the last, the all and the only, in this work.

2. Hence those doctrines and schemes of divinity that are in any respect opposite to such an absolute and universal dependence on God, derogate from his glory, and thwart the design of our redemption. And such are those schemes that put the creature in God's stead, in any of the mentioned respects, that exalt man into the place of either Father, Son, or Holy Ghost, in any thing pertaining to our redemption. However they may allow of a dependence of the redeemed on God, yet they deny a dependence that is so *absolute* and universal. They own an entire dependence of God for *some* things, but not for others; they own that we depend on God for the gift and acceptance of a Re-

deemer, but deny so absolute a dependence on him for the obtaining of an *interest* in the Redeemer. They own an absolute dependence on the Father for giving his Son, and on the Son for working out redemption, but not so entire a dependence on the Holy Ghost for *conversion*, and a being in Christ, and so coming to a title to his benefits. They own a dependence on God for *means* of grace, but not absolutely for the benefit and success of those means; a partial dependence on the power of God, for obtaining and exercising holiness, but not a mere dependence on the arbitrary and sovereign grace of God. They own a dependence on the free grace of God for a reception into his favour, so far that it is without any proper merit, but not as it is without being attracted, or moved with any excellency. They own a partial dependence on Christ, as he through whom we have life, as having purchased new terms of life, but still hold that the righteousness through which we have life is inherent in ourselves, as it was under the first covenant. Now whatever scheme is inconsistent with our *entire* dependence on God for all, and of having all of him, through him, and in him, it is repugnant to the design and tenor of the gospel, and robs it of that which God accounts its lustre and glory.

3. Hence we may learn a reason why faith is that by which we come to have an interest in this redemption; for there is included in the nature of faith, a sensible acknowledgment of *absolute dependence* on God in this affair. It is very fit that it should be required of all, in order to their having the benefit of this redemption, that they should be sensible of, and acknowledge, their dependence on God for it. It is by this means that God hath contrived to glorify himself in redemption; and it is fit that he should at least have this glory of those that are the subjects of this redemption, and have the benefit of it.—Faith is a sensibleness of what is real in the work of redemption; and the soul that believes doth entirely depend on God for all salvation, in its own sense and act. Faith abases men, and exalts God; it gives all the glory of redemption to him alone. It is necessary in order to saving faith, that man should be emptied of himself, be sensible that he is " wretched, and miserable, and poor, and blind, and naked." Humility is a great ingredient of true faith: he that truly receives redemption, receives it as a little child, Mark x. 15. " Whosoever shall not receive the kingdom of heaven

as a little child, he shall not enter therein." It is the delight of a believing soul to abase itself and exalt God alone: that is the language of it, Psalm cxv. 1. "Not unto us, O Lord, not unto us, but to thy name give glory."

4. Let us be exhorted to exalt God alone, and ascribe to him all the glory of redemption. Let us endeavour to obtain, and increase in, a sensibleness of our great dependence on God, to have our eye to him alone, to mortify a self-dependent and self-righteous disposition. Man is naturally exceeding prone to exalt himself, and depend on his own power or goodness; as though from himself he must expect happiness. He is prone to have respect to enjoyments alien from God and his Spirit, as those in which happiness is to be found.—But this doctrine should teach us to exalt God *alone*; as by trust and reliance, so by praise. *Let him that glorieth, glory in the Lord.* Hath any man hope that he is converted, and sanctified, and that his mind is endowed with true excellency and spiritual beauty? that his sins are forgiven, and he received into God's favour, and exalted to the honour and blessedness of being his child, and an heir of eternal life? let him give God all the glory; who alone makes him to differ from the worst of men in this world, or the most miserable of the damned in hell. Hath any man much comfort and strong hope of eternal life, let not his hope lift him up, but dispose him the more to abase himself, to reflect on his own exceeding unworthiness of such a favour, and to exalt God alone. Is any man eminent in holiness, and abundant in good works, let him take nothing of the glory of it to himself, but ascribe it to him whose " workmanship we are, created in Christ Jesus unto good works."

Sermon III

GOD MAKES MEN SENSIBLE OF THEIR MISERY BEFORE HE REVEALS HIS MERCY AND LOVE

HOSEA v. 15

I will go and return to my place, till they acknowledge their offence, and seek my face: in their affliction they will seek me early.

IN the preceding part of the chapter is threatened the destruction of Ephraim. Ephraim, in the prophets, generally means the ten tribes, or the kingdom of Israel, as distinguished from the kingdom of Judah. When we read of Ephraim and Judah in the prophets, thereby is meant the whole people of Israel of the twelve tribes, as in verse 12 of this chapter, "Therefore will I be unto Ephraim as a moth, and to the house of Judah as rottenness." By Judah is meant the two tribes of Judah and Benjamin, which were under the king of Judah; and by Ephraim is meant the ten tribes under the king of Israel. Ephraim is put for the whole kingdom of Israel, because Samaria, the seat of the kingdom, the royal city, was in that tribe. In the verse immediately preceding the text it is declared in what a terrible manner God was about to deal with Ephraim. "For I will be unto Ephraim as a lion, and as a young lion to the house of Judah; I, even I, will tear and go away, and none shall rescue him." In the text God declares how he would deal with them after he had torn as a lion, etc. And here,

1. God declares how he would withdraw from them. "I will go and return to my place;" when I have torn as a lion. I will go away; I will leave them in that condition. I will depart from them, and they shall see no more of me.

2. What God will wait for in them before he returns to them to show them mercy. There are three things here signified.

1. That they should be sensible of their guilt. "Till they

acknowledge their offence." It is in the original, "till they become guilty." That is, till they become guilty in their own eyes,
till they are sensible of their guilt; in the same sense as the same
expression is used in Rom. iii. 19. "That every mouth may be
stopped, and all the world may become guilty before God:"
that is, become guilty in their own eyes.

2. That they would be sensible of their misery, implied in the
expression, "in their affliction they shall seek me." Their
calamity was brought upon them, before God had torn them,
and left them. But in their pride and perverseness, they were
not well sensible of their own miserable condition, as this prophet
observes in chapter vii. 9.

3. That they should be sensible of their need of God's help,
which is implied in their seeking God's face, and seeking him
early; that is, with great care and earnestness. Before, they
would not seek God; they were not sensible of their helplessness,
as we learn in the verse but one preceding the text. "When
Ephraim saw his sickness, and Judah his wound, then went
Ephraim to the Assyrian, and sent to king Jareb." But as we
are there told, he could not heal him, nor cure his wound. And
notwithstanding all the help he could afford, God wounded him,
tore him as a young lion; and, as he declares, would leave him,
and he should cease going to any other, and should be sensible
that no other could heal, and accordingly come to him for healing.

Doctrine. That it is God's manner to make men sensible of
their misery and unworthiness, before he appears in his mercy
and love to them.

I. That it is ordinarily thus with respect to the bestowment of
great and signal mercies.

II. That it is particularly so with respect to revealing his love
and mercy to their souls.

I. This is God's ordinary way before great and signal expressions of his mercy and favour. He very commonly so orders it
in his providence, and so influences men by his Spirit, that they
are brought to see their miserable condition as they are in themselves, and to despair of help from themselves, or from an arm
of flesh, before he appears for them, and also makes them sensible
of their sin, and their unworthiness of God's help. This appears
from the account which the Scriptures give us of God's dealings

with his people. Joseph, before his great advancement in Egypt, must lie in the dungeon to humble him, and prepare him for such honour and prosperity. The children of Jacob, before Joseph reveals himself to them, and they receive that joy, and honour, and prosperity, which were consequent thereupon, pass through a train of difficulties and anxieties, till at last they are reduced to distress, and are brought to reflect upon their guilt, and to say, that they were verily guilty concerning their brother. God humbled them in his providence, and then an end was put to all their difficulties, and their sorrow was turned into joy upon Joseph's revealing himself to them. Jacob, before he hears the joyful news of Joseph's being yet alive, must be brought into great distress at the parting with Benjamin, and supposed loss of Simeon. He was reduced to great straits in his mind. He says in Gen. xlii. 36. "All these things are against me." But soon after this he had these gladsome tidings brought to him, "Joseph is yet alive, and he is governor over all the land of Egypt." And to confirm it, he sees the waggons and the noble presents, which Joseph sent to him: so that he was now brought to say, "It is enough; Joseph my son is yet alive. I will go and see him before I die." And so with the children of Israel in Egypt. Their bondage must wax more and more extreme. Their bondage had been very extreme. But yet Pharaoh gives commandment that more work should be laid upon them, and the task-masters tell them they must get their straw where they can find it; and nothing of their work should be diminished. And quickly upon this was their deliverance. So when the children of Israel were brought to the Red sea, the Egyptians pursued them, and were just at their heels, and they were reduced to the utmost distress, they see that they must assuredly perish, unless God work a miracle for them; for they were shut up on all sides: the Red sea was before them, and the army of the Egyptians encompassing them round behind. And they cried unto the Lord. And then God wonderfully appeared for their help, and made them pass through the Red sea, and put songs of deliverance into their mouths.

So before God brought the children of Israel into Canaan, he led them about in a great and terrible wilderness through a train of difficulties and temptations for forty years, that he might teach them their dependence on him, and the sinfulness of

their own hearts. Deut. xxxii. 10. "He found him in a desert
land, and in the waste howling wilderness; he led him about, he
instructed him, he kept him as the apple of his eye." God
brought them into those trials and difficulties in the wilderness
to humble them, and let them see what was in their hearts, that
they might be convinced of their own perverseness by the many
discoveries of it under those temptations, and so that they might
be sensible that it was not for their righteousness that God made
them his people, and gave them Canaan, seeing it was so evident
that they were a stiff-necked people. Deut. viii. 2, 3. "And thou
shalt remember all the way which the Lord thy God led thee
these forty years in the wilderness, to humble thee, and to prove
thee, to know what was in thine heart, whether thou wouldest
keep his commandments, or no. And he humbled thee and
suffered thee to hunger, and fed thee with manna, which thou
knewest not, neither did thy fathers know; that he might make
thee know that man doth not live by bread only, but by every
word that proceedeth out of the mouth of the Lord doth man
live." And 15, 16, 17. "Who led thee through that great and
terrible wilderness, wherein were fiery serpents, and scorpions,
and drought, where there was no water; who brought thee forth
water out of the rock of flint; who fed thee in the wilderness with
manna, which thy fathers knew not, that he might humble thee,
and that he might prove thee, to do thee good at thy latter end;
and thou say in thine heart, My power and the might of my
hand hath gotten me this wealth." And so we have examples of
this from time to time in the history of the Judges. When Israel
revolted, God gave them into the hands of their enemies. He let
them continue in their hands, till they were reduced to great
distress, and saw that they were in a helpless condition, and were
brought to reflect on themselves, and to cry unto the Lord. And
then God raised them up a deliverer. And when they cried unto
God, he would not deliver them till he had humbled them, and
brought them to own their unworthiness, and to own that they
were in God's hands. Judges x. beginning with the 10th verse.
"And the children of Israel cried unto the Lord, saying, We have
sinned against thee, both because we have forsaken our God, and
also served Balaam. And the Lord said unto the children of
Israel, Did not I deliver you from the Egyptians, and from the
Amorites, from the children of Ammon, and from the Philis-

tines? The Zidonians also, and the Amalekites, and the Maon-
ites, did oppress you; and ye cried to me, and I delivered you out
of their hand. Yet ye have forsaken me, and served other gods;
wherefore I will deliver you no more. Go and cry unto the gods
which ye have chosen; let them deliver you in the time of your
tribulation. And the children of Israel said unto the Lord, We
have sinned; do thou unto us whatsoever seemeth good unto
thee; deliver us only, we pray thee, this day. And they put away
the strange gods from among them, and served the Lord; and
his soul was grieved for the misery of Israel." And this is the
method in which God declared from the beginning he would
proceed with his people. Lev. xxvi. 40, etc. "If they shall confess their iniquity, and the iniquity of their fathers, with their
trespass which they trespassed against me, and that also they
have walked contrary unto me; and that I also have walked contrary unto them, and have brought them into the land of their
enemies; if then their uncircumcised hearts be humbled, and
they then accept of the punishment of their iniquity; then will
I remember my covenant with Jacob, and also my covenant with
Isaac, and also my covenant with Abraham will I remember;
and I will remember the land. The land also shall be left of
them, and shall enjoy her sabbaths, while she lieth desolate
without them; and they shall accept the punishment of their
iniquity; because, even because they despised my judgments, and
because their soul abhorred my statutes. And yet for all that,
when they be in the land of their enemies, I will not cast them
away, neither will I abhor them, to destroy them utterly, and to
break my covenant with them; for I am the Lord their God. But
I will for their sakes remember the covenant of their ancestors,
whom I brought forth out of the land of Egypt in the sight of
the heathen, that I might be their God." It is God's manner,
when he will bestow signal blessings in answer to prayer, to make
men seek them, and pray for them with a sense of sin and
misery. As 1 Kings viii. 38, 39. "What prayer and supplication
soever be made by any man, or by all thy people Israel, which
shall know every man the plague of his own heart, and spread
forth his hands toward this house; then hear thou in heaven, thy
dwelling-place, and forgive, and do, and give to every man according to his ways, whose heart thou knowest; for thou, even thou
only, knowest the hearts of all the children of men." By know-

ing the plague of their own hearts is meant both their sin and misery. Being sensible of their misery is included, as is evident from the manner of expressing the same petition of Solomon's prayer, as it is related in 2 Chron. vi. 29. " Then what prayer or supplication soever shall be made of any man, or of all thy people Israel, when every man shall know his own sore and his own grief." By which is probably meant his misery and his sin, which is the foundation of it. Paul gives us an account how God brought him to have despair in himself before a great deliverance, which he experienced. 2 Cor. i. 9, 10. " But we had the sentence of death in ourselves, that we should not trust in ourselves, but in God, which raiseth the dead; who delivered us from so great a death." How did Christ humble the woman of Canaan, or bring her to the exercise and expression of a sense of her own unworthiness before he answered her, and healed her daughter! When she continued to cry, after he answered her not a word, and seemed to take no notice of her, and his disciples desired him to send her away, and when she continued crying after him, he gave a very humbling answer, saying, It is not meet to take the children's bread, and to cast it to dogs. And when she took it well, as owning that being called a dog was not too bad, and owning that she was therefore unworthy of children's bread, she only sought the crumbs, then Christ answered her request. And the experience of God's people in all ages corresponds with those examples. It is God's usual method before remarkable discoveries of his mercy and love to them, especially by spiritual mercies, in a special manner to humble them, and make them sensible of their misery and helplessness in themselves, and of their vileness and unworthiness, either by some remarkably humbling dispensation of his providence or influence of his Spirit. We are come now,

II. To show particularly that it is God's manner to make men sensible of their misery and unworthiness before he reveals his saving love and mercy to their souls. The mercy of God, which he shows to a sinner when he brings him home to the Lord Jesus Christ, is the greatest and most wonderful exhibition of mercy and love, of which men are ever the subjects. There are other things, in which God greatly expresses his mercy and goodness to men, many temporal favours. The mercies already mentioned, which God bestowed upon his people of old: his advancing

Joseph in Egypt, his deliverance of the children of Israel out of Egypt, his leading them through the Red sea on dry land, his bringing them into Canaan, and driving out the heathen from before them, his delivering them from time to time from the hands of their enemies, were great mercies; but they were not equal to this of his people from under the guilt and dominion of sin. Several of them were typical of this; and as God would thus prepare men for the bestowment of those less mercies by making them sensible of their guilt and misery, so especially will he so do, before he makes known to them this great love of his in Jesus Christ. When God designs to show mercy to sinners, it is his manner thus to begin with them.

He first brings them to reflect upon themselves, and consider and be sensible what they are, and what condition they are in. What has already been said proves this. There is a harmony between God's dispensations. And as we see that this is God's manner of dealing with men when he gives them other great and remarkable mercies and manifestations of his favour, it is a confirmation that it is his method of proceeding with the souls of men, when about to reveal his mercy and love to them in Jesus Christ.

1. God makes men consider and be sensible of what sin they are guilty. Before, it may be, they were very regardless of this. They went on sinning, and never reflected upon what they did; never considered or regarded what or how many sins they committed. They saw no cause why they should trouble their minds about it. But when God convinces them, he brings them to reflect upon themselves; he sets their sins in order before their eyes. He brings their old sins to their minds, so that they are fresh in their memory—things which they had almost forgotten. And many things, which they used to regard as light offences, which were not wont to be a burden to their consciences, nor to appear worthy to be taken notice of, they are now made to reflect upon. Thus they discover of what a multitude of transgressions they have been guilty, which they have heaped up till they are grown up to heaven. There are some sins especially, of which they have been guilty, which are ever before them, so that they cannot get them out of their minds. Sometimes when men are under conviction, their sins follow them, and haunt them like a spectre. God makes them sensible of the sin of their hearts, how

corrupt and depraved their hearts are. And there are two ways in which he does this. One is by setting before them the sins of their lives. They are so set in order before them, they appear so many and so aggravated, that they are convinced what a fountain of corruption there is in their hearts. Their sinful natures appear by their sinful lives. There is sin enough, which every man has committed, to convince him, that he is sold under sin, that his heart is full of nothing but corruption, if God by his Spirit leads him rightly to consider it.

Another way which God sometimes makes use of, is, to leave men to such internal workings of corruption under the temptations which they have in their terrors and fears of hell, as shows them what a corrupt and wicked heart they have. God sometimes brings this good out of this evil, to make men see the corruption of their nature by the workings of it under temptations, which they have in their terrors about damnation. God leads them through the wilderness to prove them, and let them know what is in their hearts, as he did the children of Israel, as we have already observed. By means of the trials which the children of Israel had in the wilderness, they might be made sensible what a murmuring, perverse, rebellious, unfaithful, and idolatrous people they were. So God sometimes makes sinners sensible what wicked hearts they have, by their experience of the exercises of corruption, while they are under convictions. Not that this will in the least excuse men for allowing such workings of corruption in their hearts, because God sometimes leaves men to be wicked, that he may afterwards turn it to their good, when he in infinite wisdom sees meet so to do. We must not go and be wicked on purpose that we may get good by it. It will be very absurd, as well as horridly presumptuous, for us so to do. Though God sometimes in his sovereign mercy makes those workings of corruption, and a spirit of opposition and enmity against God, a means of showing them the vileness of their own hearts, and so to turn to their good. So God oftentimes is provoked thereby utterly to withdraw and forsake them, after the example of those murmurers, whose carcasses fell in the wilderness, of whom God sware in his wrath that they should never enter into his rest. And they who allow themselves therein, are the most likely so to provoke God. But it is God's manner to show men the plague of their own hearts by some means or other, before he reveals his redeeming love to their souls. While sinners are unconvinced, sin lies hid. They take no notice of it. But God makes the law effectual to bring men's own sins of heart and life to be reflected on, and observed. Romans vii. 9. " I was alive without the law once, but when the commandment came, sin revived." Then sin appeared and came to light, which was not before observed. Joseph's revealing himself to his brethren, is probably typical of Christ's revealing himself to the soul of a sinner, making known himself in his love, and in his near relation of a brother, and a redeemer of his soul. But before Joseph revealed himself to them, they were made to reflect upon themselves, and, say, " we are verily guilty."

2. God convinces sinners of the dreadful danger they are in by reason of their sin. Having their sins set before them, God makes them sensible of the relation which their sin has to misery. And here are two things of which they are convinced about their danger.

1. God makes them sensible that his displeasure is very dreadful. Before they heard often about the anger of God, and the fierceness of his wrath; but they were not moved by it. But now they are made sensible that it is a dreadful thing to fall into the hands of the living God. They are made in some measure sensible of the dreadfulness of hell. They are led with fixedness of impression to think what a dismal thing it will be to have God an enraged enemy, setting to work the misery of a soul, and how dismal it will be to dwell in such torment for ever without hope. Isaiah xxxiii. 14. " The sinners in Zion are afraid; fearful- ness hath surprised the hypocrites. Who among us shall dwell with the devouring fire? who among us shall dwell with everlasting burnings?" Other sinners are told of hell, but convinced sinners often have hell, as it were, in their view. Their being impressed with a sense of the dreadfulness of its misery, is the cause why it works upon their imagination oftentimes; and it will seem as though they saw the dismal flames of hell; as though they saw God in implacable wrath exerting his fury upon them; as though they heard the cries and shrieks of the damned.

2. They are made in some measure sensible of the connexion there is between their sins and that wrath, or how their sin and guilt exposes them to that wrath, of the dreadfulness of which they have such lively apprehensions, and so fear takes hold of

them. They are afraid that will be their portion. And they are sensible that they are in a miserable and doleful condition by reason of sin. Many things in the Scriptures make it evident that this is God's method. The account we have of our first parents confirms it. They had a sense of guilt and danger, before Christ was revealed to them. They were guilty, and were afraid of God's wrath, and ran and hid themselves. They were terribly afraid when they heard God coming. And doubtless their sense of their guilt and fear, when they were brought before God, and were called to an account, and God asked them what they had done, and whether they had eaten of that tree, whereof he commanded them that they should not eat, prepared them for a discovery of mercy. God made them sensible of their guilt and danger before he revealed to them the covenant of grace. And it is probable that their reflecting upon what God said about the seed of the woman bruising the serpent's head, soon wrought faith; that it was not long before the discovery God made of a merciful design towards them was a means of true consolation and hope to them. Joseph's brethren were brought into great distress for fear of their lives before Joseph revealed himself to them. Those who were converted by Peter's sermon were first pricked in their hearts in a sense of their guilt and their danger. Acts ii. 37. And Paul, before he had his first comfort, trembled, and was astonished. Acts ix. 6. And continued three days and three nights, and neither ate nor drank, which expressed his great distress. The jailer, before he was converted, was in terror. He called for a light, and sprang in, and came trembling, and fell down before Paul and Silas. Acts xvi. 29, 30. Christ's invitation is made more especially to the weary and heavy laden; which doubtless has respect, at least partly, to labouring and being weary with a sense of guilt and danger. We read when David was in the cave, that every one who was in distress, was gathered unto him. 1 Sam. xxii. 1. This doubtless was written as typifying Jesus Christ, and the referring of those who were in fear and distress unto him. The expression of flying for refuge, by which coming to Christ is signified, implies, that before they come, they are in fear of some evil. They apprehend themselves in danger, and this fear gives wings to their feet. Prov. xviii. 10. " The name of the Lord is a strong tower." The voice of God to a sinner, when he gives him true comfort, is a still small voice. But this voice is preceded by a strong wind, and a terrible earthquake, and fire, as it was in Horeb when Elijah was there. 1 Kings xix. 11, 12. "And, behold, the Lord passed by, and a great and strong wind rent the mountains and brake in pieces the rocks before the Lord; but the Lord was not in the wind; and after the wind an earthquake; but the Lord was not in the earthquake; and after the earthquake a fire; but the Lord was not in the fire; and after the fire a still small voice."

Another thing in the Scriptures, which seems to evince this, is the frequent comparison made between the church spiritually bringing forth Christ, and a woman in travail, in pain to be delivered. John xvi. 21. and Revelation xii. 2. The conversion of a sinner is represented by the same thing. It is bringing forth Christ in the heart. Paul speaks of men's regeneration as of Christ being brought forth in them. Gal. iv. 19. And therefore Christ calls believers his mother. Matt. xii. 49, 50. "And he stretched forth his hand toward his disciples, and said, Behold my mother and my brethren! For whosoever shall do the will of my Father which is in heaven, the same is my brother, and sister, and mother."

Hosea v. 15. "I will go and return to my place till they acknowledge their offence, and seek my face: in their affliction they will seek me early." (Till they shall be guilty, in the original.)

Doctrine. That it is God's manner to make men sensible of their misery and unworthiness, before he appears in his mercy and love to them.

III. They are made sensible of the desert of their sin; that their sin deserves that wrath of God to which it exposes them. They are not only sensible of the dreadfulness of God's wrath, how fearful a thing it would be to fall into the hands of the living God, and to sustain the eternal expressions of his fierce anger, as well as of the connexion between their sins and this wrath, and how their sins expose them to it; but God is also wont, before he comforts them, to show them that their sins deserve this wrath. By a clear discovery of the connexion between their sin and God's wrath, they are sensible of their danger of hell; of which many are in a measure sensible, who are wholly insensible of their desert of hell. The threatenings of the law make them afraid indeed, that God will punish sins; yet they have no thorough apprehension of their desert of the punishment threatened; and

therefore many, who are afraid, murmur against God. They
charge him foolishly with being hard and cruel. But it is God's
manner before he speaks peace to them, and reveals his redeeming love and mercy in Jesus Christ, to make them sensible that
they also deserve it. Thus Matt. xviii. 24, 25, 26. " And when he
had begun to reckon, one was brought unto him which owed
him ten thousand talents. But forasmuch as he had not to pay,
his lord commanded him to be sold, and his wife and children
and all that he had, and payment to be made. The servant
therefore fell down and worshipped him, saying, Lord, have
patience with me, and I will pay thee all. Then the lord of that
servant was moved with compassion, and loosed him, and for-
gave him the debt." Very commonly when men are first made
sensible of their danger, their mouths are open against God and
his dealings; that is, their hearts are full of murmurings. But it
is God's manner before he comforts and reveals his mercy and
love to them, to stop their mouths, and make them acknowledge
their guilt, or their desert of the threatened punishment. Rom.
iii, 19, 20. "Now we know that what things soever the law saith,
it saith to them who are under the law, that every mouth may
be stopped, and all the world may become guilty before God.
Therefore, by the deeds of the law there shall no flesh be justified
in his sight; for by the law is the knowledge of sin." God would
convince men of their guilt before he reveals a pardon to them.
Now a man cannot be said to be thoroughly sensible of his guilt,
till he is sensible that he deserves hell. A man must be sensible
that he is guilty of death, or guilty of damnation, to use the
scriptural mode of expression, before God will reveal to him his
freedom from damnation. A sense of guilt consists in two things
—in a sense of sin, and in a sense of the relation which sin has to
punishment. Now the relation which sin has to punishment, is
also twofold: first, the connexion which it has with punishment,
by which it exposes to it, and brings it; and secondly, its desert
of punishment. When a man is truly convinced of his desert of
the punishment to which his sin exposes him, then he may be
said to be thoroughly sensible of his guilt. Then he is become
guilty, in the sense of our text, and in the sense of Rom. iii. 20.

Inquiry. How is it that a sinner is made sensible of his desert
of God's wrath? A natural man may have a sense of this, though
not the same sense which a person may have after conversion;

because a natural man cannot have a true sight of sin, and of the evil of it. A man cannot truly know the evil of sin against God, except it be by a discovery of his glory and excellence; and then he will be sensible how great an evil it is to sin against him. Yet it cannot be denied that natural men are capable of a conviction of their desert of hell, or that their consciences may be convinced of it without a sight of God's glory. The consciences of wicked men will also be convinced of the justice of their sentence and of their punishment at the day of judgment; and doubtless will echo to the sentence of the Judge, and condemn them to the same punishment. Here, therefore, we would inquire how it is that a natural man may be made sensible of this. 1. We shall show what is the principle assisted. 2. How it is assisted. And 3. What are the chief external means which are used in order to this.

1. What principle in man is assisted in convincing him of his desert of eternal punishment? No new principle is infused. Natural men have only natural principles; and therefore all that is done by the Spirit of God before regeneration is by assisting natural principles. To observe, therefore, in answer to this inquiry,

That the principle, which is assisted in making natural men sensible of their desert of wrath, is natural conscience. Though man has lost a principle of love to God, and all spiritual principles, by the fall, yet natural conscience remains. Now there are two things, which are the proper work of natural conscience. One is to give man a sense of right and wrong. A natural man has no sense of the beauty and amiableness of virtue, or of the turpitude and odiousness of vice. But yet every man has that naturally within, which testifies to him that some things are right, and others wrong. Thus if a man steals, or commits murder, there is something within, which tells him that he has done wrong; he knows that he has not done right. Rom. ii. 14, 15. "For when the Gentiles, which have not the law, do by nature the things contained in the law, these having not the law, are a law unto themselves; which show the work of the law written in their hearts, their conscience also bearing witness, and their thoughts the mean while accusing, or else excusing, one another." And the other work of natural conscience is to suggest the relation there is between right and wrong, and a retribution. Man has that in him, which suggests to him, when he has done ill, a relation between that ill and punishment. If a man has done that which his conscience tells him is wrong, is unjust, his conscience tells him that he deserves to be punished for it. Thus natural conscience has a twofold power; a teaching, or accusing, and a condemning power. The Spirit of God, therefore, assists natural conscience the more thoroughly to do this, its work, and so convinces a man of sin. Conscience naturally suggests, when he has done a known evil, that he deserves punishment; and being assisted to its work thoroughly, a man is convinced that he deserves eternal punishment. Though natural conscience does remain in the man since the fall, yet it greatly needs assistance in order to its work. It is greatly hindered in doing its work by sin. Every thing in man, which is part of his perfection, is hindered and impaired by sin. A faculty of reason remains since the fall, but it is greatly impaired and blinded. So natural conscience remains, but sin, in a great degree, stupifies it, and hinders it in its work. Now when God convinces a sinner, he assists his conscience against the stupefaction of sin, and helps it to do its work more freely and fully. The Spirit of God works immediately upon men's consciences. In conviction their consciences are awakened. They are convinced in their consciences. Their consciences smite them and condemn them.

2. It may be inquired, How God assists natural conscience so as to convince the sinner of his desert of hell? I answer,

1. In general, it is by light. The whole work of God is carried on in the heart of man from his first convictions to his conversion by light. It is by discoveries which are made to his soul. But by what light is it, that a sinner is made sensible that he deserves God's wrath? It is some discovery that he has, which makes him sensible of the heinousness of disobeying and casting contempt upon God. The light which gives evangelical humiliation, and which makes man sensible of the hateful and odious nature of sin, is a discovery of God's glory and excellence and grace. But what is it which a natural man sees of God, which makes him sensible that sin against God deserves his wrath; for he sees nothing of the excellence and loveliness of God's glory and grace? I answer,

2. Particularly, it seems to be a discovery of God's awful and terrible greatness. Natural men cannot see any thing of God's

loveliness, his amiable and glorious grace, or any thing which should attract their love; but they may see his terrible greatness to excite their terror. Wicked men in another world, though they do not see his loveliness and grace, yet they see his awful greatness, and that makes them sensible of the heinousness of sin. The damned in hell are sensible of the heinousness of their sin. Their consciences declare it to them. And they are made sensible of it by what they see of the awful greatness of that Being, against whom they have sinned. And wicked men in this world are capable of being made sensible of the heinousness of sin the same way. If a wicked soul is capable while wicked of receiving the discoveries of God's terrible majesty in another world, it is capable of it in this. God may, if he pleases, make wicked men sensible of the same thing here. And in this way natural men may be so made sensible of the heinousness of sin, as to be convinced that they deserve hell; as is evident in that it is by this very means, that wicked men will be made sensible of the justice of their punishment in another world, and at the day of judgment. For then the wicked will see so much of the awful greatness of God, the Judge, that it will convince their consciences what a heinous thing it was in them to disobey and contemn such a God, and will convince them that they therefore deserve his wrath. Which shows that wicked men are capable of being convinced in the same way. A wicked man, while a wicked man, is capable of hearing the thunders, and seeing the devouring fire, of mount Sinai; that is, he is capable of being made sensible of that terrible majesty and greatness of God, which was discovered at the giving of the law. But this brings me to the

3. Thing, *viz.* the principal outward means, which the Spirit of God makes use of in this work of convincing men of their desert of hell. And that is the law. The Spirit of God in all his work upon the souls of men, works by his word. And in this whole work of conviction of sin, that part of the word is principally made use of; *viz.* the Law. It is the law which makes men sensible of their sin; and it is the law, attended with its awful threatenings and curses, which gives a sense of the awful greatness, the authority, the power, the jealousy of God. Wicked men are made sensible of the tremendous greatness of God, as it were, in the same manner in which the children of Israel were; *viz.* by the thunders, and earthquake, and devouring fire, and

sound of the trumpet, and terrible voice at mount Sinai. All the people who were in the camp trembled, and they said, Let not God speak with us, lest we die. So that it is the law, which God makes use of in assisting the natural conscience to do its work. Gal. ii. 24. " Wherefore the law was our schoolmaster to bring us to Christ." It is the law which God makes use of, to make men sensible of their guilt, and to stop their mouths. Rom. iii. 19. " Now we know that whatsoever things the law saith, it saith to them that are under the law, that every mouth may be stopped, and all the world may become guilty before God." It is the law, which kills men as to trusting in their own righteousness. " For I was alive without the law once, but when the commandment came, sin revived, and I died." Gal. ii. 19. " For I through the law am dead to the law." Conviction, which precedes conversion, is of sin and misery. But men are not thoroughly sensible of their sin or guilt, till they are sensible they deserve hell; nor thoroughly sensible of their misery, till they are sensible they are helpless.

4. It is God's manner to make men sensible of their helplessness in their own strength. It is usual with sinners, when they are first made sensible of their danger of hell, to attempt by their own strength to save themselves. They in some measure see their danger, and endeavour to work out their own deliverance. They are striving to make themselves better. They strive to convert themselves, to work their hearts into a believing frame, and to exercise a saving trust in Christ. Having heard that if ever they believe, they must put their trust in Christ, and in him alone, for salvation, they think they will trust in Christ and cast their souls upon him. And this they endeavour to do in their own strength. This is very common with persons upon a sick bed, when they are afraid that they shall die and go to hell, and are told that they must put their trust in Christ alone for salvaion. They attempt to do it in their own strength. So sinners will be striving without a sense of their insufficiency in themselves to bring their own hearts to love God, and to choose him for their portion, and to repent of their sins. Or they strive to make themselves better, that so God may be more willing to convert them and give them his grace, and enable them to believe in Christ, and love God, and repent of their sins. But before God appears to them as their help and deliverance, it is his manner to

make them sensible that they are utterly helpless in themselves. They are brought to despair of help from themselves. There is a death to all their hopes from themselves. Rom. vii. 9. Before God opens the prison doors, he makes them see that they are shut up, that they are close prisoners, and that there is no way in which they can escape. Christ tells us in Isa. lxi. 1 that he was sent to bind up the broken-hearted, and to proclaim liberty to captives, and the opening of the prison to them that are bound. Christ was sent to open the prison to them that are not only really, but sensibly, bound. Gal. iii. 23. "But before faith came, we were kept under the law, shut up unto the faith, that should afterwards be revealed." God makes men sensible that they are in a forlorn condition, that they are wretched, and miserable, and blind, and naked, before he comforts them. Christ tells us in John ix. 39. "For judgment I am come into the world, that they which see not, might see; and that they which see, might be made blind;" meaning, partly at least, by those that see, those who think they see; having respect to the Pharisees, who were proud of their knowledge; and by the blind, those who are sensibly blind. This is emblematically represented by Saul's blindness before his first comfort. He was blind till Ananias came to him to open his eyes; probably designed to intimate to us, that before God opens the eyes of men in conversion, he makes them sensibly blind. God brings men to this despair in their own strength in these ways.

1. God oftentimes makes use of men's own experience to convince them that they are helpless in themselves. When they first set out in seeking salvation, it may be they thought it an easy thing to be converted. They thought they should presently bring themselves to repent of their sins, and believe in Christ, and accordingly they strove in their own strength with hopes of success. But they were disappointed. And so God suffers them to go on striving to open their own eyes, and mend their own hearts. But they find no success. They have been striving to see for a long time, yet they are as blind as ever; and can see nothing. It is all Egyptian darkness. They have been striving to make themselves better; but they are bad as ever. They have often striven to do something which is good, to be in the exercise of good affections, which should be acceptable to God; but they have no success. And it seems to them, that instead of growing

E

better, they grow worse and worse; their hearts are fuller of wicked thoughts than they were at first; they see no more likelihood of their conversion than there was at first. So God suffers them to strive in their own strength, till they are discouraged, and despair of helping themselves. The prodigal son first strove to fill his belly with the husks which the swine did eat. But when he despaired of being helped in that way, then he came to himself, and entertained thoughts of returning to his father's house.

2. God sometimes, by a particular assistance of the understanding, enables men to see so much of their own hearts, as at once causes them to despair of helping themselves. He sometimes convinces them by their own trials, suffering them to try a long time to effect their own salvation, until they are discouraged. But God, if he pleases, can convince men without such endeavours of their own; and sometimes he does so; as must be the case in many sudden conversions, of which the instances are not unfrequent. By revealing to them their own hearts, he sometimes enables them to perceive that they are so remote from the exercise of love to God, of faith, and of every other christian grace, as well as from the possession of the least degree of spiritual light, that they despair of ever bringing themselves to it. They perceive that within their souls all is darkness as darkness itself, and as the shadow of death, and that it is too much for them to cause light. They find themselves dead to any thing good, and therefore despair of bringing themselves to the performance of gracious acts. Thus we have shown that it is God's ordinary manner, before he reveals his redeeming mercy to the souls of men, to make them sensible of their sinfulness and danger, of their desert of the divine wrath, and of their utter helplessness in themselves. This we have shown to be most accordant with the Holy Scriptures, as well as with God's method of dealing with mankind in other things. And we have shown in an imperfect manner how, and by what means, it is, that God thus convinces men. This work is what Christ speaks of, as one part of the work of the Holy Ghost. John xvi. 8. "When he is come, he will convince the world of sin, and of righteousness, and of judgment." It is God's manner to convince men of sin, before he convinces them of righteousness.

I come now to show the reasons of the doctrine.

The propriety of such a method of proceeding is very obvious.

How agreeable to the divine wisdom does it seem, that the sinner should be brought to such a conviction of his danger and misery, as to perceive his utter incapacity to help himself by any strength or contrivance of his own, and his entire unworthiness of God's help, and desert of his wrath; and that he should be brought to acknowledge that God, in the exercise of his holy sovereignty, may with perfect justice deal thus with him before he appears in his pardoning mercy and love as his helper and friend. A man who is converted is successively in two exceedingly different states; first, a very miserable, wretched state of condemnation; and then in a blessed condition, a state of justification. How agreeable, therefore, does it seem to the divine wisdom, that such a man should be conscious of this: first, of his miserable, condemned state, and then of his happy state; that, as he is really first guilty, and under a deep desert of hell, before he is really pardoned and admitted to God's favour, so he should first be conscious that he is guilty, and under such a desert of hell, before he is conscious of being the object of pardoning and redeeming mercy and grace. But the propriety of God's thus dealing with the souls of men will appear perhaps better by considering the following reasons:

1. It is the will of God, that the discoveries of his terrible majesty, and awful holiness and justice, should accompany the discoveries of his grace and love, in order that he may give to his creatures worthy and just apprehensions of himself. It is the glory of God, that these attributes are united in the divine nature, that as he is a being of infinite mercy and love and grace, so he is a being of infinite and tremendous majesty, and awful holiness and justice. The perfect and harmonious union of these attributes in the divine nature, is what constitutes the chief part of their glory. God's awful and terrible attributes, and his mild and gentle attributes, reflect glory one on the other; and the exercise of the one is in perfect consistency and harmony with that of the other. If there were the exercise of the mild and gentle attributes without the other, if there were love and mercy and grace in inconsistency with God's authority and justice and infinite hatred of sin, it would be no glory. If God's love and grace did not harmonize with his justice and the honour of his majesty, far from being an honour, they would be a dishonour to God. Therefore as God designs to glorify himself when he makes

discoveries of the one, he will also make discoveries of the other. When he makes discoveries of his love and grace, it shall appear that they harmonize with those other attributes; otherwise his true glory would not be discovered. If men were sensible of the love of God without a sense of those other attributes, they would be exposed to have improper and unworthy apprehensions of God, as though he were gracious to sinners in such a manner as did not become a Being of infinite majesty and infinite hatred of sin. And as it would expose to unworthy apprehensions of God, so it would expose the soul in some respects to behave unsuitably towards God. There would not be a due reverence blended with love and joy. Such discoveries of love, without answerable discoveries of awful greatness, would dispose the soul to come with an undue boldness to God. The very nature and design of the gospel show that this is the will of God, that those who have the discoveries of his love, should also have the discoveries of those other attributes. For this was the very end of Christ's laying down his life, and coming into the world, to render the glory of God's authority, holiness, and justice, consistent with his grace in pardoning and justifying sinners, that while God thus manifested his mercy, we might not conceive any unworthy thoughts of him with respect to those other attributes. Seeing, therefore, that this is the very end of Christ's coming into the world, we may conclude that those who are actually redeemed by Christ, and have a true discovery of Christ made to their souls, have a discovery of God's terribleness and justice to prepare them for the discovery of his love and mercy. God, of old, before the death and suffering of Christ were so fully revealed, was ever careful that the discoveries of both should be together, so that men might not apprehend God's mercy in pardoning sin and receiving sinners, to the disparagement of his justice. When God proclaimed his name to Moses, in answer to his desire that he might see God's glory, he indeed proclaimed his mercy: "The Lord, the Lord God, gracious and merciful, long-suffering, and abundant in goodness and truth; keeping mercy for thousands, forgiving iniquity, and transgression, and sin." But he did not stop here, but also proclaimed his holy justice and vengeance; "and that will by no means clear the guilty; visiting the iniquity of the fathers upon the children, and upon the children's children unto the third and fourth generation." Thus they are joined together again in the fourth commandment. "For I, the Lord thy God, am a jealous God, visiting the iniquity of the fathers upon the children unto the third and fourth generation of them that hate me." Thus we find them joined together in passages too numerous to be mentioned. When God was about to speak to Elijah in Horeb, he was first prepared for such a familiar conversing with God by awful manifestations of the divine majesty. First there was a wind, which rent the rocks, and then an earthquake, and then a devouring fire. 1 Kings xix. 11, 12. God is careful even in heaven, where the discoveries of his love and grace are given in such an exalted degree, also to provide means for a proportional sense of his terribleness, and the dreadfulness of his displeasure, by their beholding it in the miseries and torments of the damned, at the same time that they enjoy his love. Even the man Christ Jesus was first made sensible of the wrath of God, before his exaltation to that transcendant height of enjoyment of the Father's love. And this is one reason that God gives sinners a sense of his wrath against their sins, and of his justice, before he gives them the discoveries of his redeeming love.

2. Unless a man be thus convinced of his sin and misery before God makes him sensible of his redeeming love and mercy, he cannot be sensible of that love and mercy as it is; *viz.* that it is free and sovereign. When God reveals his redeeming grace to men, and makes them truly sensible of it, he would make them sensible of it as it is. God's grace and love towards sinners is in itself very wonderful, as it redeems from dreadful wrath. But men cannot be sensible of this until they perceive in some adequate degree how dreadful the wrath of God is. God's redeeming grace and love in Christ is free and sovereign, as it is altogether without any worthiness in those who are the objects of it. But men cannot be sensible of this, until they are sensible of their own unworthiness. The grace of God in Christ is glorious and wonderful, as it is not only as the objects of it are without worthiness, but as they deserve the everlasting wrath and displeasure of God. But they cannot be sensible of this until they are made sensible that they deserve God's eternal wrath. The grace of God in Christ is wonderful, as it saves and redeems from so many and so great sins, and from the punishment they have deserved. But sinners cannot be sensible of this till they are in some measure sensible of their sinfulness, and brought to reflect

upon the sins of their lives, and to see the wickedness of their hearts. It is the glory of God's grace in Christ, that it is so free and sovereign. And doubtless it is the will of God, that when he reveals his grace to the soul, it should be seen in its proper glory, though not perfectly. When men see the glory of God's grace aright, they see it as free and unmerited, and contrary to the demerit of their sins. All who have a spiritual understanding of the grace of God in Christ, have a perception of the glory of that grace. But the glory of the divine grace appears chiefly in its being bestowed on the sinner when he is in a condition so exceedingly miserable and necessitous. In order, therefore, that the sinner may be sensible of this glory, he must first be sensible of the greatness of his misery, and then of the greatness of the divine mercy. The heart of man is not prepared to receive the mercy of God in Christ, as free and unmerited, till he is sensible of his own demerit. Indeed the soul is not capable of receiving a revelation or discovery of the redeeming grace of God in Christ, as redeeming grace, without being convinced of sin and misery. He must see his sin and misery before he can see the grace of God in redeeming him from that sin and misery.

3. Until the sinner is convinced of his sin and misery, he is not prepared to receive the redeeming mercy and grace of God, as through a Mediator; because he does not see his need of a Mediator till he sees his sin and misery. If there were, on the part of God, any exercise of absolute and immediate mercy towards sinners bestowed without any satisfaction or purchase, the soul might possibly see that without a conviction of its sin and misery. But there is not. All God's mercy to sinners is through a Saviour. The redeeming mercy and grace of God is mercy and grace in Christ. And when God discovers his mercy to the soul, he will discover it as mercy in a Saviour; and it is his will that the mercy should be received as in and through a Saviour, with a full consciousness of its being through his righteousness and satisfaction. It is the will of God, that as all the spiritual comforts which his people receive are in and through Christ, so they should be sensible that they receive them through Christ, and that they can receive them in no other way. It is the will of God, that his people should have their eyes directed to Christ, and should depend upon him for mercy and favour, that whenever they receive comforts through his purchase, they should receive them as from

him. And that because God would glorify his Son as Mediator, as the glory of man's salvation belongs to Christ, so it is the will of God that all the people of Christ, all who are saved by him, should receive their salvation as of him, and should attribute the glory of it to him; and that none who will not give the glory of salvation to Christ, should have the benefit of it. Upon this account God insists upon it, and it is absolutely necessary, that a sinner's conviction of his sin, and misery, and helplessness in himself, should precede or accompany the revelation of the re-deeming love and grace of God. I shall also mention two other ends which are hereby attained.

4. By this means the redeeming mercy and love of God are more highly prized and rejoiced in, when discovered. By the previous discoveries of danger, misery, and helplessness, and desert of wrath, the heart is prepared to embrace a discovery of mercy. When the soul stands trembling at the brink of the pit, and despairs of any help from itself, it is prepared joyfully to receive tidings of deliverance. If God is pleased at such a time to make the soul hear his still small voice, his call to himself and to a Saviour, the soul is prepared to give it a joyful reception. The gospel then, if it be heard spiritually, will be glad tidings indeed; the most joyful which the sinner ever heard. The love of God and of Christ to the world, and to him in particular, will be admired, and Christ will be most precious. To remember what danger he was in, what seas surrounded him; and then to reflect how safe he now is in Christ, and how sufficient Christ is to defend him, and to answer all his wants, will cause the greater exultation of soul. God, in this method of dealing with the souls of his elect, consults their happiness, as well as his own glory. And it increases happiness, to be made sensible of their misery and unworthiness, before God comforts them; for their comfort, when they receive it, is so much the sweeter.

5. The heart is more prepared and disposed to praise God for it. This follows from the reasons already mentioned; as they are hereby made sensible how free and sovereign the mercy of God is towards them, and how great his grace in saving them; and as they more highly prize the mercy and love of God made known to them: all will dispose them to magnify the name of God, to exalt the love of God the Father in giving his Son to them, and to exalt Jesus Christ by their praise, who laid down

his life for them to redeem them from all iniquity. They are ready to say, How miserable should I have been, had not God had pity upon me, and provided me a Saviour! In what a miserable condition should I have been, had not Christ loved me, and given himself for me! I must have endured that dreadful wrath of God; I must have suffered the punishment which I had deserved by all that great sin and wickedness of which I have been guilty.

APPLICATION

I. This subject admits of an application to unconverted sinners. If it be so, as has been represented, then let me exhort you to seek those convictions. Though you are at present sinners, and have no terrifying sense of your danger of hell, yet I presume to say concerning most of you at least, that you do not intend to go to hell. When you happen to think about another world, you flatter yourself, that in some way or other you shall escape eternal misery; or at least, you do not think of it with a willingness to be damned. But if it be, that you do not suffer eternal damnation, you have a great work to do before you die. It ordinarily is a very difficult work, especially to those who have gone on for a considerable time in ways of wickedness under the means of grace. If you are ever truly converted, you must be convinced of your misery and unworthiness; you must be guilty in your own sense. Begin your work, then, and seek to be made sensible of your misery and unworthiness. Make haste, and set about this work speedily. You may defer it so long, that it will be too late. It may be too late, if you delay, in these two ways. It may be too late, as you may be overtaken with death, before you set about it, as thousands and millions have been before you. And if you should not die before you begin, yet it may be too late, as you may never have an opportunity to get through. Some persons are a long time under convictions, before they are converted. There are some, whom God suffers to continue a long time seeking salvation in their own strength before he makes them despair of help from themselves. They continue many years trusting in their own righteousness, as it were, wandering from mountain to hill, from one hold to another, seeking rest and safety. They are

a long time building castles in the air. They sometimes flatter
themselves from one consideration, and sometimes from another.
And if you should delay, there is danger that you may not have
time. Some are many years under fears of damnation, and are
seeking salvation. And there are many for whom death is too
quick. Here we will consider briefly what are the occasions of the
stupidity and senselessness of sinners; and thence shall take occasion to warn those, who would seek the convictions of God's Spirit.

1. Some provoke God to withhold the strivings and convincing
influences of his Spirit. Some provoke God to give them up to
hardness of heart. God lets them alone, and intends to let them
alone. Hosea iv. 16. " Ephraim is joined to idols; let him alone."
Psalm lxxxi. 11, 12. "But my people would not hearken to my
voice; and Israel would none of me. So I gave them up to their
own hearts' lust; and they walked in their own counsels."

Hosea v. 15.—I will go and return to my place, till they acknowledge their offence, and seek my face; in their affliction they will
seek me early.

Doctrine. It is God's manner to make men sensible of their
misery and unworthiness, before he appears in his mercy and
love to them; particularly before he appears in his redeeming
love and mercy to their souls.

Second use. To exhort those, who have some convictions of sin
and danger, that they do not lose them. If you have the strivings
of God's Spirit, God has met with you, led you to reflect upon
your sins, and rendered you sensible that you are in danger of
hell; and so made you concerned about your soul, and put you
upon seeking salvation. Take heed that you do not lose your
convictions, and grow senseless of eternal things, and negligent
of your soul's concern, that you do not return to your former
careless way of living, that you do not return to your former sins.
Here consider,

1. That there is danger in it. It is not all who are under concern for their souls, and who, by the strivings of God's Spirit, are
put upon seeking and striving for salvation, who hold out. There
are many more, who set out at the beginning of the race, who do
not hold out to the end. Many things intervene between the
beginning and the end of the race, which divert, and stop, and

turn back many who commenced well. There are many, who seem to be under strong convictions, and to be very earnest in seeking, whose convictions are but short-lived. And some, who seem to be much concerned about salvation for a considerable time, it may be for years together, yet by degrees grow careless and negligent. There is much in your own heart which tends to stupify you. It is the natural tendency of sin and lust to stupify the conscience. And as corruption is reigning as yet in your heart, it will ever be ready to exert itself in such acts as will have a great tendency to drive away your convictions. And Satan is doubtless diligently watching over you, striving in all ways to abate, and to take off, your convictions. He joins in with the sloth and lusts of your heart to persuade to negligence, and to turn your mind to other things. And the world is full of objects which tend to take off your mind from the soul's concern, and are constantly, as it were, endeavouring to take possession of your mind, and to drive out the concerns of another world.

2. Consider, if you lose your convictions, it will be no advantage to you that ever you had them, as to any furtherance of your salvation. Whatever terrors you have been under about damnation, to whatever reflections you have been brought upon your sins, whatever strong desires you have had after deliverance, and whatever earnest prayers you have made, it will all be lost. What you have suffered of fear and concern will turn to no good account; and what you have done, the pains you have taken, will be utterly lost. When you have strove against sin, and laboured in duty, have stemmed the stream, and have proceeded a considerable way up the hill, and made some progress towards the kingdom of heaven, when once you have lost your convictions, you will be as far from salvation as you were before you began; you will lose all the ground you have gained; you will go quite down to the bottom of the hill; the stream will immediately carry you back. All will be lost; you had as good never have had those convictions, as to have had them, and then to lose them.

3. You do not know that you shall ever have such an opportunity again. God is now striving with you by his Spirit. If you should lose the strivings of his Spirit, it may be that God's Spirit would never return again. If you are under convictions, you have a precious opportunity, which, if you knew the worth of it, you would esteem as better than any temporal advantages. You have

a price in your hands to get wisdom, which is more valuable than gold or silver. It is a great privilege to live under means of grace, to enjoy the word and ordinances of God, and to know the way of salvation. It is a greater thing still to live under a powerful dispensation of the means of grace under a very instructive, convincing ministry. But it is a much greater privilege still to be the subject of the convincing influences of the Spirit of God. If you have these, you have a precious advantage in your hands. And if you lose it, it is questionable whether you ever have the like advantage again. We are counselled to seek the Lord while he may be found, and to call upon him while he is near. Isa. lv. 6. A time in which God's Spirit is striving with a man by convictions of his sin and danger, is especially such a time, that is a sinner's best opportunity. It is especially a day of salvation. God may be said to be near, when he pours out his Spirit upon many in the place where a person dwells. It is prudence for all then to be calling upon God as being near at such a time. But especially is God near, at a time when he is pouring out his Spirit in immediately convincing and awakening a man's own soul. If therefore God's Spirit is now at work with you, you have a precious opportunity. Take heed that you do not by any means let it slip. It may doubtless be said concerning many, that they have missed their opportunity. Most men, who live under the gospel, have a special opportunity. There is a certain season, which God appoints for them, which is, above all others, a day of grace with them, when men have a very fair opportunity for securing eternal salvation, if they did but know it, and had hearts for it. But the misery of man is great upon him; for man knoweth not his time. The wise man tells us, Eccl. viii. 6, 7. that "To every purpose there is time and judgment, therefore the misery of man is great upon him. For he knoweth not that which shall be." And again, ix. 12. "Man knoweth not his time." If the Spirit of God is now striving with you, it may be it is your time; and it may be your only time. Be wise, therefore, and understand the things which belong to your peace, before they are hid from your eyes. You have not the influences of the Spirit of God in your own power. You cannot have convictions and awakenings when you please. God is sovereign as to the bestowment of them. If you are ready to flatter yourself, that although you neglect now, when you are young, yet you shall be awakened again; that is a vain and groundless presumption. It is a difficult thing for a man who has been going on in a sinful course, to reform. There are a great many difficulties in the way of thorough reformation. If you therefore have reformed, and returned again to your former sin, you will have all those difficulties to overcome again.

4. If you lose your convictions, and return again to a way of allowed sinning, there will be less probability of your salvation, than there was before you had any convictions. Backsliding is a very dangerous and pernicious thing to men's souls, and is often spoken of as such in God's word; which was signified in that awful dispensation of God turning Lot's wife into a pillar of salt, to be a standing emblem of the danger of looking back after one has set out in a way of religion. The ill to which they are subject, who lose their convictions, is not merely the loss of their convictions. Their convictions are not only a means of no good to them, but they turn to much ill. It would have been better for them that they had never had them. For they are now set more remote from salvation than they were before. For having risen some considerable way towards heaven, and falling back, they sink lower, and farther down towards hell, than ever they were. The way to heaven is now blocked up with greater difficulties than ever it was. Their hearts now are become harder for light, and convictions being once conquered, they evermore are an occasion of a greater hardness of heart than there was before. Yea, there is no one thing whatsoever, which has so great a tendency to it. Man's heart is hardened by losing convictions, as iron is hardened by being heated and cooled. If you are awakened, and afterwards lose your convictions, it will be a harder thing to awaken you again. If there were only that you are growing older, there would be less probability of your being awakened again; for as persons grow older they grow less and less susceptible of convictions; evil habits grow stronger and more deeply rooted in the heart. You greatly offend God by quenching his Spirit, and returning as a dog to his vomit, and as a sow that was washed to her wallowing in the mire. And there is danger that God will say concerning you, as he did concerning Jerusalem, Ezek. xxiv. 13. "Because I have purged thee, and thou wast not purged, thou shalt not be purged from thy filthiness any more, till I have caused my fury to rest upon thee." If you return again to your wicked course, if you should go to hell at last, you

will lament that ever you have had any convictions; you will find
your punishment so much the heavier. And if you should be
hereafter awakened, and set about striving for salvation, yet you
will probably find harder work in it; you do but make work for
yourself by your backsliding. You will not only have all to do
over again which you have done, and which you must have done,
if you had gone on, but there will be new work for repentance.
There probably must be greater and more dreadful terrors; and
it may be, a much longer time spent in seeking and striving, a
more difficult work with your own headstrong corruptions. If
you were but sensible of one half of the disadvantages of backsliding, and the many woes and calamities in which it will in-
volve you, you would be careful not to lose your convictions.

5. Consider the encouragement there is in Scripture to per-
severe in seeking salvation, as in Hos. vi. 3. "Then shall we know
if we follow on to know the Lord." Thence we may gather, that
God usually gives success to those who diligently, and constantly,
and perseveringly seek conversion. And that you be the better
directed in taking care not to lose your convictions, it is con-
venient that you should be aware of those things which are
common occasions of persons losing their convictions. I shall
therefore briefly mention some of them.

1. Persons falling into sin is very often the occasion of their
losing their convictions. Some temptation prevails, so that they
are drawn into some sin. Some lust upon some occasion has been
stirred up, and they have been overcome by their sinful appetites,
and have provoked God to anger. It may be they have been
drawn into some criminal act of sensuality, and so have quenched
the Spirit. Or they have got into some quarrel with some persons.
Their spirits are disturbed, and heated with malice and revenge,
and they have acted sinfully, or have sinfully expressed themselves, and have driven away the Spirit of God. These are the
most ready ways to put an end to convictions.

2. Sometimes there happens some diverting occasion; there is
some incident which for the present diverts their minds. Their
minds are taken off from their business for a short time. They
are drawn into company. It may be they see something which
revives a desire of worldly enjoyments and entertainments; or
they are engaged in some exercise and business, which diverts
their minds. And so afterwards they are more careless than they

were before. They are not so strict in attending private duties; and carelessness and stupidity by degrees steal upon them, till they wholly lose their convictions.

3. Some change in their circumstances takes off their minds from the concerns of their souls. Their minds are diverted by the new circumstances with which they are attended; or are taken up with new pleasures and enjoyments, or with new cares and business, in which they are involved. It may be they grow richer. They prosper in the world, and their worldly good things crowd in, and take possession of their minds. Or worldly cares are increased upon them, and they have so many things to look after, that their minds are taken up, and they have not time to look after their souls.

Sermon IV*

PRESSING INTO THE KINGDOM OF GOD

LUKE XVI. 16

*The law and the prophets were until John: since that time
the kingdom of God is preached, and every man presseth
into it.*

IN these words two things may be observed: *First*, Wherein
the work and office of John the Baptist consisted, *viz.* in preaching the kingdom of God, to prepare the way for its introduction
to succeed the law and the prophets.   By the law and the
prophets, in the text, seems to be intended the ancient dispensation under the Old Testament, which was received from Moses
and the prophets.   These are said to be *until John*; not that the
revelations given by them are out of use since that time, but that
the state of the church, founded and regulated under God by
them, the dispensation of which they were the ministers, and
wherein the church depended mainly on light received from
them, fully continued till John.   He first began to introduce
the New-Testament dispensation, or gospel-state of the church;
which, with its glorious, spiritual, and eternal privileges and
blessings, is often called the kingdom of heaven, or kingdom of
God.   John the Baptist preached, that the kingdom of God was
at hand.   "Repent," says he, "for the kingdom of heaven is at
hand:"—"Since that time," says Christ, "the kingdom of God
is preached."   John the Baptist first began to preach it; and then,
after him, Christ and his disciples preached the same.   Thus
Christ preached, Matt. iv. 17.   "From that time Jesus began to
preach, and to say, Repent, for the kingdom of heaven is at
hand."   So the disciples were directed to preach, Matt. x. 7.
"And, as ye go, preach, saying, The kingdom of heaven is at

* Preached at Northampton during the Awakenings of 1734-1735.

hand." It was not John the Baptist, but Christ, that fully
brought in, and actually established, this kingdom of God; but
he, as Christ's forerunner to prepare his way before him, did the
first thing that was done towards introducing it. The old dispensation was abolished, and the new brought in by degrees;
as the night gradually ceases, and gives place to the increasing
day which succeeds in its room. First the day-star arises; next
follows the light of the sun itself, but dimly reflected, in the
dawning of the day; but this light increases, and shines more and
more, and the stars that serve for light during the foregoing night,
gradually go out, and their light ceases, as being now needless,
till at length the sun rises, and enlightens the world by his own
direct light, which increases as he ascends higher above the
horizon, till the day-star itself gradually disappears; agreeable to
what John says of himself, John iii. 30. "He must increase, but
I must decrease." John was the forerunner of Christ, and har-
binger of the gospel-day; much as the morning-star is the forerunner of the sun. He had the most honourable office of any of
the prophets; the other prophets foretold Christ to come, he revealed him as already come, and had the honour to be that servant who should come immediately before him, and actually
introduce him, and even to be the instrument concerned in his
solemn inauguration, as he was baptizing him. He was the
greatest of the prophets that came before Christ, as the morning-
star is the brightest of all the stars, Matt. xi. 11. He came to
prepare men's hearts to receive that kingdom of God which
Christ was about more fully to reveal and erect. Luke i. 17. "To
make ready a people prepared for the Lord."

Secondly, We may observe wherein his success appeared, *viz.*
in that since he began his ministry, every man pressed into that
kingdom of God which he preached. The greatness of his success appeared in two things:

1. In the generalness of it, with regard to the subject, or the
persons in whom the success appeared; *every man*. Here is a
term of universality; but it is not to be taken as universal with
regard to individuals, but kinds; as such universal terms are often
used in Scripture. When John preached, there was an extraordinary pouring out of the Spirit of God that attended his
preaching. An uncommon awakening, and concern for salvation, appeared on the minds of all sorts of persons; and even in

the most unlikely persons, and those from whom such a thing might least be expected; as the Pharisees, who were exceeding proud, and self-sufficient, and conceited of their own wisdom and righteousness, and looked on themselves fit to be teachers of others, and used to scorn to be taught; and the Sadducees, who were a kind of infidels, that denied any resurrection, angel, or spirit, or any future state. So that John himself seems to be surprised to see them come to him, under such concern for their salvation; as in Matt. iii. 7. "But when he saw many of the Pharisees and Sadducees come to his baptism, he said unto them, O generation of vipers, who hath warned you to flee from the wrath to come?" And besides these, the publicans, who were some of the most infamous sort of men, came to him, inquiring what they should do to be saved. And the soldiers, who were doubtless a very profane, loose, and profligate sort of persons, made the same inquiry, Luke iii. 12, and 14. "Then came also publicans to be baptized, and said unto him, Master, what shall we do? And the soldiers likewise demanded of him, saying, And what shall we do?"

2. His success appeared in the manner in which his hearers sought the kingdom of God; they pressed into it. It is elsewhere set forth by their being violent for the kingdom of heaven, and taking it by force. Matt. xi. 12. "From the days of John the Baptist until now, the kingdom of heaven suffers violence, and the violent take it by force."

The DOCTRINE that I observe from the words is this.—"It concerns every one that would obtain the kingdom of God, to be pressing into it."—In discoursing on this subject, I would,

First, Show *what* is that way of seeking salvation that seems to be pointed forth in the expression of *pressing into the kingdom of God.*

Secondly, Give the reasons *why* it concerns every one that would obtain the kingdom of God, to seek it in this way.—And then make application.

I. I would show what manner of seeking salvation seems to be denoted by " pressing into the kingdom of God."

1. This expression denotes *strength of desire.* Men in general who live under the light of the gospel, and are not atheists, de-

F

sire the kingdom of God; that is, they desire to go to heaven rather than to hell. Most of them indeed are not much concerned about it; but on the contrary, live a secure and careless life. And some who are many degrees above these, being under some degrees of the awakenings of God's Spirit, yet are not pressing into the kingdom of God. But they that may be said to be truly so, have strong desires to get out of a natural condition, and to get an interest in Christ. They have such a conviction of the misery of their present state, and of the extreme necessity of obtaining a better, that their minds are as it were possessed with and wrapped up in concern about it. To obtain salvation is desired by them above all things in the world. This concern is so great that it very much shuts out other concerns. They used before to have the stream of their desires after other things, or, it may be, had their concern divided between this and them; but when they come to answer the expression in the text, of *pressing into the kingdom of God*, this concern prevails above all others; it lays other things low, and does in a manner engross the care of the mind. This seeking eternal life should not only be one concern that our souls are taken up about with other things; but salvation should be sought as the one thing needful, Luke x. 42. And as the one thing that is desired, Psalm xxvii. 4.

2. Pressing into the kingdom of heaven denotes earnestness and *firmness of resolution*. There should be strength of resolution, accompanying strength of desire, as it was in the psalmist, in the place just now referred to; " one thing have I desired, and that will I seek after." In order to a thorough engagedness of the mind in this affair, both these must meet together. Besides desires after salvation, there should be an earnest resolution in persons to pursue this good as much as lies in their power; to do all that in the use of their utmost strength they are able to do, in an attendance on every duty, and resisting and militating against all manner of sin, and to continue in such a pursuit.

There are two things needful in a person, in order to these strong resolutions; there must be a sense of the great importance and necessity of the mercy sought, and there must also be a sense of opportunity to obtain it, or the encouragement there is to seek it. The strength of resolution depends on the sense which God gives to the heart of these things. Persons without such a sense, may seem to themselves to take up resolutions; they may, as it

were, force a promise to themselves, and say within themselves,
"I will seek as long as I live, I will not give up till I obtain,"
when they do but deceive themselves. Their hearts are not in it;
neither do they indeed take up any such resolution as they seem
to themselves to do. It is the resolution of the mouth more than
of the heart; their hearts are not strongly bent to fulfil what their
mouth says. The firmness of resolution lies in the fulness of the
disposition of the heart to do what is resolved to be done. Those
who are pressing into the kingdom of God, have a disposition of
heart to do every thing that is required, and that lies in their
power to do, and to continue in it. They have not only earnestness, but steadiness of resolution: they do not seek with a waver-
ing unsteady heart, by turns or fits, being off and on; but it is
the constant bent of the soul, if possible, to obtain the kingdom
of God.

3. By pressing into the kingdom of God is signified *greatness
of endeavour*. It is expressed in Eccles. ix. 10. by doing what our
hand finds to do *with our might*. And this is the natural and
necessary consequence of the two forementioned things. Where
there is strength of desire, and firmness of resolution, there will
be answerable endeavours. Persons thus engaged in their hearts
will "strive to enter in at the strait gate," and will be violent for
heaven; their practice will be agreeable to the counsel of the wise
man, in Prov. ii. at the beginning, "My son, if thou wilt receive
my words, and hide my commandments with thee; so that thou
incline thine ear unto wisdom, and apply thine heart to understanding; yea, if thou criest after knowledge, and liftest up thy
voice for understanding; if thou seekest her as silver, and search-
est for her as for hid treasures; then shalt thou understand the
fear of the Lord, and find the knowledge of God." Here the
earnestness of desire and strength of resolution is signified by
inclining the ear to wisdom, and applying the heart to understanding; and the greatness of endeavour is denoted by crying
after knowledge, and lifting up the voice for understanding;
seeking her as silver, and searching for her as for hid treasures:
such desires and resolutions, and such endeavours, go together.

4. Pressing into the kingdom of God denotes an engagedness
and earnestness, that is *directly about that business* of getting
into the kingdom of God. Persons may be in very great exercise
and distress of mind, and that about the condition of their souls;

their thoughts and cares may be greatly engaged and taken up about things of a spiritual nature, and yet not be pressing into the kingdom of God, nor towards it. The exercise of their minds is not directly about the work of *seeking* salvation, in a diligent attendance on the means that God hath appointed in order to it, but something else that is beside their business; it may be about God's decrees and secret purposes, prying into them, searching for signs whereby they may determine, or at least conjecture, what they are before God makes them known by their accomplishment. They distress their minds with fears that they be not elected, or that they have committed the unpardonable sin, or that their day is past, and that God has given them up to judicial and final hardness, and never intends to show them mercy; and therefore, that it is in vain for them to seek salvation. Or they entangle themselves about the doctrine of original sin, and other mysterious doctrines of religion that are above their comprehension. Many persons that seem to be in great distress about a future eternal state, get much into a way of perplexing themselves with such things as these. When it is so, let them be never so much concerned and engaged in their minds, they cannot be said to be pressing towards the kingdom of God; because their exercise is not in their *work*, but rather that which tends to *hinder* them in their work. If they are violent, they are only working violently to *entangle* themselves, and lay blocks in their own way; their pressure is not forwards. Instead of getting along, they do but lose their time, and worse than merely lose it; instead of fighting with the giants that stand in the way to keep them out of Canaan, they spend away their time and strength in conflicting with shadows that appear by the way-side.

Hence we are not to judge of the hopefulness of the way that persons are in, or of the probability of their success in seeking salvation, only by the greatness of the concern and distress that they are in; for many persons have needless distresses that they had much better be without. It is thus very often with persons overrun with the distemper of melancholy; whence the adversary of souls is wont to take great advantage. But then are persons in the most likely way to obtain the kingdom of heaven, when the intent of their minds, and the engagedness of their spirits, is about their *proper work* and business, and all the bent of their souls is to attend on God's means, and to do what he commands and directs them to. The apostle tells us, 1 Cor. ix. 26. "that he did not fight as those that beat the air." Our time is short enough; we had not need to spend it in that which is nothing to the purpose. There are real difficulties and enemies enough for persons to encounter, to employ all their strength; they had not need to waste it in fighting with phantoms.

5. By pressing into the kingdom of God is denoted a *breaking through opposition and difficulties*. There is in the expression a plain intimation of difficulty. If there were no opposition, but the way was all clear and open, there would be no need of pressing to get along. They therefore that are pressing into the kingdom of God, go on with such engagedness, that they break through the difficulties that are in their way. They are so set for salvation, that those things by which others are discouraged, and stopped, and turned back, do not stop them, but they press through them. Persons ought to be so resolved for heaven, that if by any means they *can* obtain, they *will* obtain. Whether those means be difficult or easy, cross or agreeable, if they are requisite means of salvation, they should be complied with. When any thing is presented to be done, the question should not be, Is it easy or hard? is it agreeable to my carnal inclinations or interest, or against them? But is it a required means of my obtaining an interest in Jesus Christ, and eternal salvation? Thus the apostle, Philip. iii. 11. "If by any means I might attain unto the resurrection of the dead." He tells us there in the context what difficulties he broke through, that he suffered the loss of all things, and was willingly made conformable even to Christ's death, though that was attended with such extreme torment and ignominy.

He that is pressing into the kingdom of God, commonly finds many things in the way that are against the grain; but he is not stopped by the cross that lies before him, but takes it up, and carries it. Suppose there be something incumbent on him to do, that is cross to his natural temper, and irksome to him on that account; suppose something that he cannot do without suffering in his estate, or that he apprehends will look odd and strange in the eyes of others, and expose him to ridicule and reproach, or any thing that will offend a neighbour, and get his ill-will, or something that will be very cross to his own carnal appetite—he will *press through such difficulties*. Every thing that is found to be a weight that hinders him in running this race he casts from him, though it be a weight of gold or pearls; yea, if it be a right hand or foot that offends him, he will cut them off, and will not stick at plucking out a right eye with his own hands. These things are insuperable difficulties to those who are not thoroughly engaged in seeking their salvation; they are stumbling-blocks that they never get over. But it is not so with him that presses into the kingdom of God. Those things (before he was thoroughly roused from his security) about which he was wont to have long parleyings and disputings with his own conscience—employing carnal reason to invent arguments and pleas of excuse—he now sticks at no longer; he has done with this endless disputing and reasoning, and presses violently through all difficulties. Let what will be in the way, heaven is what he must and will obtain, not if he can without difficulty, but if it be possible. He meets with temptation: the devil is often whispering in his ear, setting allurements before him, magnifying the difficulties of the work he is engaged in, telling him that they are insuperable, and that he can never conquer them, and trying all ways in the world to discourage him; but still he presses forward. God has given and maintains such an earnest spirit for heaven, that the devil cannot stop him in his course; he is not at leisure to lend an ear to what he has to say.—I come now,

II. To show *why* the kingdom of heaven should be sought in this manner.—It should be thus sought,

1. On account of the *extreme necessity* we are in of getting into the kingdom of heaven. We are in a perishing necessity of it; without it we are utterly and eternally lost. Out of the kingdom of God is no safety; there is no other hiding-place; this is the only city of refuge, in which we can be secure from the avenger that pursues all the ungodly. The vengeance of God will pursue, overtake, and eternally destroy, them that are not in this kingdom. All that are without this enclosure will be swallowed up in an overflowing fiery deluge of wrath. They may stand at the door and knock, and cry, Lord, Lord, open to us, in vain; they will be thrust back; and God will have no mercy on them; they shall be eternally left of him. His fearful vengeance will seize them; the devils will lay hold of them; and all evil come upon them; and there will be none to pity or help; their case will be utterly desperate, and infinitely doleful. It will be a gone case with them;

all offers of mercy and expressions of divine goodness will be finally withdrawn, and all hope will be lost. God will have no kind of regard to their well-being; will take no care of them to save them from any enemy, or any evil; but himself will be their dreadful enemy, and will execute wrath with fury, and will take vengeance in an inexpressibly dreadful manner. Such as shall be in this case will be lost and undone indeed! They will be sunk down into perdition, infinitely below all that we can think. For who knows the power of God's anger? And who knows the misery of that poor worm, on whom that anger is executed without mercy?

2. On account of the shortness and *uncertainty of the opportunity* for getting into this kingdom. When a few days are past, all our opportunity for it will be gone. Our day is limited. God has set our bounds, and we know not where. While persons are out of this kingdom, they are in danger every hour of being overtaken with wrath. We know not how soon we shall get past that line, beyond which there is no work, device, knowledge, nor wisdom; and therefore we should do what we have to do with our might, Eccles. ix. 10.

3. On account of the *difficulty* of getting into the kingdom of God. There are innumerable difficulties in the way, such as few conquer; most of them that try have not resolution, courage, earnestness, and constancy enough; but they fail, give up, and perish. The difficulties are too many and too great for them that do not violently press forward. They never get along, but stick by the way; are turned aside, or turned back, and ruined. Matt. vii. 14. " Strait is the gate, and narrow is the way, which leadeth unto life, and few there be that find it." Luke xiii. 24. " Strive to enter in at the strait gate; for many, I say unto you, will seek to enter in, and shall not be able."

4. The *possibility* of obtaining. Though it be attended with so much difficulty, yet it is not a thing impossible. Acts viii. 22. " If perhaps the thought of thine heart may be forgiven thee." 2 Tim. ii. 25. " If peradventure God will give them repentance to the acknowledging of the truth." However sinful a person is, and whatever his circumstances are, there is, notwithstanding a possibility of his salvation. He himself is capable of it, and God is able to accomplish it, and has mercy sufficient for it; and there is sufficient provision made through Christ, that God may

do it consistent with the honour of his majesty, justice, and truth. So that there is no want either of sufficiency in God, or capacity in the sinner, in order to this. The greatest and vilest, most blind, dead, hard-hearted sinner living, is a subject capable of saving light and grace. Seeing therefore there is such necessity of obtaining the kingdom of God, and so short a time, and such difficulty, and yet such a possibility, it may well induce us to press into it. Jonah iii. 8, 9.

5. It is meet that the kingdom of heaven should be thus sought, because of the *great excellency* of it. We are willing to seek earthly things, of trifling value, with great diligence, and through much difficulty; it therefore certainly becomes us to seek that with great earnestness which is of infinitely greater worth and excellence. And how well may God expect and require it of us, that we should seek it in such a manner, in order to our obtaining it!

6. Such a manner of seeking is *needful to prepare* persons for the kingdom of God. Such earnestness and thoroughness of endeavours, is the ordinary means that God makes use of to bring persons to an acquaintance with themselves, to a sight of their own hearts, to a sense of their own helplessness, and to a despair in their own strength and righteousness. And such engagedness and constancy in seeking the kingdom of heaven, prepare the soul to receive it the more joyfully and thankfully, and the more highly to prize and value it when obtained. So that it is in mercy to us, as well as for the glory of his own name, that God has appointed such earnest seeking, to be the way in which he will bestow the kingdom of heaven.

APPLICATION

The use I would make of this doctrine, is of *exhortation* to all Christless persons to press into the kingdom of God. Some of you are inquiring what you shall do? You seem to desire to know what is the way wherein salvation is to be sought, and how you may be likely to obtain it. You have now heard the way that the holy word directs to. Some are seeking, but it cannot be said of them that they are *pressing* into the kingdom of heaven. There are many that in time past have sought salvation, but not in this manner, and so they never obtained, but are now gone to hell.

Some of them sought it year after year, but failed of it, and perished at last. They were overtaken with divine wrath, and are now suffering the fearful misery of damnation, and have no rest day or night, having no more opportunity to seek, but must suffer and be miserable throughout the never-ending ages of eternity. Be exhorted, therefore, not to seek salvation as they did, but let the kingdom of heaven suffer violence from you.

Here I would first answer an *objection* or two, and then proceed to give some *directions* how to press into the kingdom of God.

Object 1. Some may be ready to say, We cannot do this of ourselves; that strength of desire, and firmness of resolution, that have been spoken of, are out of our reach. If I endeavour to resolve and to seek with engagedness of spirit, I find I fail; my thoughts are presently off from the business, and I feel myself dull, and my engagedness relaxed, in spite of all I can do.

Ans. 1. Though earnestness of mind be not immediately in your power, yet the consideration of what has been now said of the *need* of it, may be a means of stirring you up to it. It is true, persons never will be thoroughly engaged in this business, unless it be by God's influence; but God influences persons by means. Persons are not stirred up to a thorough earnestness without some considerations that move them to it. And if persons can but be made sensible of the necessity of salvation, and also duly consider the exceeding difficulty of it, and the greatness of the opposition, and how short and uncertain the time is, but yet are sensible that they have an opportunity, and that there is a possibility of their obtaining, they will need no more in order to their being thoroughly engaged and resolved in this matter. If we see persons slack and unresolved, and unsteady, it is because they do not enough consider these things.

2. Though strong desires and resolutions of mind be not in your power, yet painfulness of endeavours is in your power. It is in your power to take pains in the use of means, yea very great pains. You can be very painful and diligent in watching your own heart, and striving against sin. Though there is all manner of corruption in the heart continually ready to work, yet you can very laboriously watch and strive against these corruptions; and it is in your power, with great diligence to attend the matter of your duty towards God and towards your neighbour. It is in your

power to attend all ordinances, and all public and private duties of religion, and to do it with your might. It would be a contradiction to suppose that a man cannot do these things with all the might he has, though he cannot do them with more might than he has. The dulness and deadness of the heart, and slothfulness of disposition, do not hinder men being able to take pains, though it hinders their being willing. That is one thing wherein your laboriousness may appear, even striving against your own dulness. That men have a dead and sluggish heart, does not argue that they be not able to take pains; it is so far from that, that it gives occasion for pains. It is one of the difficulties in the way of duty, that persons have to strive with, and that gives occasion for struggling and labour. If there were no difficulties attended seeking salvation, there would be no occasion for striving; a man would have nothing to strive about. There is indeed a great deal of difficulty attending all duties required of those that would obtain heaven. It is an exceeding difficult thing for them to keep their thoughts; it is a difficult thing seriously, or to any good purpose, to consider matters of the greatest importance; it is a difficult thing to hear, or read, or pray attentively. But it does not argue that a man cannot strive in these things because they are difficult; nay, he could not strive therein if there were not difficulty in them. For what is there excepting difficulties that any can have to strive or struggle with in any affair or business? Earnestness of mind, and diligence of endeavour, tend to promote each other. He that has a heart earnestly engaged, will take pains; and he that is diligent and painful in all duty, probably will not be so long before he finds the sensibleness of his heart and earnestness of his spirit greatly increased.

Object. 2. Some may object, that if they are earnest, and take a great deal of pains, they shall be in danger of trusting to what they do; they are afraid of doing their duty for fear of making a righteousness of it.

Ans. There is ordinarily no kind of seekers that trust so much to what they do, as slack and dull seekers. Though all seeking salvation, that have never been the subjects of a thorough humiliation, do trust in their own righteousness; yet some do it much more fully than others. Some though they *trust* in their own righteousness, yet are not *quiet* in it. And those who are most disturbed in their self-confidence, (and therefore in the likeliest way to be wholly brought off from it,) are not such as go on in a remiss way of seeking, but such as are most earnest and thoroughly engaged; partly because in such a way conscience is kept more sensible. A more awakened conscience will not rest so quietly in moral and religious duties, as one that is less awakened. A dull seeker's conscience will be in a great measure satisfied and quieted with his own works and performances; but one that is thoroughly awakened cannot be stilled or pacified with such things as these. In this way persons gain much more knowledge of themselves, and acquaintance with their own hearts, than in a negligent, slight way of seeking; for they have a great deal more experience of themselves. It is experience of ourselves, and finding what we are, that God commonly makes use of as the means of bringing us off from all dependence on ourselves. But men never get acquaintance with themselves so fast, as in the most earnest way of seeking. They that are in this way have more to engage them to think of their sins, and strictly to observe themselves, and have much more to do with their own hearts, than others. Such a one has much more experience of his own weakness, than another that does not put forth and try his strength; and will therefore sooner see himself dead in sin. Such a one, though he hath a disposition continually to be flying to his own righteousness, yet finds rest in nothing; he wanders about from one thing to another, seeking something to ease his disquieted conscience; he is driven from one refuge to another, goes from mountain to hill, seeking rest and finding none; and therefore will the sooner prove that there is no rest to be found, nor trust to be put, in any creature whatsoever.

It is therefore quite a wrong notion that some entertain, that the more they do, the more they shall depend on it. Whereas the reverse is true; the more they do, or the more thorough they are in seeking, the less will they be likely to rest in their doings, and the sooner will they see the vanity of all that they do. So that persons will exceedingly miss it, if ever they neglect to do any duty either to God or man, whether it be any duty of religion, justice, or charity, under a notion of its exposing them to trust in their own righteousness. It is very true, that it is a common thing for persons, when they earnestly seek salvation, to trust in the pains that they take: but yet commonly those that go on in a more slight way, trust a great deal more securely to their dull services, than he that is pressing into the kingdom of God does to his earnestness. Men's slackness in religion, and their trust in their own righteousness, strengthen and establish one another. Their trust in what they have done, and what they now do, settles them in a slothful rest and ease, and hinders their being sensible of their need of rousing up themselves and pressing forward. And on the other hand, their negligence tends so to benumb them, and keep them in such ignorance of themselves, that the most miserable refuges are stupidly rested in as sufficient. Therefore we see, that when persons have been going on for a long time in such a way, and God afterwards comes more thoroughly to awaken them, and to stir them up to be in good earnest, he shakes all their old foundations, and rouses them out of their old resting-places; so that they cannot quiet themselves with those things that formerly kept them secure.

I would now proceed to give some *directions* how you should press into the kingdom of God.

1. Be directed to sacrifice *every thing* to your soul's eternal interest. Let seeking this be so much your bent, and what you are so resolved in, that you will make every thing give place to it. Let nothing stand before your resolution of seeking the kingdom of God. Whatever it be that you used to look upon as a convenience, or comfort, or ease, or thing desirable on any account, if it stands in the way of this great concern, let it be dismissed without hesitation; and if it be of that nature that it is likely always to be a hinderance, then wholly have done with it, and never entertain any expectation from it more. If in time past you have, for the sake of worldly gain, involved yourself in more care and business than you find to be consistent with your being so thorough in the business of religion as you ought to be, then get into some other way, though you suffer in your worldly interest by it. Or if you have heretofore been conversant with company that you have reason to think have been and will be a snare to you, and a hinderance to this great design in any wise, break off from their society, however it may expose you to reproach from your old companions, or let what will be the effect of it. Whatever it be that stands in the way of your most advantageously seeking salvation—whether it be some dear sinful pleasure, or strong carnal appetite, or credit and honour, or the good-will of some persons whose friendship you desire, and whose

esteem and liking you have highly valued—and though there be danger, if you do as you ought, that you shall be looked upon by them as odd and ridiculous, and become contemptible in their eyes—or if it be your ease and indolence, and aversion to continual labour; or your outward convenience in any respect, whereby you might avoid difficulties of one kind or other—*let all go;* offer up all such things together, as it were, in one sacrifice, to the interest of your soul. Let nothing stand in competition with this, but make every thing to fall before it. If the flesh must be crossed, then cross it, spare it not, crucify it, and do not be afraid of being too cruel to it. Gal. v. 24. "They that are Christ's, have crucified the flesh, with the affections and lusts." Have no dependence on any worldly enjoyment whatsoever. Let salvation be the one thing with you. This is what is certainly required of you: and this is what many stick at; this giving up other things for salvation, is a stumbling-block that few get over. While others pressed into the kingdom of God at the preaching of John the Baptist, Herod was pretty much stirred up by his preaching. It is said, he heard him, and observed him, and did many things; but when he came to tell him that he must part with his beloved Herodias, here he stuck; this he never would yield to, Mark vii. 18-20. The rich young man was considerably concerned for salvation; and accordingly was a very strict liver in many things: but when Christ came to direct him to go and sell all that he had, and give to the poor, and come and follow him, he could not find in his heart to comply with it, but went away sorrowful. He had great possessions, and set his heart much on his estate, and could not bear to part with it. It may be, if Christ had directed him only to give away a considerable part of his estate, he would have done it; yea, perhaps, if he had bid him part with half of it, he would have complied with it: but when he directed him to throw up all, he could not grapple with such a proposal. Herein the straitness of the gate very much consists; and it is on this account that so many seek to enter in, and are not able. There are many that have a great mind to salvation, and spend part of their time in wishing that they had it, but they will not comply with the necessary means.

2. Be directed to *forget the things that are behind;* that is, not to keep thinking and making much of what you have done, but let your mind be wholly intent on what you have to do. In some

sense you ought to look back; you should look back on your sins. Jer. ii. 23. " See thy way in the valley, know what thou hast done." You should look back on the wretchedness of your religious performances, and consider how you have fallen short in them; how exceedingly polluted all your duties have been, and how justly God might reject and loathe them, and you for them. But you ought not to spend your time in looking back, as many persons do, thinking how much they have done for their salvation; what great pains they have taken, how that they have done what they can, and do not see how they can do more; how long a time they have been seeking, and how much more they have done than others, and even than such and such who have obtained mercy. They think with themselves how hardly God deals with them, that he does not extend mercy to them, but turns a deaf ear to their cries; and hence discourage themselves, and complain of God. Do not thus spend your time in looking on what is past, but look forward, and consider what is before you; consider what it is that you can do, and what it is necessary that you should do, and what God calls you still to do, in order to your own salvation. The apostle, in the 3rd chapter to the Philippians, tells us what things he did while a Jew, how much he had to boast of, if any could boast; but he tells us, that he forgot those things, and all others that were behind, and reached forth towards the things that were before, pressing forwards towards the mark for the prize of the high calling of God in Christ Jesus.

3. Labour to get your *heart thoroughly disposed* to go on and hold out to the end. Many that seem to be earnest have not a heart thus disposed. It is a common thing for persons to appear greatly affected for a little while; but all is soon past away, and there is no more to be seen of it. Labour therefore to obtain a thorough willingness and preparation of spirit, to continue seeking, in the use of your utmost endeavours, without limitation; and do not think your whole life too long. And in order to this, be advised to two things.

(1.) Remember that if ever God bestows a mercy upon you, he will use his sovereign pleasure about the *time when.* He will bestow it on some in a little time, and on others not till they have sought it long. If other persons are soon enlightened and comforted, while you remain long in darkness, there is no other way but for you to wait. God will act arbitrarily in this matter, and you cannot help it. You must even be content to wait, in a way of laborious and earnest striving, till his time comes. If you refuse, you will but undo yourself; and when you shall hereafter find yourself undone, and see that your case is past remedy, how will you condemn yourself for foregoing a great probability of salvation, only because you had not patience to hold out, and were not willing to be at the trouble of a persevering labour! And what will it avail before God or your own conscience to say that you could not bear to be obliged to seek salvation so long, when God bestowed it on others that sought it but for a very short time? Though God may have bestowed the testimonies of his favour on others in a few days or hours after they have begun earnestly to seek it, how does that alter the case as to you, if there proves to be a necessity of your laboriously seeking many years before you obtain them? Is salvation less worth taking a great deal of pains for, because, through the sovereign pleasure of God, others have obtained it with comparatively little pains? If there are two persons, the one of which has obtained converting grace with comparative ease, and another that has obtained it after continuing for many years in the greatest of most earnest labours after it, how little difference does it make at last, when once salvation is obtained! Put all the *labour* and pains, the long-continued difficulties and strugglings, of the one in the scale against salvation, and how little does it subtract; and put the ease with which the other has obtained in the scale with salvation, and how little does it add! What is either added or subtracted is lighter than vanity, and a thing worthy of no consideration, when compared with that infinite benefit that is obtained. Indeed if you were ten thousand years, and all that time should strive and press forward with as great earnestness as ever a person did for one day, all this would bear no proportion to the importance of the benefit; and it will doubtless appear little to you, when once you come to be in actual possession of eternal glory, and to see what that eternal misery is which you have escaped. You must not think much of your pains, and of the length of time; you must press towards the kingdom of God, and do your utmost to hold out to the end, and learn to make no account of it when you have done. You must undertake the business of seeking salvation upon these terms, and with no other expectations than this, that if ever God bestows mercy it will be in his own time; and not only so, but also that when you have done all, God will not hold himself obliged to show you mercy at last.

(2.) Endeavour now thoroughly to weigh in your mind the difficulty, and to *count the cost* of perseverance in seeking salvation. You that are now setting out in this business, (as there are many here who have very lately set about it;—Praised be the name of God that he has stirred you up to it!) be exhorted to attend this direction. Do not undertake in this affair with any other thought but of giving yourself wholly to it for the remaining part of your life, and going through many and great difficulties in it. Take heed that you do not engage secretly upon this condition, that you shall obtain in a little time, promising yourself that it shall be within this present season of the pouring out of God's Spirit, or with any other limitation of time whatsoever. Many, when they begin, (seeming to set out very earnestly,) do not expect that they shall need to seek very long, and so do not prepare themselves for it. And therefore, when they come to find it otherwise, and meet with unexpected difficulty, they are found unguarded, and easily overthrown. But let me advise you all who are now seeking salvation, not to entertain any self-flattering thoughts; but weigh the utmost difficulties of perseverance, and be provided for them, having your mind fixed in it to go through them, let them be what they will. Consider now beforehand, how tedious it would be, with utmost earnestness and labour, to strive after salvation for many years, in the mean time receiving no joyful or comfortable evidence of your having obtained. Consider what a great temptation to discouragement there probably would be in it; how apt you would be to yield the case; how ready to think that it is in vain for you to seek any longer, and that God never intends to show you mercy, in that he has not yet done it; how apt you would be to think with yourself, "What an uncomfortable life do I live! how much more unpleasantly do I spend my time than others that do not perplex their minds about the things of another world, but are at ease, and take the comfort of their worldly enjoyments!" Consider what a temptation there would probably be in it, if you saw others brought in that began to seek the kingdom of heaven long after you, rejoicing in a hope and sense of God's favour, after but little pains and a short time of awakening; while you, from day to day, and from year to year, seemed to labour in vain. Prepare for such temptations now. Lay in beforehand for such trials and difficulties, that you may not think any strange thing has happened when they come.

I hope that those who have given attention to what has been said, have by this time conceived, in some measure, what is signified by the expression in the text, and after what manner they ought to press into the kingdom of God. Here is this to induce you to a compliance with what you have been directed to; if you sit still, you die; if you go backward, behold you shall surely die; if you go forward, you may live. And though God has not bound himself to any thing that a person does while destitute of faith, and out of Christ, yet there is great probability that in a way of hearkening to this counsel you will live; and that by pressing onward, and persevering, you will at last, as it were by violence, take the kingdom of heaven. Those of you who have not only heard the directions given, but shall through God's merciful assistance, practise according to them, are those that probably will overcome. These we may well hope at last to see standing with the Lamb on mount Sion, clothed in white robes, with palms in their hands; when all your labour and toil will be abundantly compensated, and you will not repent that you have taken so much pains, and denied yourself so much, and waited so long. This self-denial, this waiting, will then look little, and vanish into nothing in your eyes, being all swallowed up in the first minute's enjoyment of that glory that you will then possess, and will uninterruptedly possess and enjoy to all eternity.

4th direction. Improve the present season of the pouring out of the Spirit of God on this town. Prudence in any affair whatsoever consists very much in minding and improving our opportunities. If you would have spiritual prosperity, you must exercise prudence in the concerns of your souls, as well as in outward concerns when you seek outward prosperity. The prudent husbandman will observe his opportunities; he will improve seed-time and harvest; he will make his advantage of the showers and shines of heaven. The prudent merchant will discern his opportunities; he will not be idle on a market-day; he is careful not to let slip his seasons for enriching himself: So will those who prudently seek the fruits of righteousness, and the merchandise of wisdom, improve their opportunities for their eternal wealth and happiness.

God is pleased at this time, in a very remarkable manner, to

G

pour out his Spirit amongst us; (glory be to his name!) You that
have a mind to obtain converting grace, and to go to heaven
when you die, now is your season! Now, if you have any sort of
prudence for your own salvation, and have not a mind to go to
hell, improve this season! Now is the accepted time! Now is
the day of salvation! You that in time past have been called
upon, and have turned a deaf ear to God's voice, and long stood
out and resisted his commands and counsels, hear God's voice
to-day, while it is called to-day! Do not harden your hearts at
such a day as this! Now you have a special and remarkable
price put into your hands to get wisdom, if you have but a heart
to improve it.

God hath his certain days or appointed seasons of exercising
both mercy and judgment. There are some remarkable times of
wrath, laid out by God for his awful visitation, and the executions of his anger; which times are called days of vengeance,
Prov. vi. 34. Wherein God will visit for sin, Exod. xxxii. 34.
And so, on the contrary, God has laid out in his sovereign counsels seasons of remarkable mercy, wherein he will manifest himself in the exercises of his grace and loving-kindness, more than
at other times. Such times in Scripture are called by way of
eminency, accepted times, and days of salvation, and also days of
God's visitation; because they are days wherein God will visit in
a way of mercy; as Luke xix. 44. "And shall lay thee even with
the ground, and thy children with thee; and they shall not leave
in thee one stone upon another; because thou knewest not the
time of thy visitation." It is such a time now in this town; it is
with us a day of God's gracious visitation. It is indeed a day of
grace with us as long as we live in this world, in the enjoyment
of the means of grace; but such a time as this is especially, and
in a distinguishing manner, a day of grace. There is a door of
mercy always standing open for sinners; but at such a day as this,
God opens an extraordinary door.

We are directed to seek the Lord while he may be found, and
to call upon him while he is near, Isa. lv. 6. If you that are
hitherto Christless, be not strangely besotted and infatuated, you
will by all means improve such an opportunity as this to get
heaven, when heaven is brought so near, when the fountain is
opened in the midst of us in so extraordinary a manner. Now is
the time to obtain a supply of the necessities of your poor perish-

ing souls! This is the way for sinners that have a mind to be converted before they die, when God is dealing forth so liberally and bountifully amongst us; when conversion and salvation work is going on amongst us from sabbath to sabbath, and many are pressing into the kingdom of God! Now do not stay behind, but press in amongst the rest! Others have been stirred up to be in good earnest, and have taken heaven by violence; be entreated to follow their example, if you would have a part of the inheritance with them, and would not be left at the great day, when they are taken!

How should it move you to consider that you have this opportunity now in your hands! You are in the actual possession of it! If it were past, it would not be in your power to recover it, or in the power of any creature to bring it back for you; but it is not past; it is now, at this day. Now is the accepted time, even while it is called to-day! Will you sit still at such a time? Will you sleep in such a harvest? Will you deal with a slack hand, and stay behind out of mere sloth, or love to some lust, or lothness to grapple with some small difficulty, or to put yourself a little out of your way, when so many are flowing to the goodness of the Lord? You are behind still; and so you will be in danger of being left behind, when the whole number is completed that are to enter in, if you do not earnestly bestir yourself! To be left behind at the close of such a season as this, will be awful—next to being left behind on that day when God's saints shall mount up as with wings to meet the Lord in the air—and will be what will appear very threatening of it.

God is now calling you in an extraordinary manner: and it is agreeable to the will and word of Christ, that I should now, in his name, call you, as one set over you, and sent to you to that end; so it is his will that you should hearken to what I say, as his voice. I therefore beseech you in Christ's stead now to press into the kingdom of God! Whoever you are, whether young or old, small or great; if you are a great sinner, if you have been a backslider, if you have quenched the Spirit, be who you will, do not stand making objections, but arise, apply yourself to your work! Do what you have to do with your might. Christ is calling you before, and holding forth his grace, and everlasting benefits, and wrath is pursuing you behind; wherefore fly for your life, and look not behind you!

But here I would particularly direct myself to several sorts of persons.

I. To those sinners who are in a measure awakened, and are concerned for their salvation. You have reason to be glad that you have such an opportunity, and to prize it above gold. To induce you to prize and improve it, consider several things.

1. God has doubtless a design now to deal forth saving blessings to a number. God has done it to some already, and it is not probable that he has yet finished his work amongst us: we may well hope still to see others brought out of darkness into marvellous light. And therefore,

2. God comes this day, and knocks at many persons' doors, and at your door among the rest. God seems to be come in a very unusual manner amongst us, upon a gracious and merciful design; a design of saving a number of poor miserable souls out of a lost and perishing condition, and of bringing them into a happy state and eternal glory! This is offered to you, not only as it has always been in the word and ordinances, but by the particular influences of the Spirit of Christ awakening you! This special offer is made to many amongst us; and you are not passed over. Christ has not forgot you; but has come to your door; and there as it were stands waiting for you to open to him. If you have wisdom and discretion to discern your own advantage, you will know that now is your opportunity.

3. How much more easily converting grace is obtained at such a time, than at other times! The work is equally easy with God at all times; but there is far less difficulty in the way as to *men* at such a time, than at other times. It is, as I said before, a day of God's gracious visitation; a day that he has as it were set apart for the more liberally and bountifully dispensing of his grace; a day wherein God's hand is opened wide. Experience shows it. God seems to be more ready to help, to give proper convictions, to help against temptations, and let in divine light. He seems to carry on his work with a more glorious discovery of his power, and Satan is more chained up than at other times. Those difficulties and temptations that persons before stuck at, from year to year, they are soon helped over. The work of God is carried on with greater speed and swiftness, and there are often instances of sudden conversion at such a time. So it was in the apostles' days, when there was a time of the most extraordinary pouring out of

the Spirit that ever was. How quick and sudden were conversions in those days! Such instances as that of the jailer abounded then, in fulfilment of that prophecy, Isa. lxvi. 7, 8. "Before she travailed, she brought forth: before her pain came, she was delivered of a man-child. Who hath heard such a thing? Who hath seen such things? For as soon as Zion travailed, she brought forth her children." So it is in some degree, whenever there is an extraordinary pouring out of the Spirit of God; more or less so, in proportion to the greatness of that effusion. There is seldom such quick work made of it at other times. Persons are not so soon delivered from their various temptations and entanglements, but are much longer wandering in a wilderness, and groping in darkness. And yet,

4. There are probably some here present that are now concerned about their salvation, that never will obtain. It is not to be supposed that all that are now moved and awakened will ever be savingly converted. Doubtless there are many now seeking that will not be able to enter. When has it been so in times past, when there has been times of great outpourings of God's Spirit, but that many who for a while have inquired with others what they should do to be saved, have failed, and afterwards grown hard and secure? All of you that are now awakened have a mind to obtain salvation, and probably hope to get a title to heaven, in the time of this present moving of God's Spirit: but yet, (though it be awful to be spoken, and awful to be thought,) we have no reason to think any other, than that some of you will burn in hell to all eternity. You all are afraid of hell, and seem at present disposed to take pains to be delivered from it; and yet it would be unreasonable to think any other, than that some of you will have your portion in the lake that burns with fire and brimstone. Though there are so many that seem to obtain so easily, having been but a little while under convictions, yet, for all that, some never will obtain. Some will soon lose the sense of things they now have; though their awakenings seem to be very considerable for the present, they will not hold; they have not hearts disposed to hold on through very many difficulties. Some that have set out for heaven, and hope as much as others to obtain, are indeed but slighty and slack, even now, in the midst of such a time as this. And others, who for the present seem to be more in earnest, will probably, before long, decline and fail, and gradually

return to be as they were before. The convictions of some seem to be great, while that which is the occasion of their convictions is new; which, when that begins to grow old, will gradually decay and wear off. Thus, it may be, the occasion of your awakening has been the hearing of the conversion of some person, or seeing so extraordinary a dispensation of Providence as this in which God now appears amongst us; but by and by the newness and freshness of these things will be gone, and so will not affect your mind as now they do; and it may be your convictions will go away with it.

Though this be a time wherein God doth more liberally bestow his grace, and so a time of greater advantage for obtaining it; yet there seems to be, upon some accounts, greater danger of backsliding, than when persons are awakened at other times. For commonly such extraordinary times do not last long; and then when they cease, there are multitudes that lose their convictions as it were together.

We speak of it as a happy thing, that God is pleased to cause such a time amongst us, and so it is indeed: but there are some to whom it will be no benefit; it will be an occasion of their greater misery; they will wish they had never seen this time; it will be more tolerable for those that never saw it, or any thing like it, in the day of judgment, than for them. It is an awful consideration, that there are probably those here, whom the great Judge will hereafter call to a strict account about this very thing, why they no better improved this opportunity, when he set open the fountain of his grace, and so loudly called upon them, and came and strove with them in particular, by the awakening influences of his Spirit; and they will have no good account to give to the Judge, but their mouths will be stopped, and they will stand speechless before him.

You had need therefore to be earnest, and very resolved in this affair, that you may not be one of those who shall thus fail, that you may so fight, as not uncertainly, and so run, as that you may win the prize.

5. Consider in what sad circumstances times of extraordinary effusion of God's Spirit commonly leave persons, when they leave them unconverted. They *find* them in a doleful, because in a natural, condition; but commonly *leave* them in a much more doleful condition. They are left dreadfully hardened, and with

a great increase of guilt, and their souls under a more strong dominion and possession of Satan. And frequently seasons of extraordinary advantage for salvation, when they pass over persons, and they do not improve them, nor receive any good in them, seal their damnation. As such seasons leave them, God for ever leaves them, and gives them up to judicial hardness. Luke xix. 41, 42. "And when he was come near, he beheld the city, and wept over it, saying, If thou hadst known, even thou, the things which belong unto thy peace! but now they are hid from thine eyes."

6. Consider, that it is very uncertain whether you will ever see such another time as this. If there should be such another time. it is very uncertain whether you will live to see it. Many that are now concerned for their salvation amongst us, will probably be in their graves, and it may be in hell, before that time; and if you should miss this opportunity, it may be so with you. And what good will that do you, to have the Spirit of God poured out upon earth, in the place where you once lived, while you are tormented in hell? What will it avail you, that others are crying, What shall I do to be saved? while you are shut up for ever in the bottomless pit, and are wailing and gnashing your teeth in everlasting burnings?

Wherefore improve this opportunity, while God is pouring out his Spirit, and you are on earth, and while you dwell in that place where the Spirit of God is thus poured out, and you yourself have the awakening influences of it, that you may never wail and gnash your teeth in hell, but may sing in heaven for ever, with others that are redeemed from amongst men, and redeemed amongst us.

7. If you should see another such time, it will be under far greater disadvantages than now. You will probably then be much older, and will have more hardened your heart; and so will be under less probability of receiving good. Some persons are so hardened in sin, and so left of God, that they can live through such a time as this, and not be much awakened or affected by it; they can stand their ground, and be but little moved. And so it may be with you, by another such time, if there should be another amongst us, and you should live to see it. The case in all probability will be greatly altered with you by that time. If you should continue Christless and graceless till then, you will be

much further from the kingdom of God, and much deeper involved in snares and misery; and the devil will probably have a
vastly greater advantage against you, to tempt and confound you.

8. We do not know but that God is now gathering in his elect,
before some great and sore judgment. It has been God's manner
before he casts off a visible people, or brings some great and destroying judgments upon them, first to gather in his elect, that
they may be secure. So it was before the casting off the Jews
from being God's people. There was first a very remarkable pouring out of the Spirit and gathering in of the elect, by the preaching of the apostles and evangelists, as we read in the beginning of
the Acts: but after this harvest and its gleanings were over, the
rest were blinded, and hardened; the gospel had little success
amongst them, and the nation was given up, and cast off from
being God's people, and their city and land was destroyed by the
Romans in a terrible manner; and they have been cast off by God
now for a great many ages, and still remain a hardened and rejected people. So we read in the beginning of the 7th chapter of
the Revelations, that God, when about to bring destroying judgments on the earth, first sealed his servants in the forehead. He
set his seal upon the hearts of the elect, gave them the saving
influences and indwelling of his Spirit, by which they were sealed
to the day of redemption. Rev. vii. 1-3. " And after these things,
I saw four angels standing on the four corners of the earth, holding the four winds of the earth, that the wind should not blow
on the earth, nor on the sea, nor on any tree. And I saw another
angel ascending from the east, having the seal of the living God:
and he cried with a loud voice to the four angels, to whom it was
given to hurt the earth and the sea, saying, Hurt not the earth,
neither the sea, nor the trees, till we have sealed the servants of
our God in their foreheads."

And this may be the case now, that God is about, in a great
measure, to forsake this land, and give up this people, and to
bring most awful and overwhelming judgments upon it, and that
he is now gathering in his elect, to secure them from the calamity.
The state of the nation, and of this land, never looked so threatening of such a thing as at this day. The present aspect of things
exceedingly threatens vital religion, and even those truths that
are especially the foundation of it, out of this land. If it should
be so, how awful will the case be with those that shall be left, and

not brought in, while God continues the influences of his
Spirit, to gather in those that are to be redeemed from amongst
us?

9. If you neglect the present opportunity, and be finally unbelieving, those that are converted in this time of the pouring
out of God's Spirit will rise up in judgment against you. Your
neighbours, your relations, acquaintance, or companions that are
converted, will that day appear against you. They will not only
be taken while you are left, mounting up with joy to meet the
Lord in the air—at his right hand with glorious saints and angels,
while you are at the left with devils—but how they will rise up
in judgment *against* you. However friendly you have been together, and have taken pleasure in one another's company, and
have often familiarly conversed together, they will then surely
appear against you. They will rise up as witnesses, and will declare what a precious opportunity you had, and did not improve;
how you continued unbelieving, and rejected the offers of a
Saviour, when those offers were made in so extraordinary a
manner, and when so many others were prevailed upon to accept
of Christ; how you was negligent and slack, and did not know the
things that belonged to your peace, in that your day. And not
only so, but they shall be your judges, as assessors with the great
Judge; and as such will appear against you; they will be with the
Judge in passing sentence upon you. 1 Cor. vi. 2. "Know ye not
that the saints shall judge the world?" Christ will admit them
to the honour of judging the world with him: "They shall sit
with Christ in his throne," Rev. iii. 21. They shall sit with Christ
in his throne of government, and they shall sit with him in his
throne of judgment, and shall be judges with him when you are
judged, and as such shall condemn you.

10. And *lastly,* You do not know that you shall live through
the present time of the pouring out of God's Spirit. You may be
taken away in the midst of it, or you may be taken away in the
beginning of it; as God in his providence is putting you in mind,
by the late instance of death in a young person in the town.*
God has of late been very awful in his dealings with us, in the
repeated deaths of young persons amongst us. This should stir
every one up to be in the more haste to press into the kingdom

* Joseph Clark's wife, a young woman lately married, that died suddenly the week before this was delivered.

of God, that so you may be safe whenever death comes. This is a blessed season and opportunity; but you do not know how little of it you may have. You may have much less of it than others; may by death be suddenly snatched away from all advantages that are here enjoyed for the good of souls. Therefore make haste, and escape for thy life. One moment's delay is dangerous; for wrath is pursuing, and divine vengeance hanging over every uncovered person.

Let these considerations move every one to be improving this opportunity, that while others receive saving good, and are made heirs of eternal glory, you may not be left behind, in the same miserable doleful circumstances in which you came into the world, a poor captive to sin and Satan, a lost sheep, a perishing, undone creature, sinking down into everlasting perdition; that you may not be one of them spoken of, Jer. xvii. 6. "That shall be like the heath in the desert, and shall not see when good comes." If you do not improve this opportunity, remember I have told you, you will hereafter lament it; and if you do not lament it in this world, then I will leave it with you to remember it throughout a miserable eternity.

II. I would address myself to such as yet remain unawakened. It is an awful thing that there should be any one person remaining secure amongst us at such a time as this; but yet it is to be feared that there are some of this sort. I would here a little expostulate with such persons.

1. When do you expect that it will be more likely that you should be awakened and wrought upon than now? You are in a Christless condition; and yet without doubt intend to go to heaven; and therefore intend to be converted some time before you die; but this is not to be expected till you are first awakened, and deeply concerned about the welfare of your soul, and brought earnestly to seek God's converting grace. And when do you intend that this shall be? How do you lay things out in your own mind, or what projection have you about this matter? Is it ever so likely that a person will be awakened, as at such a time as this? How do we see many, who before were secure, now roused out of their sleep, and crying, What shall I do to be saved? But you are yet secure! Do you flatter yourself that it will be more likely you should be awakened when it is a dull and dead time? Do you lay matters out thus in your own mind, that

though you are senseless when others are generally awakened, that yet you shall be awakened when others are generally senseless? Or do you hope to see another such time of the pouring out of God's Spirit hereafter? And do you think it will be more likely that you should be wrought upon then, than now? And why do you think so? Is it because then you shall be so much older than you are now, and so that your heart will be grown softer and more tender with age? or because you will then have stood out so much longer against the calls of the gospel, and all means of grace? Do you think it more likely that God will give you the needed influences of his Spirit then, than now, because then you will have provoked him so much more, and your sin and guilt will be so much greater? And do you think it will be any benefit to you, to stand it out through the present season of grace, as proof against the extraordinary means of awakening there are? Do you think that this will be a good preparation for a saving work of the Spirit hereafter?

2. What means do you expect to be awakened by? As to the awakening awful things of the word of God, you have had those set before you times without number, in the most moving manner that the dispensers of the word have been capable of. As to particular solemn warnings, directed to those that are in your circumstances, you have had them frequently, and have them now from time to time. Do you expect to be awakened by awful providences? Those also you have lately had, of the most awakening nature, one after another. Do you expect to be moved by the deaths of others? We have lately had repeated instances of these. There have been deaths of old and young: the year has been remarkable for the deaths of young persons in the bloom of life; and some of them very sudden deaths. Will the conversion of others move you? There is indeed scarce any thing that is found to have so great a tendency to stir persons up as this: and this you have been tried with of late in frequent instances; but are hitherto proof against it. Will a general pouring out of the Spirit, and seeing a concern about salvation amongst all sorts of people, do it? This means you now have, but without effect. Yea, you have all these things together; you have the solemn warnings of God's word, and awful instances of death, and the conversion of others, and see a general concern about salvation: but all together do not move you to any great concern about your own precious,

immortal, and miserable soul. Therefore consider by what means it is that you expect ever to be awakened.

You have heard that it is probable some who are now awakened, will never obtain salvation; how dark then does it look upon you that remain stupidly unawakened! Those who are not moved at such a time as this, come to adult age, have reason to fear whether they are not given up to judicial hardness. I do not say they have reason to *conclude* it, but they have reason to fear it. How dark doth it look upon you, that God comes and knocks at so many persons' doors, and misses yours! that God is giving the strivings of his Spirit so generally amongst us, while you are left senseless!

3. Do you expect to obtain salvation without ever seeking it? If you are sensible that there is a necessity of your seeking in order to obtaining, and ever intend to seek, one would think you could not avoid it at such a time as this. Inquire therefore, whether you intend to go to heaven, living all your days a secure, negligent, careless life.—Or,

4. Do you think you can bear the damnation of hell? Do you imagine that you can tolerably endure the devouring fire, and everlasting burnings? Do you hope that you shall be able to grapple with the vengeance of God Almighty, when he girds himself with strength, and clothes himself with wrath? Do you think to strengthen yourself against God, and to be able to make your part good with him? 1 Cor. x. 22. "Do we provoke the Lord to jealousy? are we stronger than he?" Do you flatter yourself that you shall find out ways for your ease and support, and to make it out tolerably well, to bear up your spirit in those everlasting burnings that are prepared for the devil and his angels? Ezek. xxii. 14. "Can thine heart endure, or can thine hands be strong, in the days that I shall deal with thee?"—It is a difficult thing to conceive what such Christless persons think, that are unconcerned at such a time.

III. I would direct myself to them who are grown considerably into years, and are yet in a natural condition. I would now take occasion earnestly to exhort you to improve this extraordinary opportunity, and press into the kingdom of God. You have lost many advantages that once you had, and now have not the same advantages that others have. The case is very different with you from what it is with many of your neighbours. You, above all, had need to improve such an opportunity. Now is the time for you to bestir yourself, and take the kingdom of heaven!—Consider,

1. Now there seems to be a door opened for old sinners. Now God is dealing forth freely to all sorts: his hand is opened wide, and he does not pass by old ones so much as he used to do. You are not under such advantages as others who are younger; but yet, so wonderfully has God ordered it, that now you are not destitute of great advantage. Though old in sin, God has put a new and extraordinary advantage into your hands. O! improve this price you have to get wisdom! You that have been long seeking to enter in at the strait gate and yet remain without, now take your opportunity and press in! You that have been long in the wilderness, fighting with various temptations, labouring under discouragements, ready to give up the case, and have been often tempted to despair, now, behold the door that God opens for you! Do not give way to discouragements now; this is not a time for it. Do not spend time in thinking that you have done what you can already, and that you are not elected, and in giving way to other perplexing, weakening, disheartening temptations. Do not waste away this precious opportunity in such a manner. You have no time to spare for such things as these; God calls you now to something else. Improve this time in seeking and striving for salvation, and not in that which tends to hinder it.—It is no time now for you to stand talking with the devil; but hearken to God, and apply yourself to that which he does now so loudly call you to.

Some of you have often lamented the loss of past opportunities, particularly the loss of the time of youth, and have been wishing that you had so good an opportunity again; and have been ready to say, "O! if I was young again, how would I improve such an advantage!" That opportunity which you have had in time past is irrecoverable; you can never have it again: but God can give you other advantages of another sort, that are very great, and he is so doing at this day. He is now putting a new opportunity into your hands; though not of the same kind with that which you once had, and have lost, yet in some respects as great of another kind. If you lament your folly in neglecting and losing past opportunities, then do not be guilty of the folly of neglecting the opportunity which God now gives you. This opportunity you could not have purchased, if you would have given all that you had in the world for it. But God is putting it into your hands himself, of his own free and sovereign mercy, without your purchasing it. Therefore when you have it, do not neglect it.

2. It is a great deal more likely with respect to such persons than others, that this is their last time. There will be a last time of special offer of salvation to impenitent sinners.—"God's Spirit shall not always strive with man," Gen. vi. 3. God sometimes continues long knocking at the doors of wicked men's hearts; but there are the *last* knocks, and the *last* calls that ever they shall have. And sometimes God's last calls are the loudest; and then if sinners do not hearken, he finally leaves them. How long has God been knocking at many of your doors that are old in sin! It is a great deal more likely that these are his last knocks. You have resisted God's Spirit in times past, and have hardened your heart once and again; but God will not be thus dealt with always. There is danger, that if now, after so long a time, you will not hearken, he will utterly desert you, and leave you to walk in your own counsels.

It seems by God's providence, as though God had yet an elect number amongst old sinners in this place, that perhaps he is now about to bring in. It looks as though there were some that long lived under Mr. Stoddard's ministry, that God has not utterly cast off, though they stood it out under such great means as they then enjoyed. It is to be hoped that God will now bring in a remnant from among them. But it is the more likely that God is now about finishing with them, one way or other, for their having been so long the subjects of such extraordinary means. You have seen former times of the pouring out of God's Spirit upon the town, when others were taken and you left, others were called out of darkness into marvellous light, and were brought into a glorious and happy state, and you saw not good when good came. How dark will your circumstances appear, if you shall also stand it out through this opportunity, and still be left behind! Take heed that you be not of those spoken of, Heb. vi. 7, 8. that are like the "earth that has rain coming oft upon it, and only bears briers and thorns." As we see there are some pieces of ground, the more showers of rain fall upon them, the more fruitful seasons there are, the more do the briers, and other useless and hurtful plants, that are rooted in them, grow and flourish. Of such ground the apostle says, "It is rejected, and is nigh unto cursing, whose end is to be burned." The way that the husband-man takes with such ground, is, to set fire to it, to burn up the growth of it.—If you miss this opportunity, there is danger that you will be utterly rejected, and that your end will be to be burned. And if this is to be, it is to be feared, that you are not far from, but nigh unto, cursing.

Those of you that are already grown old in sin, and are now under awakenings, when you feel your convictions begin to go off, if ever that should be, then remember what you have now been told; it may well then strike you to the heart!

IV. I would direct the advice to those that are young, and now under their first special convictions. I would earnestly urge such to improve this opportunity, and press into the kingdom of God. —Consider two things,

1. You have all manner of advantages now centering upon you. It is a time of great advantage for all; but your advantages are above others. There is no other sort of persons that have now so great and happy an opportunity as you have.—You have the great advantage that is common to all who live in this place, *viz.* That now it is a time of the extraordinary pouring out of the Spirit of God. And have you not that great advantage, the awakening influences of the Spirit of God on you in particular? and besides, you have this peculiar advantage, that you are now in your youth. And added to this, you have another unspeakable advantage, that you are now under your first convictions. Happy is he that never has hardened his heart, and blocked up his own way to heaven by backsliding, and has now the awakening in-fluences of God's Spirit, if God does but enable him thoroughly to improve them! Such above all in the world bid fair for the kingdom of God. God is wont on such, above any kind of persons, as it were easily and readily to bestow the saving grace and comforts of his Spirit. Instances of speedy and sudden con-version are most commonly found among such. Happy are they that have the Spirit of God with them, and never have quenched it, if they did but know the price they have in their hands!

If you have a sense of your necessity of salvation, and the great worth and value of it, you will be willing to take the surest way to it, or that which has the greatest probability of success; and that certainly is, thoroughly to improve your first convictions. If you do so, it is not likely that you will fail; there is the greatest probability that you will succeed.—What is it not worth, to have such an advantage in one's hands for obtaining eternal life? The present season of the pouring out of God's Spirit, is the first that many of you who are now under awakenings have ever seen, since you came to years of understanding. On which account, it is the greatest opportunity that ever you have had, and probably by far the greatest that ever you will have. There are many here present who wish they had such an opportunity, but they never can obtain it; they cannot buy it for money; but you have it in your possession, and can improve it if you will. But yet,

2. There is on some accounts greater danger that such as are in your circumstances will fail of thoroughly improving their convictions, with respect to stedfastness and perseverance, than others. Those that are young are more unstable than elder persons. They who never had convictions before, have less experience of the difficulty of the work they have engaged in; they are more ready to think that they shall obtain salvation easily, and are more easily discouraged by disappointments; and young persons have less reason and consideration to fortify them against temptations to backsliding. You should therefore labour now the more to guard against such temptations. By all means make but one work of seeking salvation! Make thorough work of it the first time! There are vast disadvantages that they bring themselves under, who have several turns of seeking with great intermissions. By such a course, persons exceedingly wound their own souls, and entangle themselves in many snares. Who are those that commonly meet with so many difficulties, and are so long labouring in darkness and perplexity, but those who have had several turns at seeking salvation; who have one while had convictions, and then have quenched them, and then have set about the work again, and have backslidden again, and have gone on after that manner? The children of Israel would not have been forty years in the wilderness, if they had held their courage, and had gone on as they set out; but they were of an unstable mind, and were for going back again into Egypt.— Otherwise, if they had gone right forward without discouragement, as God would have led them, they would have soon entered and taken possession of Canaan. They had got to the very

borders of it when they turned back, but were thirty-eight years after that, before they got through the wilderness. Therefore, as you regard the interest of your soul, do not run yourself into a like difficulty, by unsteadiness, intermission, and backsliding; but press right forward, from henceforth, and make but one work of seeking, converting, and pardoning grace, however great, and difficult, and long a work that may be.

H

Sermon V*

THE JUSTICE OF GOD IN THE DAMNATION
OF SINNERS

ROM. III. 19

—That every mouth may be stopped—

THE main subject of the doctrinal part of this epistle is the free grace of God in the salvation of men by Jesus Christ; especially as it appears in the doctrine of justification by faith alone. And the more clearly to evince this doctrine, and show the reason of it, the apostle, in the first place, establishes that point, that no flesh living can be justified by the deeds of the law. And to prove it, he is very large and particular in showing that all mankind, not only the Gentiles, but Jews, are under sin, and so under the condemnation of the law; which is what he insists upon from the beginning of the epistle to this place. He first begins with the Gentiles; and in the first chapter shows that they are under sin, by setting forth the exceeding corruptions and horrid wickedness that overspread the Gentile world: and then through the second chapter, and the former part of his third chapter, to the text and following verse, he shows the same of the Jews, that they also are in the same circumstances with the Gentiles in this regard. They had a high thought of themselves, because they were God's covenant people, and circumcised, and the children of Abraham. They despised the Gentiles as polluted, condemned, and accursed; but looked on themselves, on account of their external privileges, and ceremonial and moral righteousness, as a pure and holy people, and the children of God; as the apostle observes in the second chapter. It was therefore strange doctrine to them, that they also were unclean and guilty in God's sight, and under the condemnation and curse of the law. The apostle therefore, on

* Preached at Northampton during the Awakenings of 1734-1735.

account of their strong prejudices against such doctrine, the more particularly insists upon it, and shows that they are no better than the Gentiles; as in the 9th verse of this chapter, "What then? are we better than they? No, in no wise; for we have before proved both Jews and Gentiles, that they are all under sin." And, to convince them of it, he produces certain passages out of their own law, or the Old Testament, (to whose authority they pretended a great regard,) from the 9th verse to our text. And it may be observed, that the apostle, *first,* cites certain passages to prove that all mankind are *corrupt,* (ver. 10-12.) " As it is written, There is none righteous, no not one : There is none that understandeth, there is none that seeketh after God : They are all gone out of the way, they are together become unprofitable, there is none that doeth good, no not one." *Secondly,* The passages he cites next, are to prove, that not only are all corrupt, but each one *wholly* corrupt, as it were all over unclean, from the crown of the head to the soles of his feet; and therefore several particular parts of the body are mentioned, the throat, the tongue, the lips, the mouth, the feet, (ver. 13-15.) " Their throat is an open sepulchre; with their tongues they have used deceit; the poison of asps is under their lips; whose mouth is full of cursing and bitterness : their feet are swift to shed blood." And, *Thirdly,* He quotes other passages to show, that each one is not only all over corrupt, but corrupt to a desperate degree, (ver. 16-18.) by affirming the most pernicious tendency of their wickedness; " Destruction and misery are in their ways." And then by denying all goodness or godliness in them; " And the way of peace have they not known : There is no fear of God before their eyes." And then, lest the Jews should think these passages of their law do not concern them, and that only the Gentiles are intended in them, the apostle shows in the text, not only that they are not exempt, but that they especially must be understood : " Now we know that whatsoever things the law saith, it saith to them who are under the law." By those that are *under* the law are meant the Jews; and the Gentiles by those that are *without* law; as appears by the 12th verse of the preceding chapter. There is special reason to understand the law, as speaking to and of them, to whom it was immediately given. And therefore the Jews would be unreasonable in exempting themselves. And if we examine the places of the Old Testament whence these passages are taken, we shall see plainly that special respect is had to the wickedness of the people of that nation, in every one of them. So that the law shuts all up in universal and desperate wickedness, *that every mouth may be stopped;* the mouths of the Jews, as well as of the Gentiles, notwithstanding all those privileges by which they were distinguished from the Gentiles.

The things that the law says, are sufficient to stop the mouths of all mankind, in two respects:

1. To stop them from boasting of their righteousness, as the Jews were wont to do; as the apostle observes in the 23rd verse of the preceding chapter.—That the apostle has respect to stopping their mouths in this respect, appears by the 27th verse of the context, "Where is boasting then? It is excluded." The law stops our mouths from making any plea for life, or the favour of God, or any positive good, from our own righteousness.

2. To stop them from making any excuse for ourselves, or objection against the execution of the sentence of the law, or the infliction of the punishment that it threatens. That this is intended, appears by the words immediately following, "That all the world may become guilty before God." That is, that they may appear to be guilty, and stand convicted before God, and justly liable to the condemnation of his law, as guilty of death, according to the Jewish way of speaking.

And thus the apostle proves, that no flesh can be justified in God's sight by the deeds of the law; as he draws the conclusion in the following verse; and so prepares the way for establishing the great doctrine of justification by faith alone, which he proceeds to do in the following part of the chapter, and of the epistle.

DOCTRINE

"It is just with God eternally to cast off and destroy sinners."—For this is the punishment which the law condemns to.—The truth of his doctrine may appear by the joint consideration of two things, *viz.* Man's *sinfulness*, and God's *sovereignty*.

I. It appears from the consideration of man's sinfulness. And that, whether we consider the infinitely evil nature of all sin, or how much sin men are guilty of.

1. If we consider the infinite evil and heinousness of sin in

general, it is not unjust in God to inflict what punishment is deserved; because the very notion of deserving any punishment is, that it may be justly inflicted. A deserved punishment and a just punishment are the same thing. To say that one *deserves* such a punishment, and yet to say that he does not *justly* deserve it, is a contradiction; and if he justly deserves it, then it may be justly *inflicted*.

Every crime or fault deserves a greater or less punishment, in proportion as the crime itself is greater or less. If any fault deserves punishment, then so much the greater the fault, so much the greater is the punishment deserved. The faulty nature of any thing is the formal ground and reason of its desert of punishment; and therefore the more any thing hath of this nature, the more punishment it deserves. And therefore the terribleness of the degree of punishment, let it be never so terrible, is no argument against the justice of it, if the proportion does but hold between the heinousness of the crime and the dreadfulness of the punishment; so that if there be any such thing as a fault infinitely heinous, it will follow that it is just to inflict a punishment for it that is infinitely dreadful.

A crime is more or less heinous, according as we are under greater or less *obligations* to the contrary. This is self-evident; because it is herein that the criminalness or faultiness of any thing consists, that it is contrary to what we are obliged or bound to, or what *ought* to be in us. So the faultiness of one being hating another, is in proportion to his obligation to love him. The crime of one being despising and casting contempt on another, is proportionably more or less heinous, as he was under greater or less obligations to honour him. The fault of disobeying another, is greater or less, as any one is under greater or less obligations to obey him. And therefore if there be any being that we are under infinite obligations to love, and honour, and obey, the contrary towards him must be infinitely faulty.

Our obligation to love, honour, and obey any being, is in proportion to his loveliness, honourableness, and authority; for that is the very meaning of the words. When we say any one is very lovely, it is the same as to say, that he is one very much to be loved. Or if we say such a one is more honourable than another, the meaning of the words is, that he is one that we are more obliged to honour. If we say any one has great authority over us, it is the same as to say, that he has great right to our subjection and obedience.

But God is a being *infinitely* lovely, because he hath infinite excellency and beauty. To have infinite excellence and beauty, is the same thing as to have infinite loveliness. He is a being of infinite greatness, majesty, and glory; and therefore he is infinitely honourable. He is infinitely exalted above the greatest potentates of the earth, and highest angels in heaven; and therefore he is infinitely more honourable than they. His authority over us is infinite; and the ground of his right to our obedience is infinitely strong; for he is infinitely worthy to be obeyed himself, and we have an absolute, universal, and infinite dependence upon him.

So that sin against God, being a violation of infinite obligations, must be a crime infinitely heinous, and so deserving infinite punishment.—Nothing is more agreeable to the common sense of mankind, than that sins committed against any one, must be proportionably heinous to the dignity of the being offended and abused; as it is also agreeable to the word of God, 1 Sam. ii. 25. "If one man sin against another, the Judge shall judge him;" (*i.e.* shall judge him, and inflict a finite punishment, such as finite judges can inflict;) "but if a man sin against the Lord, who shall entreat for him?" This was the aggravation of sin that made Joseph afraid of it, Gen. xxxix. 9. "How shall I commit this great wickedness, and sin against God?" This was the aggravation of David's sin, in comparison of which he esteemed all others as nothing, because they were infinitely exceeded by it. Psalm li. 4. "Against thee, thee only have I sinned."—The *eternity* of the punishment of ungodly men renders it infinite: and it renders it no more than infinite; and therefore renders it no more than proportionable to the heinousness of what they are guilty of.

If there be *any* evil or faultiness in sin against God, there is certainly *infinite* evil: for if it be any fault at all, it has an infinite aggravation, *viz.* that it is against an infinite object. If it be ever so small upon other accounts, yet if it be any thing, it has one infinite dimension; and so is an infinite evil. Which may be illustrated by this: if we suppose a thing to have infinite length, but no breadth and thickness, (a mere mathematical line,) it is nothing: but if it have *any* breadth and thickness, though never so small, and infinite length, the quantity of it is infinite; it exceeds the quantity of any thing, however broad, thick, and long, wherein these dimensions are all finite.

So that the objections made against the *infinite* punishment of sin, from the necessity, or rather previous certainty, of the futurition of sin, arising from the unavoidable original corruption of nature, if they argue any thing, argue against *any* faultiness at all: for if this necessity or certainty leaves *any* evil at all in sin, that fault must be *infinite* by reason of the infinite object.

But every such objector as would argue from hence, that there is no fault at all in sin, confutes himself, and shows his own insincerity in his objection. For at the same time that he objects, that men's acts are necessary, and that this kind of necessity is inconsistent with faultiness in the act, his own practice shows that he does not believe what he objects to be true: otherwise why does he at all *blame* men? Or why are such persons at all displeased with men, for abusive, injurious, and ungrateful acts towards them? Whatever they pretend, by this they show that indeed they do believe that there is no necessity in men's acts that is inconsistent with blame. And if their objection be this, that this previous certainty is by God's own ordering, and that where God orders an antecedent certainty of acts, he tranfers all the fault from the actor on himself; their practice shows, that at the same time they do not believe this, but fully believe the contrary: for when they are abused by men, they are displeased with *men*, and not with *God* only.

The light of nature teaches all mankind, that when an injury is *voluntary* it is faulty, without any consideration of what there might be previously to determine the futurition of that evil act of the will. And it really teaches this as much to those that object and cavil most as to others; as their universal practice shows. By which it appears, that such objections are insincere and perverse. Men will mention others' corrupt nature when they are injured, as a thing that aggravates their crime, and that wherein their faultiness partly consists. How common is it for persons, when they look on themselves greatly injured by another, to inveigh against him, and aggravate his baseness, by saying, "He is a man of a most perverse spirit: he is naturally of a selfish, niggardly, or proud and haughty temper: he is one of a base and vile disposition." And yet men's natural and corrupt dispositions are mentioned as an excuse for them, with respect to their sins against God, as if they rendered them blameless.

2. That it is just with God eternally to cast off wicked men, may more abundantly appear, if we consider how much sin they are guilty of. From what has been already said, it appears, that if men were guilty of sin but in one particular, that is sufficient ground of their eternal rejection and condemnation. If they are *sinners*, that is enough. Merely this, might be sufficient to keep them from ever lifting up their heads, and cause them to smite on their breasts, with the publican that cried, "God be merciful to me a sinner." But sinful men are full of sin; principles and acts of sin: their guilt is like great mountains, heaped one upon another, till the pile is grown up to heaven. They are totally corrupt, in every part, in all their faculties; in all the principles of their nature, their understanding, and wills; and in all their dispositions and affections. Their heads, their hearts, are totally depraved; all the members of their bodies are only instruments of sin; and all their senses, seeing, hearing, tasting, etc., are only inlets and outlets of sin, channels of corruption. There is nothing but sin, no good at all. Rom. vii. 18. "In me, that is, in my flesh, dwells no good thing." There is all manner of wickedness. There are the seeds of the greatest and blackest crimes. There are principles of all sorts of wickedness against men; and there is all wickedness against God. There is pride; there is enmity; there is contempt; there is quarrelling; there is atheism; there is blasphemy. There are these things in exceeding strength; the heart is under the power of them, is sold under sin, and is a perfect slave to it. There is hard-heartedness, hardness greater than that of a rock, or an adamant-stone. There is obstinacy and perverseness, incorrigibleness and inflexibleness in sin, that will not be overcome by threatenings or promises, by awakenings or encouragements, by judgments or mercies, neither by that which is terrifying nor that which is winning. The very blood of God our Saviour will not win the heart of a wicked man.

And there are actual wickednesses, without number or measure. There are breaches of every command, in thought, word, and deed: a life full of sin; days and nights filled up with sin; mercies abused and frowns despised; mercy and justice, and all the divine perfections, trampled on; and the honour of each person in the Trinity trod in the dirt. Now if one sinful word or thought has so much evil in it, as to deserve eternal destruction, how do they deserve to be eternally cast off and destroyed, that are guilty of so much sin!

II. If with man's sinfulness, we consider God's *sovereignty*, it may serve further to clear God's justice in the eternal rejection and condemnation of sinners, from men's cavils and objections. I shall not now pretend to determine precisely, what things are, and what things are not, proper acts and exercises of God's holy sovereignty; but only, that God's sovereignty extends to the following things.

1. That such is God's sovereign power and right, that he is originally under no *obligation* to keep men from sinning; but may in his providence permit and *leave* them to sin. He was not obliged to keep either angels or men from falling. It is *unreasonable* to suppose, that God should be obliged, if he makes a reasonable creature capable of knowing his will, and receiving a law from him, and being subject to his moral government, at the same time to make it *impossible* for him to sin, or break his law. For if God be obliged to this, it destroys all use of any commands, laws, promises, or threatenings, and the very notion of any moral government of God over those reasonable creatures. For to what purpose would it be, for God to give such and such laws, and declare his holy will to a creature, and annex promises and threatenings to move him in his duty, and make him careful to perform it, if the creature at the same time has this to think of, that God is *obliged* to make it *impossible* for him to break his laws? How can God's threatenings move to care or watchfulness, when, at the same time, God is obliged to render it impossible that he should be exposed to the threatenings? Or, to what purpose is it for God to give a law at all? For according to this supposition, it is God, and not the creature, that is under law. It is the lawgiver's care, and not the subject's, to see that his law is obeyed; and this care is what the lawgiver is absolutely obliged to! If God be *obliged* never to *permit* a creature to fall, there is an end of all divine laws, or government, or authority of God over the creature; there can be no manner of use of these things.

God *may permit* sin, though the being of sin will *certainly* ensue on that permission: and so, by permission, he may dispose and order the event. If there were any such thing as chance, or mere contingence, and the very notion of it did not carry a gross absurdity, (as might easily be shown that it does,) it would have been very unfit that God should have left it to mere chance, whether man should fall or no. For chance, if there should be any such thing, is undesigning and blind. And certainly it is more fit that an event of so great importance, and which is attended with such an infinite train of great consequences, should be disposed and ordered by infinite *wisdom*, than that it should be left to blind *chance*.

If it be said, that God need not have interposed to render it impossible for man to sin, and yet not leave it to mere contingence or blind chance neither; but might have left it with man's *free will*, to determine whether to sin or no: I answer, if God did leave it to man's free will, without any *sort of disposal, or ordering* [or rather, *adequate cause*] in the case, whence it should be previously *certain* how that free will should determine, then still that first determination of the will must be merely contingent or by chance. It could not have any antecedent act of the will to determine it; for I speak now of the very first act or motion of the will, respecting the affair that may be looked upon as the prime ground and highest source of the event. To suppose this to be determined by a foregoing act is a contradiction. God's disposing this determination of the will by his *permission*, does not at all infringe the liberty of the creature. It is in no respect any more inconsistent with liberty, than mere chance or contingence. For if the determination of the will be from blind, undesigning chance, it is no more from the agent himself, or from the will itself, than if we suppose, in the case, a wise, divine disposal by permission.

2. It was fit that it should be at the ordering of the divine wisdom and good pleasure, whether every particular man should stand for himself, or whether the first father of mankind should be appointed as the moral and federal head and representative of the rest. If God has not liberty in this matter to determine either of these two as he pleases, it must be because determining that the first father of man should represent the rest, and not that every one should stand for himself, is *injurious* to mankind. For if it be not injurious, how is it unjust? But it is not injurious to mankind; for there is nothing in the nature of the case itself, that makes it better that each man should stand for himself, than

that all should be represented by their common father; as the least reflection or consideration will convince any one. And if there be nothing in the nature of the thing that makes the former better for mankind than the latter, then it will follow, that they are not hurt in God's choosing and appointing the latter, rather than the former; or, which is the same thing, that it is not injurious to mankind.

3. When men are fallen, and become sinful, God by his sovereignty has a right to determine about their redemption as he pleases. He has a right to determine whether he will redeem any or not. He might, if he had pleased, have left all to perish, or might have redeemed all. Or, he may redeem some, and leave others; and if he doth so, he may take whom he pleases, and leave whom he pleases. To suppose that all have forfeited his favour, and deserved to perish, and to suppose that he may not leave any one individual of them to perish, implies a contradiction; because it supposes that such a one has a claim to God's favour, and is not justly liable to perish; which is contrary to the supposition.

It is meet that God should order all these things according to his own pleasure. By reason of his greatness and glory, by which he is infinitely above all, he is worthy to be sovereign, and that his pleasure should in all things take place. He is worthy that he should make himself his end, and that he should make nothing but his own wisdom his rule in pursuing that end, without asking leave or counsel of any, and without giving account of any of his matters. It is fit that he who is absolutely perfect, and infinitely wise, and the Fountain of all wisdom, should determine every thing [that he effects] by his own will, even things of the greatest importance. It is meet that he should be thus sovereign, because he is the first being, the eternal being, whence all other beings are. He is the Creator of all things; and all are absolutely and universally dependent on him; and therefore it is meet that he should act as the sovereign possessor of heaven and earth.

APPLICATION

In the improvement of this doctrine, I would chiefly direct myself to sinners who are afraid of damnation, in a use of conviction. This may be matter of conviction to you, that it would be just and righteous with God eternally to reject and destroy you. This is what you are in danger of. You who are a Christless sinner, are a poor condemned creature: God's wrath still abides upon you; and the sentence of condemnation lies upon you. You are in God's hands, and it is uncertain what he will do with you. You are afraid what will become of you. You are afraid that it will be your portion to suffer eternal burnings; and your fears are not without grounds; you have reason to tremble every moment. But be you never so much afraid of it, let eternal damnation be never so dreadful, yet it is just. God may nevertheless do it, and be righteous, and holy, and glorious. Though eternal damnation be what you cannot bear, and how much soever your heart shrinks at the thoughts of it, yet God's justice may be glorious in it. The dreadfulness of the thing on your part, and the greatness of your dread of it, do not render it the less righteous on God's part. If you think otherwise, it is a sign that you do not see yourself, that you are not sensible what sin is, nor how much of it you have been guilty of. Therefore for your conviction, be directed,

First, To look over your past life: inquire at the mouth of conscience, and hear what that has to testify concerning it. Consider what you are, what light you have had, and what means you have lived under: and yet how you have behaved yourself! What have those many days and nights you have lived been filled up with? How have those years that have rolled over your heads, one after another, been spent? What has the sun shone upon you for, from day to day, while you have improved his light to serve Satan by it? What has God kept your breath in your nostrils for, and given you meat and drink, that you have spent your life and strength, supported by them, in opposing God, and rebellion against him?

How *many* sorts of wickedness have you not been guilty of! How manifold have been the abominations of your life! What profaneness and contempt of God has been exercised by you! How little regard have you had to the Scriptures, to the word preached, to sabbaths, and sacraments! How profanely have you talked, many of you, about those things that are holy! After what manner have many of you kept God's holy day, not regarding the holiness of the time, nor caring what you thought of in it! Yea, you have not only spent the time in worldly, vain,

and unprofitable thoughts, but immoral thoughts; pleasing yourself with the reflection on past acts of wickedness, and in contriv-
ing new acts.   Have not you spent much holy time in gratifying
your lusts in your imaginations; yea, not only holy time, but the
very time of God's public worship, when you have appeared in
God's more immediate presence?   How have you not only not
attended to the worship, but have in the mean time been feasting
your lusts, and wallowing yourself in abominable uncleanness!
How many sabbaths have you spent, one after another, in a most
wretched manner!   Some of you not only in worldly and wicked
thoughts, but also a very wicked outward behaviour!   When you
on sabbath-days have got along with your wicked companions,
how has holy time been treated among you!   What kind of conversation has there been!   Yea, how have some of you, by a very
indecent carriage, openly dishonoured and cast contempt on the
sacred services of God's house, and holy day!   And what you
have done some of you alone, what wicked practices there have
been in secret, even in holy time, God and your own consciences
know.

And how have you behaved yourself in the time of family
prayer!   And what a trade have many of you made of absenting
yourselves from the worship of the families you belong to, for the
sake of vain company!   And how have you continued in the
neglect of secret prayer! therein wilfully living in a known sin,
going abreast against as plain a command as any in the Bible!
Have you not been one that has cast off fear, and restrained
prayer before God?

What wicked carriage have some of you been guilty of towards
your parents!   How far have you been from paying that honour
to them which God has required!   Have you not even harboured
ill-will and malice towards them? and when they have displeased
you, have wished evil to them? yea, and shown your vile spirit in
your behaviour? and it is well if you have not mocked them
behind their backs; and, like the accursed Ham and Canaan, as
it were, derided your parents' nakedness instead of covering it,
and hiding your eyes from it.   Have not some of you often dis-
obeyed your parents, yea, and refused to be subject to them?   Is
it not a wonder of mercy and forbearance, that the proverb has
not before now been accomplished on you, Prov. xxx. 17. "The
eye that mocketh at his father, and refuseth to obey his mother,

the ravens of the valley shall pick it out, and the young eagles shall eat it?"

What revenge and malice have you been guilty of towards your neighbours! How have you indulged this spirit of the devil, hating others, and wishing evil to them, rejoicing when evil befell them, and grieving at others' prosperity, and lived in such a way for a long time! Have not some of you allowed a passionate furious spirit, and behaved yourselves in your anger more like wild beasts than like Christians?

What covetousness has been in many of you! Such has been your inordinate love of the world, and care about the things of it, that it has taken up your heart; you have allowed no room for God and religion; you have minded the world more than your eternal salvation. For the vanities of the world you have neglected reading, praying, and meditation; for the things of the world you have broken the sabbath; for the world you have spent a great deal of your time in quarrelling. For the world you have envied and hated your neighbour; for the world you have cast God, and Christ, and heaven, behind your back; for the world you have sold your own soul. You have as it were drowned your soul in worldly cares and desires; you have been a mere earthworm, that is never in its element but when grovelling and buried in the earth.

How much of a spirit of *pride* has appeared in you, which is in a peculiar manner the spirit and condemnation of the devil! How have some of you vaunted yourselves in your apparel! others in their riches! others in their knowledge and abilities! How has it galled you to see others above you! How much has it gone against the grain for you to give others their due honour! And how have you shown your pride by setting up your wills in opposing others, and stirring up and promoting division, and a party spirit in public affairs.

How *sensual* have you been! Are there not some here that have debased themselves below the dignity of human nature, by wallowing in sensual filthiness, as swine in the mire, or as filthy vermin feeding with delight on rotten carrion? What intemperance have some of you been guilty of! How much of your precious time have you spent away at the tavern, and in drinking companies, when you ought to have been at home seeking God and your salvation in your families and closets!

And what abominable *lasciviousness* have some of you been guilty of! How have you indulged yourself from day to day, and from night to night, in all manner of unclean imaginations! Has not your soul been filled with them, till it has become a hold of foul spirits, and a cage of every unclean and hateful bird? What foul-mouthed persons have some of you been, often in lewd and lascivious talk and unclean songs, wherein were things not fit to be spoken! And such company, where such conversation has been carried on, has been your delight. And with what unclean acts and practices have you defiled yourself! God and your own consciences know what abominable lasciviousness you have practised in things not fit to be named, when you have been alone; when you ought to have been reading, or meditating, or on your knees before God in secret prayer. And how have you corrupted others, as well as polluted yourselves! What vile uncleanness have you practised in company! What abominations have you been guilty of in the dark! Such as the apostle doubtless had respect to in Eph. v. 12. " For it is a shame even to speak of those things that are done of them in secret." Some of you have corrupted others, and done what in you lay to undo their souls, (if you have not actually done it,) and by your vile practices and example have made room for Satan, invited his presence, and established his interest, in the town where you have lived.

What *lying* have some of you been guilty of, especially in your childhood! And have not your heart and lips often disagreed since you came to riper years? What fraud, and deceit, and unfaithfulness, have many of you practised in your own dealings with your neighbours, of which your own heart is conscious, if you have not been noted by others.

And how have some of you behaved yourselves in your *family* relations! How have you neglected your children's souls! And not only so, but have corrupted their minds by your bad examples; and instead of training them up in the nurture and admonition of the Lord, have rather brought them up in the devil's service!

How have some of you attended that sacred ordinance of the Lord's supper without any manner of serious preparation, and in a careless slighty frame of spirits, and chiefly to comply with custom! Have you not ventured to put the sacred symbols of the body and blood of Christ into your mouth, while at the same time you lived in ways of known sins, and intended no other than still to go on in the same wicked practices? And, it may be, have sat at the Lord's table with rancour in your heart against some of your brethren that you have sat therewith. You have come even to that holy feast of love among God's children, with the leaven of malice and envy in your heart; and so have eat and drank judgment to yourself.

What stupidity and sottishness has attended your course of wickedness; which has appeared in your obstinacy under awakening dispensations of God's word and providence. And how have some of you backslidden after you have set out in religion, and quenched God's Spirit after he had been striving with you! And what unsteadiness, and slothfulness, and long misimprovement of God's strivings with you, have you been chargeable with!

Now, can you think when you have thus behaved yourself, that God is *obliged* to show you mercy? Are you not after all this ashamed to talk of its being hard with God to cast you off? Does it become one who has lived such a life to open his mouth to excuse himself, to object against God's justice in his condemnation, or to complain of it as hard in God not to give him converting and pardoning grace, and make him his child, and bestow on him eternal life? or to talk of his duties and great pains in religion, as if such performances were worthy to be accepted, and to draw God's heart to such a creature? If this has been your manner, does it not show how little you have considered yourself, and how little a sense you have had of your own sinfulness?

Secondly, Be directed to consider, if God should eternally reject and destroy you, what an agreeableness and exact mutual answerableness there would be between God so dealing with you, and your spirit and behaviour. There would not only be an equality, but a similitude. God declares, that his dealings with men shall be suitable to their disposition and practice. Psalm xviii. 25, 26. "With the merciful man, thou wilt show thyself merciful; with an upright man, thou wilt show thyself upright; with the pure, thou wilt show thyself pure; and with the froward, thou wilt show thyself froward." How much soever you dread damnation, and are affrighted and concerned at the thoughts of it; yet if God should indeed eternally damn you, you would be met with but in your own way; you would be dealt with exactly according to your own dealing. Surely it is but fair that you should be made to buy in the same measure in which you sell.

Here I would particularly show,—1. That if God should eternally destroy you, it would be agreeable to your treatment of *God*. 2. That it would be agreeable to your treatment of *Jesus Christ*. 3. That it would be agreeable to your behaviour towards your *neighbours*. 4. That it would be according to your own foolish behaviour towards *yourself*.

I. If God should for ever cast you off, it would be exactly agreeable to your treatment of *him*. That you may be sensible of this, consider,

1. You never have exercised the least degree of love to God; and therefore it would be agreeable to your treatment of him if he should never express any love to you. When God converts and saves a sinner, it is a wonderful and unspeakable manifestation of divine love. When a poor lost soul is brought home to Christ, and has all his sins forgiven him, and is made a child of God, it will take up a whole eternity to express and declare the greatness of that love. And why should God be *obliged* to express such wonderful love to you, who never exercised the least degree of love to him in all your life? You never have loved God, who is infinitely glorious and lovely; and why then is God under *obligation* to love you, who are all over deformed and loathsome as a filthy worm, or rather a hateful viper? You have no benevolence in your heart towards God; you never rejoiced in God's happiness; if he had been miserable, and that had been possible, you would have liked it as well as if he were happy; you would not have cared how miserable he was, nor mourned for it, any more than you now do for the devil's being miserable. And why then should God be looked upon as obliged to take so much care for your happiness, as to do such great things for it, as he doth for those that are saved? Or why should God be called hard, in case he should not be careful to save you from misery? You care not what becomes of God's glory; you are not distressed how much soever his honour seems to suffer in the world: and why should God care any more for your welfare? Has it not been so, that if you could but promote your private interest, and gratify your own lusts, you cared not how much the glory of God suffered? And why may not God advance his own glory in the ruin of your welfare, not caring how much your interest suffers

I

by it? You never so much as stirred one step, sincerely making the glory of God your end, or acting from real respect to him; and why then is it hard if God do not do such great things for you, as the changing of your nature, raising you from spiritual death to life, conquering the powers of darkness for you, translating you out of the kingdom of darkness into the kingdom of his dear Son, delivering you from eternal misery, and bestowing upon you eternal glory? You were not willing to deny yourself for God; you never cared to put yourself out of your way for Christ; whenever any thing cross or difficult came in your way, that the glory of God was concerned in, it has been your manner to shun it, and excuse yourself from it. You did not care to hurt yourself for Christ, whom you did not see worthy of it; and why then must it be looked upon as a hard and cruel thing, if Christ has not been pleased to spill his blood and be tormented to death for such a sinner.

2. You have slighted God; and why then may not God justly slight you? When sinners are sensible in some measure of their misery, they are ready to think it hard that God will take no more notice of them; that he will see them in such a lamentable distressed condition, beholding their burdens and tears, and seem to slight it, and manifest no pity to them. Their souls they think are precious: it would be a dreadful thing if they should perish, and burn in hell for ever. They do not see through it, that God should make so light of their salvation. But then, ought they not to consider, that as their souls are precious, so is God's honour precious? The honour of the infinite God, the great God of heaven and earth, is a thing of as great importance, (and surely may justly be so esteemed by God,) as the happiness of you, a poor little worm. But yet you have slighted that honour of God, and valued it no more than the dirt under your feet. You have been told that such and such things were contrary to the will of a holy God, and against his honour; but you cared not for that. God called upon you, and exhorted you to be more tender of his honour; but you went on without regarding him. Thus have you slighted God! And yet, is it hard that God should slight you? Are you more honourable than God, that he must be obliged to make much of you, how light soever you make of him and his glory?

And you have not only slighted God in time past, but you

slight him still. You indeed now make a pretence and show of
honouring him in your prayers, and attendance on other external
duties, and by sober countenance, and seeming devoutness in
your words and behaviour; but it is all mere dissembling. That
downcast look and seeming reverence, is not from any honour
you have to God in your heart, though you would have God take
it so. You who have not believed in Christ, have not the least
jot of honour to God; that show of it is merely forced, and what
you are driven to by fear, like those mentioned in Psalm lxvi. 3.
" Through the greatness of thy power shall thine enemies submit
themselves to thee." In the original it is, " shall lie unto thee;"
that is, yield feigned submission, and dissemble respect and
honour to thee. There is a rod held over you that makes you
seem to pay such respect to God. This religion and devotion,
even the very appearance of it, would soon be gone, and all vanish
away, if that were removed. Sometimes it may be you weep in
your prayers, and in your hearing sermons, and hope God will
take notice of it, and take it for some honour; but he sees it to be
all hypocrisy. You weep for yourself; you are afraid of hell; and
do you think that that is worthy of God to take much notice of
you, because you can cry when you are in danger of being
damned; when at the same time you indeed care nothing for
God's honour.

Seeing you thus disregard so great a God, is it a heinous thing
for God to slight you, a little, wretched, despicable creature; a
worm, a mere nothing, and less than nothing; a vile insect, that
has risen up in contempt against the Majesty of heaven and
earth?

3. Why should God be looked upon as obliged to bestow salvation upon you, when you have been so ungrateful for the mercies
he has bestowed upon you already? God has tried you with a
great deal of kindness, and he never has sincerely been thanked
by you for any of it. God has watched over you, and preserved
you, and provided for you, and followed you with mercy all your
days; and yet you have continued sinning against him. He has
given you food and raiment, but you have improved both in the
service of sin. He has preserved you while you slept; but when
you arose, it was to return to the old trade of sinning. God, notwithstanding this ingratitude, has still continued his mercy; but
his kindness has never won your heart, or brought you to a more

grateful behaviour towards him. It may be you have received many remarkable mercies, recoveries from sickness, or preservations of your life when exposed by accidents, when if you had died, you would have gone directly to hell; but you never had any true thankfulness for any of these mercies. God has kept you out of hell, and continued your day of grace, and the offers of salvation, so long a time; while you did not regard your own salvation so much as in secret to ask God for it. And now God has greatly added to his mercy to you, by giving you the strivings of his Spirit, whereby a most precious opportunity for your salvation is in your hands. But what thanks has God received for it? What kind of returns have you made for all this kindness? As God has multiplied mercies, so have you multiplied provocations.

And yet now are you ready to quarrel for mercy, and to find fault with God, not only that he does not bestow more mercy, but to contend with him, because he does not bestow infinite mercy upon you, heaven with all it contains, and even himself, for your eternal portion. What ideas have you of yourself, that you think God is *obliged* to do so much for you, though you treat him ever so ungratefully for his kindness wherewith you have been followed all the days of your life.

4. You have voluntarily chosen to be with Satan in his enmity and opposition to God; how justly therefore might you be with him in his punishment! You did not choose to be on God's side, but rather chose to side with the devil, and have obstinately continued in it, against God's often repeated calls and counsels. You have chosen rather to hearken to Satan than to God, and would be with him in his work. You have given yourself up to him, to be subject to his power and government, in opposition to God; how justly therefore may God also give you up to him, and leave you in his power, to accomplish your ruin! Seeing you have yielded yourself to his will, to do as he would have you, surely God may leave you in his hands to execute his will upon you. If men will be with God's enemy, and on his side, why is God obliged to redeem them out of his hands, when they have done his work? Doubtless you would be glad to serve the devil, and be God's enemy while you live, and then to have God your friend, and deliver you from the devil, when you come to die. But will God be unjust if he deals otherwise by you? No, surely! It will be altogether and perfectly just, that you should have your

portion with him with whom you have chosen to work; and that
you should be in his possession to whose dominion you have
yielded yourself; and if you cry to God for deliverance, he may
most justly give you that answer, Judges x. 14. " Go to the gods
which you have chosen."

5. Consider how often you have refused to hear God's calls to
you, and how just it would therefore be, if he should refuse to
hear you when you call upon him. You are ready, it may be, to
complain that you have often prayed, and earnestly begged of
God to show you mercy, and yet have no answer to prayer: One
says, I have been constant in prayer for so many years, and God
has not heard me. Another says, I have done what I can; I have
prayed as earnestly as I am able; I do not see how I can do more;
and it will seem hard if after all I am denied. But do you consider how often God has called, and you have denied him? God
has called earnestly and for a long time; he has called and called
again in his word, and in his providence, and you have refused.
You were not uneasy for fear you should not show regard enough
to his calls. You let him call as loud and as long as he would;
for your part, you had no leisure to attend to what he said; you
had other business to mind; you had these and those lusts to
gratify and please, and worldly concerns to attend; you could not
afford to stand considering of what God had to say to you. When
the ministers of Christ have stood and pleaded with you, in his
name, sabbath after sabbath, and have even spent their strength
in it, how little were you moved!   It did not alter you, but you
went on still as you used to do; when you went away, you returned again to your sins, to your lasciviousness, to your vain
mirth, to your covetousness, to your intemperance, and that has
been the language of your heart and practice, Exod. v. 2. " Who
is the Lord, that I should obey his voice?" Was it no crime for
you to refuse to hear when God called? And yet is it now very
hard that God does not hear your earnest calls, and that though
your calling on God be not from any respect to him, but merely
from self-love? The devil would beg as earnestly as you, if he
had any hope to get salvation by it, and a thousand times as
earnestly, and yet be as much of a devil as he is now. Are your
calls more worthy to be heard than God's? Or is God more
obliged to regard what you say to him, than you to regard his
commands, counsels, and invitations to you? What can be more

justice than this, Prov. i. 24, etc. " Because I have called, and ye refused, I have stretched out my hand, and no man regarded; but ye have set at nought all my counsel, and would none of my reproof: I will also laugh at your calamity, I will mock when your fear cometh; when your fear cometh as desolation, and your destruction cometh as a whirlwind; when distress and anguish cometh upon you. Then shall they call upon me, but I will not answer; they shall seek me early, but they shall not find me."

6. Have you not taken encouragement to sin against God, on that very presumption, that God would show you mercy when you sought it? And may not God justly refuse you that mercy that you have presumed upon? You have flattered yourself, that though you did so, yet God would show you mercy when you cried earnestly to him for it: how righteous therefore would it be in God, to disappoint such a wicked presumption! It was upon that very hope that you dared to affront the Majesty of heaven so dreadfully as you have done; and can you now be so sottish as to think that God is obliged not to frustrate that hope?

When a sinner takes encouragement to neglect secret prayer which God has commanded, to gratify his lusts, to live a carnal vain life, to thwart God, to run upon him, and contemn him to his face, thinking with himself, " If I do so, God would not damn me; he is a merciful God, and therefore when I seek his mercy he will bestow it upon me;" must God be accounted hard because he will not do according to such a sinner's presumption?

Cannot he be excused from showing such a sinner mercy when he is pleased to seek it, without incurring the charge of being unjust? if this be the case, God has no liberty to vindicate his own honour and majesty; but must lay himself open to all manner of affronts, and yield himself up to the abuses of vile men, though they disobey, despise, and dishonour him, as much as they will; and when they have done, his mercy and pardoning grace must not be in his own power and at his own disposal, but he must be obliged to dispense it at their call. He must take these bold and vile contemners of his Majesty, when it suits them to ask it, and must forgive all their sins, and not only so, but must adopt them into his family, and make them his children, and bestow eternal glory upon them. What mean, low, and strange thoughts have such men of God, who think thus of him! Consider, that you have injured God the more, and have been the worse enemy to him, for his being a merciful God. So have you treated that attribute of God's mercy! How just is it therefore that you never should have any benefit of that attribute!

There is something peculiarly heinous in sinning against the mercy of God more than other attributes. There is such base and horrid ingratitude, in being the worse to God because he is a being of infinite goodness and grace, that it above all things renders wickedness vile and detestable. This ought to win us, and engage us to serve God better; but instead of that, to sin against him the more, has something inexpressibly bad in it, and does in a peculiar manner enhance guilt, and incense wrath; as seems to be intimated, Rom. ii. 4, 5. "Or despisest thou the riches of his goodness, and forbearance, and long-suffering; not knowing that the goodness of God leadeth thee to repentance? But after thy hardness and impenitent heart, treasurest up unto thyself wrath against the day of wrath, and revelation of the righteous judgment of God."

The greater the mercy of God is, the more should you be engaged to love him, and live to his glory. But it has been contrariwise with you; the consideration of the mercies of God being so exceeding great, is the thing wherewith you have encouraged yourself in sin. You have heard that the mercy of God was without bounds, that it was sufficient to pardon the greatest sinner, and you have upon that very account ventured to be a very great sinner. Though it was very offensive to God, though you heard that God infinitely hated sin, and that such practices as you went on in were exceeding contrary to his nature, will, and glory, yet that did not make you uneasy; you heard that he was a very merciful God, and had grace enough to pardon you, and so cared not how offensive your sins were to him. How long have some of you gone on in sin, and what great sins have some of you been guilty of, on that presumption! Your own conscience can give testimony to it, that this has made you refuse God's calls, and has made you regardless of his repeated commands. Now, how righteous would it be if God should swear in his wrath, that you should never be the better for his being infinitely merciful!

Your ingratitude has been the greater, that you have not only abused the attribute of God's mercy, taking encouragement from it to continue in sin, but you have also presumed that God would exercise infinite mercy to you in particular; which consideration should have especially endeared God to you. You have taken encouragement to sin the more, from that consideration, that Christ came into the world and died to save sinners; such thanks has Christ had from you, for enduring such a tormenting death for his enemies! Now, how justly might God refuse that you should ever be the better for his Son's laying down his life! It was because of these things that you put off seeking salvation. You would take the pleasures of sin still longer, hardening yourself because mercy was infinite, and it would not be too late, if you sought it afterwards; now, how justly may God disappoint you in this, and so order it that it shall be too late.

7. How have some of you risen up against God, and in the frame of your minds opposed him in his sovereign dispensations! And how justly upon that account might God oppose you, and set himself against you! You never yet would submit to God; never willingly comply, that God should have dominion over the world, and that he should govern it for his own glory, according to his own wisdom. You, a poor worm, a potsherd, a broken piece of an earthen vessel, have dared to find fault and quarrel with God. Isaiah xlv. 9. "Woe to him that strives with his Maker. Let the potsherd strive with the potsherds of the earth: shall the clay say to him that fashioned it, What makest thou?" But yet you have ventured to do it. Rom. ix. 20. "Who art thou, O man, that repliest against God?" But yet you have thought you were big enough; you have taken upon you to call God to an account, why he does thus and thus; you have said to Jehovah, What doest thou?

If you have been restrained by fear from openly venting your opposition and enmity of heart against God's government, yet it has been in you; you have not been quiet in the frame of your mind; you have had the heart of a viper within, and have been ready to spit your venom at God. It is well if sometimes you have not actually done it, by tolerating blasphemous thoughts and malignant risings of heart against him; yea, and the frame of your heart in some measure appeared in impatient and fretful behaviour.—Now, seeing you have thus opposed God, how just is it that God should oppose you! Or is it because you are so much better, and so much greater than God, that it is a crime for him to make that opposition against you which you make against him? Do you think that the liberty of making opposition is your exclusive prerogative, so that you may be an enemy to God, but God must by no means be an enemy to you, but must be looked upon under obligation nevertheless to help you, and save you by his blood, and bestow his best blessings upon you?

Consider how in the frame of your mind you have thwarted God in those very exercises of mercy towards others that you are seeking for yourself. God exercising his infinite grace towards your neighbours, has put you into an ill frame, and it may be, set you in a tumult of mind. How justly therefore may God refuse ever to exercise that mercy towards you! Have you not thus opposed God showing mercy to others, even at the very time when you pretended to be earnest with God for pity and help for yourself? yea, and while you were endeavouring to get something wherewith to recommend yourself to God? And will you look to God still with a challenge of mercy, and contend with him for it notwithstanding? Can you who have such a heart, and have thus behaved yourself, come to God for any other than mere *sovereign mercy*?

II. If you should for ever be cast off by God, it would be agreeable to your treatment of *Jesus Christ*. It would have been just with God if he had cast you off for ever, without ever making you the offer of a Saviour. But God hath not done that; he has provided a Saviour for sinners, and offered him to you, even his own Son Jesus Christ, who is the only Saviour of men. All that are not forever cast off are saved by him. God offers men salvation through him, and has promised us, that if we come to him, we shall not be cast off. But you have treated, and still treat, this Saviour after such a manner, that if you should be eternally cast off by God, it would be most agreeable to your behaviour towards him; which appears by this, *viz.* " That you reject Christ, and will not have him for your Saviour."

If God offers you a Saviour from deserved punishment, and you will not receive him, then surely it is just that you should go without a Saviour. Or is God obliged, because you do not like *this* Saviour, to provide you another? He has given an infinitely honourable and glorious person, even his only-begotten Son, to be a sacrifice for sin, and so provided salvation; and this Saviour is offered to you: now if you refuse to accept him, is God therefore unjust if he does not save you? Is he obliged to save you in a way of *your* own choosing, because you do not like the way of

his choosing? Or will you charge Christ with injustice because
he does not become your Saviour, when at the same time you
will not have him when he offers himself to you, and beseeches
you to accept of him as your Saviour?

I am sensible that by this time many persons are ready to
object against this. If all should speak what they now think, we
should hear a murmuring all over the meeting-house, and one
and another would say, " I cannot see how this can be, that I am
not willing that Christ should be my Saviour, when I would give
all the world that he was my Saviour: how is it possible that I
should not be willing to have Christ for my Saviour, when this
is what I am seeking after, and praying for, and striving for, as
for my life?"

Here therefore I would endeavour to convince you, that you
are under a gross mistake in this matter. And, 1*st*, I would
endeavour to show the grounds of your mistake. And, 2*dly*, To
demonstrate to you, that you have rejected, and do wilfully reject,
Jesus Christ.

1*st*, That you may see the weak grounds of your mistake, consider,

1. There is a great deal of difference between a willingness not
to be damned, and a being willing to receive Christ for your
Saviour. You have the former; there is no doubt of that: no-
body supposes that you *love misery* so as to choose an eternity
of it; and so doubtless you are willing to be saved from eternal
misery. But that is a very different thing from being willing to
come to Christ: persons very commonly mistake the one for the
other, but they are quite two things. You may love the deliverance, but hate the deliverer. You tell of willingness; but consider
what is the object of that willingness. It does not respect Christ;
the way of salvation by him is not at all the object of it; but it is
wholly terminated on your escape from misery. The inclination
of your will goes no further than self, it never reaches Christ.
You are willing not to be miserable; that is, you love yourself,
and there your will and choice terminate. And it is but a vain
pretence and delusion to say or think, that you are willing to
accept of Christ.

2. There is certainly a great deal of difference between a forced
compliance and a free willingness. Force and freedom cannot
consist together. Now that willingness, whereby you think you

are willing to have Christ for a Saviour, is merely a forced thing. Your heart does not go out after Christ of itself, but you are forced and driven to seek an interest in him.   Christ has no share at all in your heart; there is no manner of closing of the heart with him.   This forced compliance is not what Christ seeks of you; he seeks a free and willing acceptance, Psalm cx. 3. " Thy people shall be willing in the day of thy power." He seeks not that you should receive him *against* your will, but *with* a free will. He seeks entertainment in your heart and choice.——And if you refuse thus to receive Christ, how just is it that Christ should refuse to receive you! How reasonable are Christ's terms, who offers to save all those that willingly, or with a good will, accept of him for their Saviour!   Who can rationally expect that Christ should force himself upon any man to be his Saviour? Or what can be looked for more reasonable, than that all who would be saved by Christ, should heartily and freely entertain him? And surely it would be very dishonourable for Christ to offer himself upon lower terms.—But I would now proceed,

2*dly*, To show that you are not willing to have Christ for a Saviour.   To convince you of it, consider,

1. How it is possible that you should be willing to accept of Christ as a Saviour from the desert of a punishment that you are not sensible you have deserved. If you are truly willing to accept of Christ as a Saviour, it must be as a sacrifice to make atonement for your guilt. Christ came into the world on this errand, to offer himself as an atonement, to answer for our desert of punishment. But how can you be willing to have Christ for a Saviour from a desert of hell, if you be not sensible that you have a desert of hell? If you have not really deserved everlasting burnings in hell, then the very offer of an atonement for such a desert is an imposition upon you. If you have no such guilt upon you, then the very offer of a satisfaction for that guilt is an injury, because it implies in it a charge of guilt that you are free from. Now therefore it is impossible that a man who is not convinced of his guilt can be willing to accept of such an offer; because he cannot be willing to accept the charge which the offer implies. A man who is not convinced that he has deserved so dreadful a punishment, cannot willingly submit to be charged with it. If he thinks he is willing, it is but a mere forced, feigned business; because in his heart he looks upon himself greatly injured; and therefore he

cannot freely accept of Christ, under that notion of a Saviour from the desert of such a punishment; for such an acceptance is an implicit owning that he does deserve such a punishment.

I do not say, but that men may be willing to be saved from an undeserved punishment; they may rather not suffer it than suffer it. But a man cannot be willing to accept one at God's hands, under the notion of a Saviour from a punishment deserved from him which he thinks he has not deserved; it is impossible that any one should freely allow a Saviour under that notion. Such an one cannot like the way of salvation by Christ; for if he thinks he has not deserved hell, then he will think that freedom from hell is a debt; and therefore cannot willingly and heartily receive it as a free gift.—If a king should condemn a man to some tormenting death, which the condemned person thought himself not deserving of, but looked upon the sentence as unjust and cruel, and the king, when the time of execution drew nigh, should offer him his pardon, under the notion of a very great act of grace and clemency, the condemned person never could willingly and heartily allow it under that notion, because he judged himself unjustly condemned.

Now by this it is evident that you are not willing to accept of Christ as your Saviour; because you never yet had such a sense of your own sinfulness, and such a conviction of your great guilt in God's sight, as to be indeed convinced that you lay justly condemned to the punishment of hell. You never were convinced that you had forfeited all favour, and were in God's hands, and at his sovereign and arbitrary disposal, to be either destroyed or saved, just as he pleased. You never yet were convinced of the sovereignty of God. Hence are there so many objections arising against the justice of your punishment from original sin, and from God's decrees, from mercy shown to others, and the like.

2. That you are not sincerely willing to accept of Christ as your Saviour, appears by this, That you never have been convinced that he is sufficient for the work of your salvation. You never had a sight or sense of any such excellency or worthiness in Christ, as should give such great value to his bood and his mediation with God, as that it was sufficient to be accepted for such exceeding guilty creatures, who have so provoked God, and exposed themselves to such amazing wrath. Saying it is so, and allowing it to be as others say, is a very different thing from being really con-

vinced of it, and a being made sensible of it in your own heart. The sufficiency of Christ depends upon, or rather consists in, his excellency. It is because he is so excellent a person that his blood is of sufficient value to atone for sin, and it is hence that his obedience is so worthy in God's sight; it is also hence that his intercession is so prevalent; and therefore those that never had any spiritual sight or sense of Christ's excellency, cannot be sensible of his sufficiency.

And that sinners are not convinced that Christ is sufficient for the work he has undertaken, appears most manifestly when they are under great convictions of their sin, and danger of God's wrath. Though it may be before they thought they could allow Christ to be sufficient, (for it is easy to allow any one to be sufficient for our defence at a time when we see no danger,) yet when they come to be sensible of their guilt and God's wrath, what discouraging thoughts do they entertain! How are they ready to draw towards despair, as if there were no hope or help for such wicked creatures as they! The reason is, They have no apprehension or sense of any other way that God's majesty can be vindicated, but only in their misery. To tell them of the blood of Christ signifies nothing, it does not relieve their sinking, despairing hearts. This makes it most evident that they are not convinced that Christ is sufficient to be their Mediator.—And as long as they are unconvinced of this, it is impossible they should be willing to accept of him as their Mediator and Saviour. A man in distressing fear will not willingly betake himself to a fort that he judges not sufficient to defend him from the enemy. A man will not willingly venture out into the ocean in a ship that he suspects is leaky, and will sink before he gets through his voyage.

3. It is evident that you are not willing to have Christ for your Saviour, because you have so mean an opinion of him, that you durst not trust his faithfulness. One that undertakes to be the Saviour of souls had need be faithful; for if he fails in such a trust, how great is the loss! But you are not convinced of Christ's faithfulness; as is evident, because at such times as when you are in a considerable measure sensible of your guilt and God's anger, you cannot be convinced that Christ is willing to accept of you, or that he stands ready to receive you, if you should come to him, though Christ so much invites you to come to him, and has so

fully declared that he will not reject you, if you do come; as particularly, John vi. 37. "Him that cometh to me, I will in no wise cast out." Now, there is no man can be heartily willing to trust his eternal welfare in the hands of an unfaithful person, or one whose faithfulness he suspects.

4. You are not willing to be saved in that way by Christ, as is evident, because you are not willing that your own goodness should be set at nought. In the way of salvation by Christ men's own goodness is wholly set at nought; there is no account at all made of it. Now you cannot be willing to be saved in a way wherein your own goodness is set at nought, as is evident, since you make much of it yourself. You make much of your prayers and pains in religion, and are often thinking of them; how considerable do they appear to you, when you look back upon them! And some of you are thinking how much more you have done than others, and expecting some respect or regard that God should manifest to what you do. Now, if you make so much of what you do yourself, it is impossible that you should be freely willing that God should make nothing of it. As we may see in other things; if a man is proud of a great estate, or if he values himself much upon his honourable office, or his great abilities, it is impossible that he should like it, and heartily approve of it, that others should make light of these things and despise them.

Seeing therefore it is so evident, that you refuse to accept of Christ as your Saviour, why is Christ to be blamed that he does not save you? Christ has offered himself to you to be your Saviour in time past, and he continues offering himself still, and you continue to reject him, and yet complain that he does not save you.—So strangely unreasonable, and inconsistent with themselves, are gospel sinners!

But I expect there are many of you that still object. Such an objection as this, is probably now in the hearts of many here present.

Object. If I am not willing to have Christ for my Saviour, I cannot make myself willing.—But I would give an answer to this objection by laying down two things, that must be acknowledged to be exceeding evident.

1. It is no excuse, that you cannot receive Christ of yourself, unless you *would* if you could. This is so evident of itself, that it scarce needs any proof. Certainly if persons would not if they

could, it is just the same thing as to the blame that lies upon them, whether they can or cannot. If you were willing, and then found that you could not, your being unable would alter the case, and might be some excuse; because then the defect would not be in your will, but only in your ability. But as long as you *will* not, it is no matter, whether you have ability or no ability.

If you are not willing to accept of Christ, it follows that you have no sincere willingness to be willing; because the will always necessarily approves of and rests in its own acts. To suppose the contrary would be to suppose a contradiction; it would be to suppose that a man's will is contrary to itself, or that he wills contrary to what he himself wills. As you are not willing to come to Christ, and cannot make yourself willing, so you have no sincere desire to be willing; and therefore may most justly perish without a Saviour. There is no excuse at all for you; for say what you will about your inability, the seat of your blame lies in your perverse *will*, that is an *enemy* to the Saviour. It is in vain for you to tell of your want of power, as long as your will is found defective. If a man should hate you, and smite you in the face, but should tell you at the same time, that he hated you so much, that he could not help choosing and willing so to do, would you take it the more patiently for that? Would not your indignation be rather stirred up the more?

2. If you would be willing if you could, that is no excuse, unless your willingness to be willing be *sincere*. That which is hypocritical, and does not come from the heart, but is merely forced, ought wholly to be set aside, as worthy of no consideration; because common sense teaches, that what is not hearty, but hypocritical, is indeed nothing, being only a show of what is not; but that which is good for nothing, ought to go for nothing. But if you set aside all that is not free, and call nothing a willingness, but a free hearty willingness, then see how the case stands, and whether or no you have not lost all your excuse for standing out against the calls of the gospel. You say you would make yourself willing to accept if you *could*; but it is not from any good principle that you are willing for that. It is not from any free inclination, or true respect to Christ, or any love to your duty, or any spirit of obedience. It is not from the influence of any real respect, or tendency in your heart, towards any thing good, or from any other principle than such as is in the hearts of devils, and

would make them have the same sort of willingness in the same circumstances. It is therefore evident, that there can be no goodness in that *would* be willing to come to Christ: and that which has no goodness, cannot be an excuse for any badness. If there be no good in it, then it signifies nothing, and weighs nothing, when put into the scales to counterbalance that which is bad.

Sinners therefore spend their time in foolish arguing and objecting, making much of that which is good for nothing, making those excuses that are not worth offering. It is in vain to keep making objections. You stand justly condemned. The blame lies at your door: Thrust it off from you as often as you will, it will return upon you. Sew fig-leaves as long as you will, your nakedness will appear. You continue wilfully and wickedly rejecting Jesus Christ, and will not have him for your Saviour, and therefore it is sottish madness in you to charge Christ with injustice that he does not save you.

Here is the sin of unbelief! Thus the guilt of that great sin lies upon you! If you never had thus treated a Saviour, you might most justly have been damned to all eternity: it would but be exactly agreeable to your treatment of God. But besides this, when God, notwithstanding, has offered you his own dear Son, to save you from this endless misery you had deserved, and not only so, but to make you happy eternally in the enjoyment of himself, you have refused him, and would not have him for your Saviour, and still refuse to comply with the offers of the gospel; what can render any person more inexcusable? If you should now perish for ever, what can you have to say?

Hereby the justice of God in your destruction appears in two respects:

1. It is more abundantly manifest that it is *just* that you should be destroyed. Justice never appears so conspicuous as it does after refused and abused mercy. Justice in damnation appears abundantly the more clear and bright, after a wilful rejection of offered salvation. What can an offended prince do more than freely offer pardon to a condemned malefactor? And if he refuses to accept of it, will any one say that his execution is unjust?

2. God's justice will appear in your *greater* destruction. Besides the guilt that you would have had if a Saviour never had been offered, you bring that great additional guilt upon you, of

most ungratefully refusing offered deliverance.   What more base and vile treatment of God can there be, than for you, when justly condemned to eternal misery, and ready to be executed, and God graciously sends his own Son, who comes and knocks at your door with a pardon in his hand, and not only a pardon, but a deed of eternal glory; I say, what can be worse, than for you, out of dislike and enmity against God and his Son, to refuse to accept those benefits at his hands?   How justly may the anger of God be greatly incensed and increased by it! when a sinner thus ungratefully rejects mercy, his last error is worse than the first; this is more heinous than all his former rebellion, and may justly bring down more fearful wrath upon him.

The heinousness of this sin of rejecting a Saviour especially appears in two things:

1. The greatness of the benefits offered: which appears in the greatness of the deliverance, which is from inexpressible degrees of corruption and wickedness of heart and life, the least degree of which is infinitely evil; and from misery that is everlasting; and in the greatness and glory of the inheritance purchased and offered.   Heb. ii. 3. "How shall we escape if we neglect so great salvation."

2. The wonderfulness of the way in which these benefits are procured and offered.   That God should lay help on his own Son, when our case was so deplorable that help could be had in no mere creature; and that he should undertake for us, and should come into the world, and take upon him our nature, and should not only appear in a low state of life, but should die such a death, and endure such torments and contempt for sinners while enemies, how wonderful is it!   And what tongue or pen can set forth the greatness of the ingratitude, baseness, and perverseness there is in it, when a perishing sinner that is in the most extreme necessity of salvation, rejects it, after it is procured in such a way as this!   That so glorious a person should be thus treated, and that when he comes on so gracious an errand!   That he should stand so long offering himself and calling and inviting, as he has done to many of you, and all to no purpose, but all the while be set at nought!   Surely you might justly be cast into hell without one more offer of a Saviour! yea, and thrust down into the lowest hell!   Herein you have exceeded the very devils; for they never rejected the offers of such glorious mercy; no, nor of any mercy

K

at all. This will be the distinguishing condemnation of gospel-sinners, John iii. 18. "He that believeth not, is condemned already, because he hath not believed in the name of the only-begotten Son of God."—That outward smoothness of your carriage towards Christ, that appearance of respect to him in your looks, your speeches, and gestures, do not argue but that you set him at nought in your heart. There may be much of these outward shows of respect, and yet you be like Judas, that betrayed the Son of man with a kiss; and like those mockers that bowed the knee before him, and at the same time spat in his face.

III. If God should for ever cast you off and destroy you, it would be agreeable to your treatment of *others*.—It would be no other than what would be exactly answerable to your behaviour towards your fellow-creatures, that have the same human nature, and are naturally in the same circumstances with you, and that you ought to love as yourself. And that appears especially in two things.

1. You have many of you been opposite in your spirit to the salvation of others. There are several ways that natural men manifest a spirit of opposition against the salvation of souls. It sometimes appears by a fear that their companions, acquaintance, and equals, will obtain mercy, and so become unspeakably happier than they. It is sometimes manifested by an uneasiness at the news of what others have hopefully obtained. It appears when persons envy others for it, and dislike them the more, and disrelish their talk, and avoid their company, and cannot bear to hear their religious discourse, and especially to receive warnings and counsels from them. And it oftentimes appears by their backwardness to entertain charitable thoughts of them, and by their being brought with difficulty to believe that they have obtained mercy, and a forwardness to listen to any thing that seems to contradict it. The devil hated to own Job's sincerity, Job i. 7, etc., and chap. ii. verses 3, 4, 5. There appears very often much of this spirit of the devil in natural men. Sometimes they are ready to make a ridicule of others' pretended godliness: they speak of the ground of others' hopes, as the enemies of the Jews did of the wall that they built. Neh. iv. 3. "Now Tobiah the Ammonite was by him, and he said, That which they build, if a fox go up, he shall even break down their stone-wall." There are many that join with Sanballat and Tobiah, and are of the

same spirit with them.   There always was, and always will be, an enmity betwixt the seed of the serpent and the seed of the woman.   It appeared in Cain, who hated his brother, because he was more acceptable to God than himself; and it appears still in these times, and in this place.   There are many that are like the elder brother, who could not bear that the prodigal when he returned should be received with such joy and good entertain-ment, and was put into a fret by it, both against his brother that had returned, and his father that made him so welcome.   Luke xv.

Thus have many of you been opposed to the salvation of others, who stand in as great necessity of it as you.   You have been against their being delivered from everlasting misery, who can bear it no better than you; not because their salvation would do you any hurt, or their damnation help you, any otherwise than as it would gratify that vile spirit that is so much like the spirit of the devil, who, because he is miserable himself, is un-willing that others should be happy.   How just therefore is it that God should be opposed to your salvation!   If you have so little love or mercy in you as to begrudge your neighbour's salva-tion, whom you have no cause to hate, but the law of God and nature requires you to love, why is God bound to exercise such infinite love and mercy to you, as to save you at the price of his own blood?   you, whom he is no way bound to love, but who have deserved his hatred a thousand and a thousand times?   You are not willing that others should be converted, who have be-haved themselves injuriously towards you; and yet, will you count it hard if God does not bestow converting grace upon you that have deserved ten thousand times as ill of God, as ever any of your neighbours have of you?   You are opposed to God's showing mercy to those that you think have been vicious persons, and are very unworthy of such mercy.   Is others' unworthiness a just reason why God should not bestow mercy on them? and yet will God be heard, if, notwithstanding all your unworthiness, and the abominableness of your spirit and practice in his sight, he does not show you mercy?   You would have God bestow liberally on you, and upbraid not; but yet when he shows mercy to others, you are ready to upbraid as soon as you hear of it: you immediately are thinking with yourself how ill they have be-haved themselves; and it may be your mouths on this occasion are open, enumerating and aggravating the sins they have been guilty of. You would have God bury all your faults, and wholly blot out all your transgressions; but yet if he bestows mercy on others, it may be you will take that occasion to rake up all their old faults that you can think of. You do not much reflect on and condemn yourself for your baseness and unjust spirit towards others, in your opposition to their salvation; you do not quarrel with yourself, and condemn yourself for this; but yet you in your heart will quarrel with God, and fret at his dispensations, because you think he seems opposed to showing mercy to you. One would think that the consideration of these things should for ever *stop your mouth*.

2. Consider how you have promoted others' damnation. Many of you, by the bad examples you have set, by corrupting the minds of others, by your sinful conversation, by leading them into or strengthening them in sin, and by the mischief you have done in human society other ways that might be mentioned, have been guilty of those things that have tended to others' damnation. You have heretofore appeared on the side of sin and Satan, and have strengthened their interest, and have been many ways accessory to others' sins, have hardened their hearts, and thereby have done what has tended to the ruin of their souls.—Without doubt there are those here present who have been in a great measure the means of others' damnation. One man may really be a means of others' damnation as well as salvation. Christ charges the scribes and Pharisees with this, Matt. xxiii. 13. "Ye shut up the kingdom of heaven against men; for ye neither go in yourselves, neither suffer ye them that are entering, to go in." We have no reason to think that this congregation has none in it who are cursed from day to day by poor souls that are roaring out in hell, whose damnation they have been the means of, or have greatly contributed to.—There are many who contribute to their own children's damnation, by neglecting their education, by setting them bad examples, and bringing them up in sinful ways. They take some care of their bodies, but take little care of their poor souls; they provide for them bread to eat, but deny them the bread of life, that their famishing souls stand in need of. And are there no such parents here who have thus treated their children? If their children be not gone to hell, no thanks to them; it is not because they have not done what has tended to their destruction. Seeing therefore you have had no

more regard to others' salvation, and have promoted their damnation, how justly might God leave you to perish yourself!

IV. If God should eternally cast you off, it would but be agreeable to your own behaviour towards *yourself*; and that in two respects:

1. In being so *careless* of your own salvation. You have refused to take care for your salvation, as God has counselled and commanded you from time to time; and why may not God neglect it, now you seek it of him? Is God obliged to be more careful of your happiness, than you are either of your own happiness or his glory? Is God bound to take that care for you, out of love to you, that you will not take for yourself, either from love to yourself, or regard to his authority? How long, and how greatly, have you neglected the welfare of your precious soul, refusing to take pains and deny yourself, or put yourself a little out of your way for your salvation, while God has been calling upon you! Neither your duty to God, nor love to your own soul, were enough to induce you to do little things for your own eternal welfare; and yet do you now expect that God should do great things, putting forth almighty power, and exercising infinite mercy for it? You were urged to take care for your salvation, and not to put it off. You were told *that* was the best time before you grew older, and that it might be, if you would put it off, God would not hear you afterwards; but yet you would not hearken; you would run the venture of it. Now how justly might God order it so, that it should be too late, leaving you to seek in vain! You were told that you would repent of it if you delayed; but you would not hear: how justly therefore may God give you cause to repent of it, by refusing to show you mercy now! If God sees you going on in ways contrary to his commands and his glory, and requires you to forsake them, and tells you that they tend to the destruction of your own soul, and therefore counsels you to avoid them, and you refuse; how just would it be if God should be provoked by it, henceforward to be as careless of the good of your soul as you are yourself!

2. You have not only neglected your salvation, but you have wilfully taken direct courses to *undo* yourself. You have gone on in those ways and practices which have directly tended to your damnation, and have been perverse and obstinate in it. You cannot plead ignorance; you had all the light set before you that

you could desire. God told you that you were undoing yourself; but yet you would do it. He told you that the path you were going in led to destruction, and counselled you to avoid it; but you would not hearken. How justly therefore may God leave you to be undone! You have obstinately persisted to travel in the way that leads to hell for a long time, contrary to God's continual counsels and commands, till it may be at length you are got almost to your journey's end, and are come near to hell's gate, and so begin to be sensible of your danger and misery; and now account it unjust and hard if God will not deliver you! You have destroyed yourself, and destroyed yourself wilfully, contrary to God's repeated counsels, yea, and destroyed yourself in fighting against God. Now therefore, why do you blame any but *yourself* if you are destroyed? If you will undo yourself in opposing God, and while God opposes you by his calls and counsels, and, it may be too, by the convictions of his Spirit, what can you object against it, if God now leaves you to be undone? You would have your own way, and did not like that God should oppose you in it, and your way was to ruin your own soul; how just therefore is it, if, now at length, God ceases to oppose you, and falls in with you, and lets your soul be ruined; and as you would destroy yourself, so should put to his hand to destroy you too! The ways you went on in had a natural tendency to your misery: if you would drink poison in opposition to God, and in contempt of him and his advice, who can you blame but yourself if you are poisoned, and so perish? If you would run into the fire against all restraints both of God's mercy and authority, you must even blame yourself if you are burnt.

Thus I have proposed some things for your consideration, which, if you are not exceeding blind, senseless, and perverse, will *stop your mouth*, and convince you that you stand justly condemned before God; and that he would in no wise deal hardly with you, but altogether *justly*, in denying you any mercy, and in refusing to hear your prayers, though you pray never so earnestly, and never so often, and continue in it never so long. God may utterly disregard your tears and moans, your heavy heart, your earnest desires, and great endeavours; and he may cast you into eternal destruction, without any regard to your welfare, denying you converting grace, and giving you over to Satan, and at last cast you into the lake that burns with fire and brimstone, to be there to eternity, having no rest day or night, for ever glorifying his justice upon you in the presence of the holy angels, and in the presence of the Lamb.

Object. But here many may still object, (for I am sensible it is a hard thing to *stop* sinners' mouths,) "God shows mercy to others that have done these things as well as I, yea, that have done a great deal worse than I."

Ans. 1. That does not prove that God is any way *bound to* show mercy to you, or them either. If God bestows it on others, he does not so because he is bound to bestow it: he might if he had pleased, with glorious justice, have denied it them. If God bestows it on some, that does not prove that he is *bound* to bestow it on *any*; and if he is bound to bestow it on none, then he is not bound to bestow it on you. God is in debt to none; and if he gives to some that he is not in debt to, because it is his pleasure, that does not bring him into debt to others. It alters not the case as to you, whether others have it, or have it not: you do not deserve damnation the less, if mercy never had been bestowed on any at all. Matt. xx. 15. "Is thine eye evil, because I am good?"

2. If this objection be good, then the exercise of God's mercy is not in his *own right,* and his grace is not his own to give. That which God may not dispose of as he pleases, is not his own: for that which is one's own, is at his own disposal: but if it be not God's own, then he is not capable of making a gift or present of it to any one; it is impossible to give what is a *debt.*—What is it that you would make of God? Must the great God be tied up, that he must not use his own pleasure in bestowing his own gifts, but if he bestows them on one, must be looked upon obliged to bestow them on another? Is not God worthy to have the same right, with respect to the gifts of his grace, that a man has to his money or goods? Is it because God is not so great, and should be more in subjection than man, that this cannot be allowed him? If any of you see cause to show kindness to a neighbour, do all the rest of your neighbours come to you, and tell you, that you owe them so much as you have given to such a man? But this is the way that you deal with God, as though God were not worthy to have as absolute a property in his goods as you have in yours.

At this rate God cannot make a present of any thing; he has

nothing of his own to bestow: if he has a mind to show peculiar favour to some, or to lay some particular persons under peculiar obligations to him, he cannot do it; because he has no special gift at his own disposal. If this be the case, why do you pray to God to bestow saving grace upon you? If God does not do fairly to deny it you, because he bestows it on others, then it is not worth your while to pray for it, but you may go and tell him that he has bestowed it on others as bad or worse than you, and so *demand* it of him as a debt. And at this rate persons never need to *thank* God for salvation, when it is bestowed; for what occasion is there to thank God for that which was not at his own disposal, and that he could not fairly have denied? The thing at bottom is, that men have low thoughts of God, and high thoughts of themselves; and therefore it is that they look upon God as having so little right, and they so much. Matt. xx. 15. " Is it not lawful for me to do what I will with mine own?"

3. God may justly show greater respect to others than to you, for you have shown greater respect to others than to God. You have rather chosen to offend God than men. God only shows a greater respect to others, who are by nature your equals, than to you; but you have shown a greater respect to those that are infinitely inferior to God than to him. You have shown a greater regard to *wicked* men than to God; you have honoured them more, loved them better, and adhered to them rather than to him. Yea, you have honoured the devil, in many respects, more than God: you have chosen his will and his interest, rather than God's will and his glory: you have chosen a little worldly pelf, rather than God: you have set more by a vile lust than by him: you have chosen these things, and rejected God. You have set your heart on these things, and cast God behind your back: and where is the injustice if God is pleased to show greater respect to others than to you, or if he chooses others and rejects you? You have shown great respect to vile and worthless things, and no respect to God's glory; and why may not God set his love on others, and have no respect to your happiness? You have shown great respect to others, and not to God, whom you are laid under infinite obligations to respect above all; and why may not God show respect to others, and not to you, who never have laid him under the least obligation?

And will you not be ashamed, notwithstanding all these things, still to open your mouth, to object and cavil about the *decrees* of God, and other things that you cannot fully understand. Let the decrees of God be what they will, that alters not the case as to your *liberty*, any more than if God had only foreknown. And why is God to blame for decreeing things? Especially since he decrees nothing but *good*. How unbecoming an infinitely wise Being would it have been to have made a world, and let things run at random, without disposing events, or fore-ordering how they should come to pass? And what is that to you, how God has fore-ordered things, as long as your constant experience teaches you that it does not hinder your doing what you choose to do. This you know, and your daily practice and behaviour amongst men declares that you are fully sensible of it, with respect to yourself and others. Still to object, because there are some things in God's dispensations above your understanding, is exceedingly unreasonable. Your own conscience charges you with great guilt, and with those things that have been mentioned, let the secret things of God be what they will. Your conscience charges you with those vile dispositions, and that base behaviour towards God, that you would at any time most highly resent in your neighbour towards you, and that not a whit the less for any concern those secret counsels and mysterious dispensations of God may have in the matter. It is in vain for you to exalt yourself against an infinitely great, and holy, and just God. If you continue in it, it will be to your eternal shame and confusion, when hereafter you shall see at whose door all the blame of your misery lies.

I will finish what I have to say to natural men in the application of this doctrine, with a *caution* not to improve the doctrine to *discouragement*. For though it would be *righteous* in God for ever to cast you off, and destroy you, yet it would also be just in God to save you, in and through Christ, who has made complete satisfaction for all sin. Rom. iii. 25, 26. " Whom God hath set forth to be a propitiation, through faith in his blood, to declare his righteousness for the remission of sins that are past, through the forbearance of God; to declare, I say, at this time his righteousness, that he might be just, and the justifier of him which believeth in Jesus." Yea, God may, through this Mediator, not only justly, but honourably, show you mercy. The blood of Christ is so precious, that it is fully sufficient to pay the debt you have contracted, and perfectly to vindicate the Divine Majesty from all the dishonour cast upon it, by those many great sins of yours that have been mentioned. It was as great, and indeed a much greater thing, for Christ to die, than it would have been for you and all mankind to have burnt in hell to all eternity. Of such dignity and excellency is Christ in the eyes of God, that, seeing he has suffered so much for poor sinners, God is willing to be at peace with them, however vile and unworthy they have been, and on how many accounts soever the punishment would be *just*. So that you need not be at all discouraged from seeking mercy, for there is enough in Christ.

Indeed it would not become the glory of God's majesty to show mercy to you, so sinful and vile a creature, for any thing that you have done; for such worthless and despicable things as your prayers, and other religious performances. It would be very dishonourable and unworthy of God so to do, and it is in vain to expect it. He will show mercy only on Christ's account, and that, according to his sovereign pleasure, on whom he pleases, when he pleases, and in what manner he pleases. You cannot bring him under *obligation* by your works; do what you will, he will not look on himself obliged. But if it be his pleasure, he can honourably show mercy through Christ to any sinner of you all, not one in this congregation excepted.—Therefore here is encouragement for you still to seek and wait, notwithstanding all your wickedness; agreeable to Samuel's speech to the children of Israel, when they were terrified with the thunder and rain that God sent, and when guilt stared them in the face, 1 Sam. xii. 20. "Fear not; ye have done all this wickedness; yet turn not aside from following the Lord, but serve the Lord with all your heart."

I would conclude this discourse by putting the godly in mind of the freeness and wonderfulness of the grace of God towards them. For such were the same of you.—The case was just so with you as you have heard; you had such a wicked heart, you lived such a wicked life, and it would have been most just with God for ever to have cast you off; but he has had mercy upon you; he hath made his glorious grace appear in your everlasting salvation. You had no love to God; but yet he has exercised unspeakable love to you. You have contemned God, and set light by him; but so great a value has God's grace set on you and your happiness, that you have been redeemed at the price of the blood of his own Son. You chose to be with Satan in his service; but yet God hath made you a joint heir with Christ of his glory. You were ungrateful for past mercies; yet God not only continued those mercies, but bestowed unspeakably greater mercies upon you. You refused to hear when God called; yet God heard you when you called. You abused the infiniteness of God's mercy to encourage yourself in sin against him; yet God has manifested the infiniteness of that mercy, in the exercises of it towards you. You have rejected Christ, and set him at nought; and yet he is become your Saviour. You have neglected your own salvation; but God has not neglected it. You have destroyed yourself; but yet in God has been your help. God has magnified his free grace towards you, and not to others; because he has chosen you, and it hath pleased him to set his love upon you.

O! what cause is here for praise! What obligations you are under to bless the Lord who hath dealt bountifully with you, and magnify his holy name! What cause for you to praise God in humility, to walk humbly before him. Ezek. xvi. 63. " That thou mayest remember and be confounded, and never open thy mouth any more, because of thy shame, when I am pacified toward thee for all that thou hast done, saith the Lord God!" You shall never open your mouth in boasting, or self-justification; but lie the lower before God for his mercy to you. You have reason, the more abundantly, to open your mouth in God's praises, that they may be continually in your mouth, both here and to all eternity, for his rich, unspeakable, and sovereign mercy to you, whereby he, and he alone, hath made you to differ from others.

Sermon VI

SAFETY, FULNESS, AND SWEET REFRESHMENT, TO BE FOUND IN CHRIST

ISAIAH XXXII. 2

And a man shall be as an hiding-place from the wind, and a covert from the tempest; as rivers of water in a dry place, as the shadow of a great rock in a weary land.

IN these words we may observe,

1. The person who is here prophesied of and commended, *viz.* the Lord Jesus Christ, the King spoken of in the preceding verse, who shall reign in righteousness. This King is abundantly prophesied of in the Old Testament, and especially in this prophecy of Isaiah. Glorious predictions were from time to time uttered by the prophets concerning that great King who was to come: there is no subject which is spoken of in so magnificent and exalted a style by the prophets of the Old Testament, as the Messiah. They saw his day and rejoiced, and searched diligently, together with the angels, into those things. 1 Peter i. 11, 12. " Searching what, or what manner of time, the Spirit of Christ which was in them did signify, when it testified beforehand the sufferings of Christ, and the glory that should follow. Unto whom it was revealed, that not unto themselves, but unto us, they did minister the things, which are now reported unto you by them that have preached the gospel unto you with the Holy Ghost sent down from heaven; which things the angels desire to look into."

We are told here that " a *man* shall be a hiding-place from the wind," etc. There is an emphasis in the words, that " a *man* " should be this. If these things had been said of God, it would not be strange under the Old Testament; for God is frequently called a hiding-place for his people, a refuge in time of trouble,

156

a strong rock, and a high tower. But what is so remarkable is, that they are said of "a *man*." But this is a prophecy of the Son of God incarnate.

2. The things here foretold of him, and the commendations given him.

"He shall be a hiding-place from the wind, and a covert from the tempest:" that is, he shall be the safety and defence of his people, to which they shall flee for protection in the time of their danger and trouble. To him they shall flee, as one who is abroad, and sees a terrible storm arising, makes haste to some shelter to secure himself; so that however furious is the tempest, yet he is safe within, and the wind and rain, though they beat never so impetuously upon the roof and walls, are no annoyance unto him.

He shall be as "rivers of water in a dry place." This is an allusion to the deserts of Arabia, which was an exceedingly hot and dry country. One may travel there many days, and see no sign of a river, brook, or spring, nothing but a dry and parched wilderness; so that travellers are ready to be consumed with thirst, as the children of Israel were when they were in this wilderness, when they were faint because there was no water. Christ Now when a man finds Jesus Christ, he is like one that has been travelling in those deserts till he is almost consumed with thirst, and who at last finds a river of cool and clear water. And Christ was typified by the river of water that issued out of the rock for the children of Israel in this desert: he is compared to a river, because there is such a plenty and fulness in him.

He is the "shadow of a great rock in a weary land." Allusion is still made to the desert of Arabia. It is not said, as the shadow of a tree, because in some places of that country, there is nothing but dry sand and rocks for a vast space together, not a tree to be seen; and the sun beats exceedingly hot upon the sands, and all the shade to be found there, where travellers can rest and shelter themselves from the scorching sun, is under some great rock. They who come to Christ find such rest and refreshment as the weary traveller in that hot and desolate country finds under the shadow of a great rock.

We propose to speak to three propositions that are explicatory of the several parts of the text.

I. There is in Christ Jesus abundant foundation of peace and safety for those who are in fear and danger. "A man shall be a hiding-place from the wind, a covert from the tempest."

II. There is in Christ provision for the satisfaction, and full contentment, of the needy and thirsty soul. He shall be "as rivers of water in a dry place."

III. There are quiet rest and sweet refreshment in Christ Jesus for him who is weary. He shall be "as the shadow of a great rock in a weary land."

I. There is in Christ Jesus abundant foundation of peace and safety for those who are in fear and danger.

The fears and dangers to which men are subject, are of two kinds; temporal and eternal. Men are frequently in distress from fear of temporal evils. We live in an evil world, where we are liable to an abundance of sorrows and calamities. A great part of our lives is spent in sorrowing for present or past evils, and in fearing those which are future. What poor, distressed creatures are we, when God is pleased to send his judgments among us? If he visits a place with mortal and prevailing sickness, what terror seizes our hearts! If any person is taken sick, and trembles for his life, or if our near friends are at the point of death, or in many other dangers, how fearful is our condition! Now there is sufficient foundation for peace and safety to those exercised with such fears, and brought into such dangers. But Christ is a refuge in all trouble; there is a foundation for rational support and peace in him, whatever threatens us. He whose heart is fixed, trusting in Christ, need not be afraid of any evil tidings. "As the mountains are round about Jerusalem," so Christ is round about them that fear him.

But it is the other kind of fear and danger to which we have a principal respect; the fear and danger of God's wrath. The fears of a terrified conscience, the fearful expectation of the dire fruits of sin, and the resentment of an angry God, these are infinitely the most dreadful. If men are in danger of those things, and are not asleep, they will be more terrified than with the fears of any outward evil. Men are in a most deplorable condition, as they are by nature exposed to God's wrath; and if they are sensible how dismal their case is, will be in dreadful fears and dismal expectations.

God is pleased to make some sensible of their true condition. He lets them see the storm that threatens them, how black the

clouds are, and how impregnated with thunder, that it is a burning tempest, that they are in danger of being speedily overtaken
by it, that they have nothing to shelter themselves from it, and
that they are in danger of being taken away by the fierceness of
his anger.

It is a fearful condition when one is smitten with a sense of the
dreadfulness of God's wrath, when he has his heart impressed
with the conviction that the great God is not reconciled to him,
that he holds him guilty of these and those sins, and that he is
angry enough with him to condemn him for ever. It is dreadful
to lie down and rise up, it is dreadful to eat and drink, and to
walk about, in God's anger from day to day. One, in such a case,
is ready to be afraid of every thing; he is afraid of meeting God's
wrath wherever he goes. He has no peace of mind, but there is
a dreadful sound in his ears; his mind is afflicted and tossed with
tempest, and not comforted, and courage is ready to fail, and the
spirit ready to sink with fear; for how can a poor worm bear the
wrath of the great God, and what would not he give for peace of
conscience, what would not he give if he could find safety! When
such fears exist to a great degree, or are continued a long time,
they greatly enfeeble the heart, and bring it to a trembling pos-
ture and disposition.

Now for such as these there is abundant foundation for peace
and safety in Jesus Christ, and this will appear from the following things: *Professional Work of Christ*

1. Christ has undertaken to save all such from what they fear,
if they come to him. It is his professional business; the work in
which he engaged before the foundation of the world. It is
what he always had in his thoughts and intentions; he undertook
from everlasting to be the refuge of those that are afraid of God's
wrath. His wisdom is such, that he would never undertake a
work for which he is not sufficient. If there were some in so
dreadful a case that he was not able to defend them, or so guilty
that it was not fit that he should save them, then he never would
have undertaken for them. Those who are in trouble and distressing fear, if they come to Jesus Christ, have this to ease them
of their fears, that Christ has promised them that he will protect
them; that they come upon his invitation; that Christ has
plighted his faith for their security if they will close with him;
and that he is engaged by covenant to God the Father that

he will save those afflicted and distressed souls that come to him.

Christ, by his own free act, has made himself the surety of such, he has voluntarily put himself in their stead; and if justice has any thing against them, he has undertaken to answer for them. By his own act, he has engaged to be responsible for them; so that if they have exposed themselves to God's wrath, and to the stroke of justice, it is not their concern, but his, how to answer or satisfy for what they have done. Let there be never so much wrath that they have deserved, they are as safe as if they never had deserved any; because he has undertaken to stand for them, let it be more or less. If they are in Christ Jesus, the storm does of course light on him, and not on them; as when we are under a good shelter, the storm, that would otherwise come upon our heads, lights upon the shelter.

2. He is chosen and appointed of the Father to this work. There needs be no fear nor jealousy, whether the Father will approve of this undertaking of Christ Jesus, whether he will accept of him as a surety, or whether he will be willing that his wrath should be poured upon his own dear Son, instead of us miserable sinners. For there was an agreement with him concerning it before the world was; it was a thing much upon God's heart, that his Son Jesus Christ should undertake this work, and it was the Father that sent him into the world. It is as much the act of God the Father as it is of the Son. Therefore, when Christ was near the time of his death, he tells the Father that he had finished the work which he gave him to do. Christ is often called God's elect, or his chosen, because he was chosen by the Father for this work; and God's anointed, for the words *Messiah* and *Christ* signify *anointed*, because he is by God appointed and fitted for this work.

3. If we are in Christ Jesus, justice and the law have their course with respect to our sins, without our hurt. The foundation of the sinner's fear and distress is the justice and the law of God; they are against him, and they are unalterable, they must have their course. Every jot and tittle of the law must be fulfilled, heaven and earth shall be destroyed rather than justice should not take place; there is no possibility of sin's escaping justice.

But yet if the distressed trembling soul who is afraid of justice, would fly to Christ, he would be a safe hiding-place. Justice and the threatening of the law will have their course as fully, while he is safe and untouched, as if he were to be eternally destroyed. Christ bears the stroke of justice, and the curse of the law falls fully upon him; Christ bears all that vengeance that belongs to the sin that has been committed by him, and there is no need of its being borne twice over. His temporal sufferings, by reason of the infinite dignity of his person, are fully equivalent to the eternal sufferings of a mere creature. And then his sufferings answer for him who flees to him as well as if they were his own, for indeed they are his own by virtue of the union between Christ and him. Christ has made himself one with them; he is the head, and they are the members. Therefore, if Christ suffers for the believer, there is no need of his suffering; and what needs he to be afraid? His safety is not only consistent with absolute justice, but it is consistent with the tenor of the law. The law leaves fair room for such a thing as the answering of a surety. If the end of punishment in maintaining the authority of the law and the majesty of the government is fully secured by the sufferings of Christ as his surety, then the law of God, according to the true and fair interpretation of it, has its course as much in the sufferings of Christ, as it would have in his own sufferings. The threatening, "thou shalt surely die," is properly fulfilled in the death of Christ, as it is fairly to be understood. Therefore if those who are afraid will go to Jesus Christ, they need to fear nothing from the threatening of the law. The threatening of the law has nothing to do with them.

4. Those who come to Christ, need not be afraid of God's wrath for their sins; for God's honour will not suffer by their escaping punishment and being made happy. The wounded soul is sensible that he has affronted the majesty of God, and looks upon God as a vindicator of his honour; as a jealous God that will not be mocked, an infinitely great God that will not bear to be affronted, that will not suffer his authority and majesty to be trampled on, that will not bear that his kindness should be abused. A view of God in this light terrifies awakened souls. They think how exceedingly they have sinned, how they have sinned against light, against frequent and long-continued calls and warnings; and how they have slighted mercy, and been guilty of turning the grace of God into lasciviousness, taking encouragement from God's mercy to go on in sin against him; and they

L

fear that God is so affronted at the contempt and slight which they have cast upon him, that he, being careful of his honour, will never forgive them, but will punish them. But if they go to Christ, the honour of God's majesty and authority will not be in the least hurt by their being freed and made happy. For what Christ has done has repaired God's honour to the full. It is a greater honour to God's authority and majesty, that, rather than it should be wronged, so glorious a person would suffer what the law required. It is surely a wonderful display of the honour of God's majesty, to see an infinite and eternal person dying for its being wronged. And then Christ by his obedience, by that obedience which he undertook for our sakes, has honoured God abundantly more than the sins of any of us have dishonoured him, how many soever, and how great soever. How great an honour is it to God's law that so great a person is willing to submit to it, and to obey it! God hates our sins, but not more than he delights in Christ's obedience which he performed on our account. This is a sweet savour to him, a savour of rest. God is abundantly compensated, he desires no more; Christ's righteousness is of infinite worthiness and merit.

5. Christ is a person so dear to the Father, that those who are in Christ need not be at all jealous of being accepted upon his account. If Christ is accepted they must of consequence be accepted, for they are in Christ, as members, as parts, as the same. They are the body of Christ, his flesh and his bones. They that are in Christ Jesus, are one spirit; and therefore, if God loves Christ Jesus, he must of necessity accept of those that are in him, and that are of him. But Christ is a person exceedingly dear to the Father, the Father's love to the Son is really infinite. God necessarily loves the Son; God could as soon cease to be, as cease to love the Son. He is God's elect, in whom his soul delighteth; he is his beloved Son, in whom he is well pleased; he loved him before the foundation of the world, and had infinite delight in him from all eternity.

A terrified conscience, therefore, may have rest here, and abundant satisfaction that he is safe in Christ, and that there is not the least danger but that he shall be accepted, and that God will be at peace with him in Christ.

6. God has given an open testimony that Christ has done and suffered enough, and that he is satisfied with it, by his raising

him from the dead. Christ, when he was in his passion, was in the hands of justice, he was God's prisoner for believers, and it pleased God to bruise him, and put him to grief and to bring him into a low state; and when he raised him from the dead, he set him at liberty, whereby he declared that it was enough. If God was not satisfied, why did he set Christ at liberty so soon? *Good Q.* he was in the hands of justice, why did not God pour out more wrath upon him, and hold him in the chains of darkness longer? God raised him up and opened the prison doors to him, because he desired no more. And now surely there is free admittance for all sinners into God's favour through this risen Saviour, there is enough done, and God is satisfied; as he has declared and sealed to it by the resurrection of Christ, who is alive, and lives for evermore, and is making intercession for poor, distressed souls that come unto him.

7. Christ has the dispensation of safety and deliverance in his own hands, so that we need not fear but that, if we are united to him, we may be safe. God has given him all power in heaven and in earth, to give eternal life to whomsoever comes to him. He is made head over all things to the church, and the work of salvation is left with himself, he may save whom he pleases, and defend those that are in him by his own power. What greater ground of confidence could God have given us than that the Mediator, who died for us, and intercedes for us, should have committed to him the dispensation of the very thing which he died to purchase and for which he intercedes?

8. Christ's love, and compassion, and gracious disposition, are such that we may be sure he is inclined to receive all who come to him. If he should not do it, he would fail of his own undertaking, and also of his promise to the Father, and to us; and his wisdom and faithfulness will not allow of that. But he is so full of love and kindness that he is disposed to nothing but to receive and defend us, if we come to him. Christ is exceedingly ready to pity us, his arms are open to receive us, he delights to receive distressed souls that come to him, and to protect them; he would gather them as a hen gathereth her chickens under her wings; it is a work that he exceedingly rejoices in, because he delights in acts of love, and pity, and mercy.

I shall take occasion from what now has been said, to invite those who are afraid of God's wrath, to come to Christ Jesus.

You are indeed in a dreadful condition. It is dismal to have God's wrath impending over our heads, and not to know how soon it will fall upon us. And you are in some measure sensible that it is a dreadful condition, you are full of fear and trouble, and you know not where to flee for help; your mind is, as it were, tossed with a tempest. But how lamentable is it, that you should spend your life in such a condition, when Christ would shelter you, as a hen shelters her chickens under her wings, if you were but willing; and that you should live such a fearful, distressed life, when there is so much provision made for your safety in Christ Jesus!

How happy would you be if your hearts where but persuaded to close with Jesus Christ! Then you would be out of all danger: whatever storms and tempests were without, you might rest securely within; you might hear the rushing of the wind, and the thunder roar abroad, while you are safe in this hiding-place. O be persuaded to hide yourself in Christ Jesus! What greater assurance of safety can you desire? He has undertaken to defend and save you, if you will come to him: he looks upon it as his work; he engaged in it before the world was, and he has given his faithful promise which he will not break; and if you will but make your flight there, his life shall be for yours; he will answer for you, you shall have nothing to do but rest quietly in him; you may stand still and see what the Lord will do for you. If there be any thing to suffer, the suffering is Christ's, you will have nothing to suffer; if there be any thing to be done, the doing of it is Christ's, you will have nothing to do but to stand still and behold it.

You will certainly be accepted of the Father if your soul lays hold of Jesus Christ. Christ is chosen and anointed of the Father, and sent forth for this very end, to save those that are in danger and fear; and he is greatly beloved of God, even infinitely, and he will accept of those that are in him. Justice and the law will not be against you, if you are in Christ; that threatening, "in the day that thou eatest thou shalt die," in the proper sense of it will not touch you. The majesty and honour of God are not against you. You need not be afraid but that you shall be justified, if you come to him; there is an act of justification already past and declared for all who come to Christ by the resurrection of Christ, and as soon as ever you come, you are by that declared free. If

Justification is Already PAST

you come to Christ it will be a sure sign that Christ loved you from all eternity, and that he died for you; and you may be sure if he died for you, he will not lose the end of his death, for the dispensation of life is committed unto him.

You need not, therefore, continue in so dangerous a condition; there is help for you. You need not stand out in the storm so long, as there is so good a shelter near you, whose doors are open to receive you. O make haste, therefore, unto that man who is a hiding-place from the wind, and a covert from the tempest!

Let this truth also cause believers more to prize the Lord Jesus Christ. Consider that it is he, and he only, who defends you from wrath, and that he is a safe defence; your defence is a high tower; your city of refuge is impregnable. There is no rock like your rock. There is none like Christ, "the God of Jeshurun, who rideth upon the heaven in thy help, and in his excellency on the sky, the eternal God is thy refuge, and underneath are everlasting arms." He in whom you trust is a buckler to all that trust in him. O prize that Saviour, who keeps your soul in safety, while thousands of others are carried away by the fury of God's anger, and are tossed with raging and burning tempests in hell! O, how much better is your case than theirs! and to whom is it owing but to the Lord Jesus Christ? Remember what was once your case, and what it is now, and prize Jesus Christ.

And let those Christians who are in doubts and fears concerning their condition, renewedly fly to Jesus Christ, who is a hiding-place from the wind, and a covert from the tempest. Most Christians are at times afraid whether they shall not miscarry at last. Such doubtings are always through some want of the exercise of faith, and the best remedy for them is a renewed resort of the soul to this hiding-place; the same act which at first gave comfort and peace, will give peace again. They that clearly see the sufficiency of Christ, and the safety of committing themselves to him to save them from what they fear, will rest in it that Christ will defend them; be directed therefore at such times to do as the psalmist. Psal. lvi. 3, 4. "What time I am afraid, I will trust in thee. In God I will praise his word; in God I have put my trust: I will not fear what flesh can do unto me."

II. There is provision in Christ for the satisfaction and full contentment of the needy and thirsty soul. This is the sense of those words in the text, "as rivers of water in a dry place," in a dry and parched wilderness, where there is a great want of water, and where travellers are ready to be destroyed with thirst, such as was that wilderness in which the children of Israel wandered. This comparison is used elsewhere in the Scriptures. Psalm lxiii. 1. "O God, thou art my God; early will I seek thee: my soul thirsteth for thee, my flesh longeth for thee in a dry and thirsty land, where no water is." Ps. cxliii. 6. "I stretch forth my hands unto thee; my soul thirsteth after thee, as a thirsty land." Those who travel in such a land, who wander in such a wilderness, are in extreme need of water; they are ready to perish for the want of it; and thus they have a great thirst and longing for it.

It is said that Christ is a river of water, because there is such a fulness in him, so plentiful a provision for the satisfaction of the needy and longing soul. When one is extremely thirsty, though it is not a small draught of water will satisfy him, yet when he comes to a river, he finds a fulness, there he may drink full draughts. Christ is like a river, in that he has a sufficiency not only for one thirsty soul, but by supplying him the fountain is not lessened; there is not the less afforded to those who come afterwards. A thirsty man does not sensibly lessen a river by quenching his thirst.

Christ is like a river in another respect. A river is continually flowing, there are fresh supplies of water coming from the fountain-head continually, so that a man may live by it, and be supplied with water all his life. So Christ is an ever-flowing fountain; he is continually supplying his people, and the fountain is not spent. They who live upon Christ, may have fresh supplies from him to all eternity; they may have an increase of blessedness that is new, and new still, and which never will come to an end.

In illustrating this second proposition, I shall inquire,

1. What it is that the soul of every man naturally and necessarily craves.

First. The soul of every man necessarily craves happiness. This is an universal appetite of human nature, that is alike in the good and the bad; it is as universal as the very essence of the soul, because it necessarily and immediately flows from that essence. It is not only natural to all mankind, but to the angels; it is universal among all reasonable, intelligent beings, in heaven, earth, or hell, because it flows necessarily from an intelligent nature. There is no rational being, nor can there be any, without a love and desire of happiness. It is impossible that there should be any creature made that should love misery, or not love happiness, since it implies a manifest contradiction; for the very notion of misery is to be in a state that nature abhors, and the notion of happiness is to be in such a state as is most agreeable to nature.

Therefore, this craving of happiness must be insuperable, and what never can be changed; it never can be overcome, or in any way abated. Young and old love happiness alike, and good and bad, wise and unwise; though there is a great variety as to men's ideas of happiness. Some think it is to be found in one thing, and some in another; yet, as to the desire of happiness in general, there is no variety. There are particular appetites that may be restrained, and kept under, and conquered, but this general appetite for happiness never can be.

Secondly. The soul of every man craves a happiness that is equal to the capacity of his nature. The soul of man is like a vessel; the capacity of the soul is as the largeness or contents of the vessel. And therefore, if man has much pleasure and happiness, yet if the vessel is not full, the craving will not cease. Every creature is restless till it enjoys what is equal to the capacity of its nature. Thus we may observe in the brutes; when they have that which is suitable to their nature, and proportional to their capacity, they are contented. Man is of such a nature, that he is capable of an exceedingly great degree of happiness; he is made of a vastly higher nature than the brutes, and therefore he must have vastly higher happiness to satisfy. The pleasures of the outward senses which content the beasts, will not content man. He has other faculties of a higher nature that stand in need of something to fill them; if the sense be satiated, yet if the faculties of the soul are not filled, man will be in a craving restless state.

It is more especially by reason of the faculty of understanding that the soul is capable of so great a happiness, and desires so much. The understanding is an exceedingly extensive faculty; it extends itself beyond the limits of earth, beyond the limits of the creation. As we are capable of understanding immensely more than we do understand, who can tell how far the understanding of men is capable of stretching itself? and as the understanding enlarges, the desire will enlarge with it. It must there-

fore be an incomprehensible object that must satisfy the soul; it
will never be contented with that, and that only, to which it can
see an end, it will never be satisfied with that happiness to which
it can find a bottom.

A man may seem to take contentment for a little while in a
finite object, but after he has had a little experience, he finds that
he wants something besides. This is very apparent from the experience of this restless craving world. Every one is inquiring,
Who will show us any good?

2. Men in their fallen state, are in very great want of this
happiness. They were once in the enjoyment of it, but mankind
are sunk to a very low estate; we are naturally poor, destitute
creatures. We came naked into the world, and our souls as well
as our bodies are in a wretched, miserable condition; we are so
far from having food to eat suitable to our nature, that we are
greedy after the husks which the swine do eat.

The poverty of man in a natural condition, appears in his dis-
contented, craving spirit; it shows that the soul is very empty,
when, like the horse-leech, it cries, " Give, give, and saith not, It
is enough." We are naturally like the prodigal, for we once were
rich, but we departed from our father's house, and have squan-
dered away our wealth, and are become poor, hungry, famishing
wretches.

Men in a natural condition may find something to gratify their
senses, but there is nothing to feed the soul; that more noble and
more essential part perishes for lack of food. They may fare
sumptuously every day, they may pamper their bodies, but the
soul cannot be fed from a sumptuous table; they may drink wine
in bowls, yet the spiritual part is not refreshed. The superior
faculties want to be supplied as well as the inferior. True poverty
and true misery consist in the want of those things of which our
spiritual part stands in need.

3. Those sinners who are thoroughly awakened, are sensible
of their great want. Multitudes of men are not sensible of their
miserable, needy condition. There are many who are thus poor,
and think themselves rich, and increased in goods. Indeed there
are no natural men that have true contentment: they are all restless, and crying, " Who will show us any good?" but multitudes
are not sensible how exceedingly necessitous is their condition.
But the thoroughly awakened soul sees that he is very far from

true happiness, that those things which he possesses will never make him happy; that for all his outward possessions he is wretched, and miserable, and poor, and blind, and naked. He becomes sensible of the short continuance and uncertainty of those things, and their insufficiency to satisfy a troubled conscience. He wants something else to give him peace and ease. If you would tell him that he might have a kingdom, it would not quiet him; he desires to have his sins pardoned, and to be at peace with his Judge. He is poor, and he becomes a beggar; he comes and cries for help. He does not thirst because he as yet sees where true happiness is to be found, but because he sees that he has it not, and cannot find it. He is without comfort, and does not know where to find it, but he longs for it. O, what would he not give, if he could find some satisfying peace and comfort!

Such are those hungry, thirsty souls that Christ so often invites to come to him. Isa. lv. 1, 2. "Ho, every one that thirsteth, come ye to the waters, and he that hath no money, come ye, buy and eat; yea, come, buy wine and milk without money and without price. Wherefore do ye spend money for that which is not bread, and your labour for that which satisfieth not? hearken diligently unto me, and eat ye that which is good, and let your soul delight itself in fatness." "If any man thirst, let him come unto me and drink; and he that is athirst, let him come and take of the water of life freely."

4. There is in Christ Jesus provision for the full satisfaction and contentment of such as these.

First. The excellency of Christ is such, that the discovery of it is exceedingly contenting and satisfying to the soul. The inquiry of the soul is after that which is most excellent. The carnal soul imagines that earthly things are excellent; one thinks riches most excellent, another has the highest esteem of honour, and to another carnal pleasure appears the most excellent; but the soul cannot find contentment in any of these things, because it soon finds an end to their excellency.

Worldly men imagine, that there is true excellency and true happiness in those things which they are pursuing. They think that if they could but obtain them, they should be happy; and when they obtain them, and cannot find happiness, they look for happiness in something else, and are still upon the pursuit.

But Christ Jesus has true excellency, and so great excellency, that when they come to see it they look no further, but the mind rests there. It sees a transcendent glory and an ineffable sweetness in him; it sees that till now it has been pursuing shadows, but that now it has found the substance; that before it had been seeking happiness in the stream, but that now it has found the ocean. The excellency of Christ is an object adequate to the natural cravings of the soul, and is sufficient to fill the capacity. It is an infinite excellency, such an one as the mind desires, in which it can find no bounds; and the more the mind is used to it, the more excellent it appears. Every new discovery makes this beauty appear more ravishing, and the mind sees no end; here is room enough for the mind to go deeper and deeper, and never come to the bottom. The soul is exceedingly ravished when it first looks on this beauty, and it is never weary of it. The mind never has any satiety, but Christ's excellency is always fresh and new, and tends as much to delight, after it has seen a thousand or ten thousand years, as when it was seen the first moment. The excellency of Christ is an object suited to the superior faculties of man, it is suited to entertain the faculty of reason and understanding, and there is nothing so worthy about which the understanding can be employed as this excellency; no other object is so great, noble, and exalted.

This excellency of Jesus Christ is the suitable food of the rational soul. The soul that comes to Christ, feeds upon this, and lives upon it; it is that bread which came down from heaven, of which he that eats shall not die; it is angels' food, it is that wine and milk that is given without money, and without price. This is that fatness in which the believing soul delights itself; here the longing soul may be satisfied, and the hungry soul may be filled with goodness. The delight and contentment that is to be found here, passeth understanding, and is unspeakable and full of glory. It is impossible for those who have tasted of this fountain, and know the sweetness of it, ever to forsake it. The soul has found the river of water of life, and it desires no other drink; it has found the tree of life, and it desires no other fruit.

Secondly. The manifestation of the love of Christ gives the soul abundant contentment. This love of Christ is exceeding sweet and satisfying, it is better than life, because it is the love of a person of such dignity and excellency. The sweetness of his love depends very much upon the greatness of his excellency; so much the more lovely the person, so much the more desirable is his love. How sweet must the love of that person be, who is the eternal Son of God, who is of equal dignity with the Father! How great a happiness must it be to be the object of the love of him who is the Creator of the world, and by whom all things consist, and who is exalted at God's right hand, and made head over principalities and powers in heavenly places, who has all things put under his feet, and is King of kings and Lord of lords, and is the brightness of the Father's glory! Surely to be beloved by him, is enough to satisfy the soul of a worm of the dust.

This love of Christ is also exceedingly sweet and satisfying from the greatness of it; it is a dying love; such love as never was before seen, and such as no other can parallel. There have been instances of very great love between one earthly friend and another; there was a surpassing love between David and Jonathan. But there never was any such love as Christ has towards believers. The satisfying nature of this love arises also from the sweet fruits of it. Those precious benefits that Christ bestows upon his people, and those precious promises which he has given them, are the fruit of this love; joy and hope are the constant streams that flow from this fountain, from the love of Christ.

Thirdly. There is provision for the satisfaction and contentment of the thirsty longing soul in Christ, as he is the way to the Father; not only from the fulness of excellency and grace which he has in his own person, but as by him we may come to God, may be reconciled to him, and may be made happy in his favour and love.

The poverty and want of the soul in its natural state consist in its being separated from God, for God is the riches and the happiness of the creature. But we naturally are alienated from God; and God is alienated from us, our Maker is not at peace with us. But in Christ there is a way for a free communication between God and us; for us to come to God, and for God to communicate himself to us by his Spirit. John xiv. 6. " Jesus saith unto him, I am the way, and the truth, and the life: no man cometh unto the Father but by me." Ephes. ii. 13, 18, 19. " But now in Christ Jesus, ye who sometimes were far off, are made nigh by the blood of Christ. For through him we both have access by one Spirit unto the Father. Now, therefore, ye are no more strangers and foreigners, but fellow-citizens with the saints, and of the household of God."

Christ by being thus the way to the Father, is the way to true happiness and contentment. John x. 9. "I am the door: by me, if any man enter in, he shall be saved, and shall go in and out, and find pasture."

Hence I would take occasion to invite needy, thirsty souls to come to Jesus. "In the last day, that great day of the feast, Jesus stood and cried, saying, If any man thirst, let him come unto me and drink." You that have not yet come to Christ, are in a poor, necessitous condition; you are in a parched wilderness, in a dry and thirsty land. And if you are thoroughly awakened, you are sensible that you are in distress and ready to faint for want of something to satisfy your souls. Come to him who is " as rivers of water in a dry place." There are plenty and fulness in him; he is like a river that is always flowing, you may live by it for ever, and never be in want. Come to him who has such excellency as is sufficient to give full contentment to your soul, who is a person of transcendent glory, and ineffable beauty, where you may entertain the view of your soul for ever without weariness, and without being cloyed. Accept of the offered love of him who is the only-begotten Son of God, and his elect, in whom his soul delighteth. Through Christ, come to God the Father, from whom you have departed by sin. He is the way, the truth, and the life; he is the door, by which if any man enters he shall be saved.

III. There are quiet rest and sweet refreshment in Christ Jesus, for those that are weary. He is " as the shadow of a great rock in a weary land."

The comparison that is used in the text is very beautiful and very significative. The dry, barren, and scorched wilderness of Arabia is a very lively representation of the misery that men have brought upon themselves by sin. It is destitute of any inhabitants but lions and tigers and fiery serpents; it is barren and parched, and without any river or spring; it is a land of drought, wherein there is seldom any rain, a land exceedingly hot and uncomfortable. The scorching sunbeams that are ready to consume the spirits of travellers, are a fit representation of terror of conscience, and the inward sense of God's displeasure.

And there being no other shade in which travellers may rest, but only here and there that of a great rock, it is a fit representation of Jesus Christ, who came to redeem us from our misery. Christ is often compared to a rock, because he is a sure foundation to builders, and because he is a sure bulwark and defence. They who dwell upon the top of a rock, dwell in a most defensible place; we read of those whose habitation is the munitions of rocks. He may also be compared to a rock, as he is everlasting and unchangeable. A great rock remains stedfast, unmoved, and unbroken by winds and storms from age to age; and therefore God chose a rock to be an emblem of Christ in the wilderness, when he caused water to issue forth for the children of Israel; and the shadow of a great rock is a most fit representation of the refreshment given to weary souls by Jesus Christ.

1. There is quiet rest and full refreshment in Christ for sinners that are weary and heavy laden with sin. Sin is the most evil and odious thing, as well as the most mischievous and fatal; it is the most mortal poison; it, above all things, hazards life, and endangers the soul, exposes to the loss of all happiness, and to the suffering of all misery, and brings the wrath of God. All men have this dreadful evil hanging about them, and cleaving fast to the soul, and ruling over it, and keeping it in possession, and under absolute command: it hangs like a viper to the heart, or rather holds it as a lion does his prey.

But yet there are multitudes, who are not sensible of their misery. They are in such a sleep that they are not very unquiet in this condition, it is not very burthensome to them, they are so sottish that they do not know what is their state, and what is like to become of them. But there are others who have their sense so far restored to them that they feel the pain, and see the approaching destruction, and sin lies like a heavy load upon their hearts; it is a load that lies upon them day and night, they cannot lay it down to rest themselves, but it continually oppresses them. It is bound fast unto them, and is ready to sink them down; it is a continual labour of heart, to support itself under this burden. Thus we read of them " that labour, and are heavy laden."

Or rather, it is like the scorching heat in a dry wilderness, where the sun beats and burns all the day long; where they have nothing to defend them; where they can find no shade to refresh themselves. If they lay themselves down to rest, it is like

lying down in the hot sands, where there is nothing to keep off the heat.

Here it may be proper to inquire who are weary and heavy laden with sin; and in what sense a sinner may be weary and burdened with sin. Sinners are not wearied with sin from any dislike to it, or dislike of it. There is no sinner that is burdened with sin in the sense in which a godly man carries his indwelling sin, as his daily and greatest burden, because he loathes it, and longs to get rid of it; he would fain be at a great distance from it, and have nothing more to do with it; he is ready to cry out as Paul did, "O wretched man that I am! who shall deliver me from the body of this death?" The unregenerate man has nothing of this nature, for sin is yet his delight, he dearly loves it. If he be under convictions, his love to sin in general is not mortified, he loves it as well as ever, he hides it still as a sweet morsel under his tongue.

But there is a difference between being weary and burdened with sin, and being weary of sin. Awakened sinners are weary with sin, but not properly weary of it.

Therefore, they are only weary of the guilt of sin, the guilt that cleaves to their consciences is that great burden. God has put the sense of feeling into their consciences, that were before as seared flesh, and it is guilt that pains them. The filthiness of sin and its evil nature, as it is an offence to a holy, gracious, and glorious God, is not a burden to them. But it is the connexion between sin and punishment, between sin and God's wrath, that makes it a burden. Their consciences are heavy laden with guilt, which is an obligation to punishment; they see the threatening and curse of the law joined to their sins, and see that the justice of God and his vengeance are against them. They are burdened with their sins, not because there is any odiousness in them, but because there is hell in them. This is the sting of sin, whereby it stings the conscience, and distresses and wearies the soul.

The guilt of such and such great sins is upon the soul, and the man sees no way to get rid of it, but he has wearisome days and wearisome nights; it makes him ready sometimes to say as the psalmist did, "O that I had wings like a dove! for then would I fly away and be at rest. Lo, then would I wander far off, and remain in the wilderness. I would hasten my escape from the windy storm and tempest."

But when sinners come to Christ, he takes away that which was their burden, or their sin and guilt, that which was so heavy upon their hearts, that so distressed their minds.

First. He takes away the guilt of sin, from which the soul before saw no way how it was possible to be freed, and which, if it was not removed, led to eternal destruction. When the sinner comes to Christ, it is all at once taken away, and the soul is left free, it is lightened of its burden, it is delivered from its bondage, and is like a bird escaped from the snare of the fowler. The soul sees in Christ a way to peace with God, and a way by which the law may be answered, and justice satisfied, and yet he may escape; a wonderful way indeed, but yet a certain and a glorious one. And what rest does it give to the weary soul to see itself thus delivered, that the foundation of its anxieties and fears is wholly removed, and that God's wrath ceases, that it is brought into a state of peace with God, and that there is no more occasion to fear hell, but that it is for ever safe!

How refreshing is it to the soul to be at once thus delivered of that which was so much its trouble and terror, and to be eased of that which was so much its burden! This is like coming to a cool shade after one has been travelling in a dry and hot wilderness, and almost fainting under the scorching heat.

And then Christ also takes away sin itself, and mortifies that root of bitterness which is the cause of all the inward tumults and disquietudes that are in the mind, that make it like the troubled sea that cannot rest, and leaves it all calm. When guilt is taken away and sin is mortified, then the foundation of fear, and trouble, and pain is removed, and the soul is left in peace and serenity.

Secondly. Christ puts strength and a principle of new life into the weary soul that comes to him. The sinner, before he comes to Christ, is as a sick man that is weakened and brought low, and whose nature is consumed by some strong distemper: he is full of pain, and so weak that he cannot walk nor stand. Therefore, Christ is compared to a physician. "But when Jesus heard that, he said unto them, They that be whole, need not a physician, but they that are sick." When he comes and speaks the word, he puts a principle of life into him that was before as dead: he gives a principle of spiritual life and the beginning of eternal life; he invigorates the mind with a communication of his own life and strength, and renews the nature and creates it again, and makes the man to be a new creature.

So that the fainting, sinking spirits are now revived, and this principle of spiritual life is a continual spring of refreshment, like a well of living water. "Whosoever drinketh of the water that I shall give him, shall never thirst; but the water that I shall give him shall be in him a well of water springing up into everlasting life." Christ gives his Spirit, that calms the mind, and is like a refreshing breeze of wind. He gives that strength whereby he lifts up the hands that hang down, and strengthens the feeble knees.

Thirdly. Christ gives to those who come to him such comfort and pleasure as are enough to make them forget all their former labour and travail. A little of true peace, a little of the joys of the manifested love of Christ, and a little of the true and holy hope of eternal life, are enough to compensate for all that toil and weariness, and to erase the remembrance of it from the mind. That peace which results from true faith passes understanding, and that joy is joy unspeakable. There is something peculiarly sweet and refreshing in this joy, that is not in other joys; and what can more effectually support the mind, or give a more rational ground of rejoicing, than a prospect of eternal glory in the enjoyment of God from God's own promise in Christ? If we come to Christ, we may not only be refreshed by resting in his shadow, but by eating his fruit: these things are the fruits of this tree. "I sat down under his shadow with great delight, and his fruit was sweet to my taste."

Before proceeding to the next particular of this proposition, I would apply myself to those that are weary; to move them to repose themselves under Christ's shadow.

The great trouble of such a state, one would think, should be a motive to you to accept of an offer of relief, and remedy. You are weary, and doubtless would be glad to be at rest; but here you are to consider,

1st. That there is no remedy but in Jesus Christ; there is nothing else will give you true quietness. If you could fly into heaven, you would not find it there; if you should take the wings of the morning, and dwell in the uttermost parts of the earth, in some solitary place in the wilderness, you could not fly from your burden. So that if you do not come to Christ, you must either continue still weary and burdened, or, which is worse, you must return to your old dead sleep, to a state of stupidity; and not only so, but you must be everlastingly wearied with God's wrath.

At hand

2d. Consider that Christ is a remedy at hand. You need not wish for the wings of a dove that you may fly afar off, and be at rest, but Christ is nigh at hand, if you were but sensible of it. Rom. x. 6, 7, 8. " But the righteousness which is of faith speaketh on this wise, Say not in thine heart, Who shall ascend into heaven? (that is, to bring Christ down from above:) or, Who shall descend into the deep? (that is, to bring up Christ again from the dead.) But what saith it? The word is nigh thee, even in thy mouth, and in thy heart; that is, the word of faith which we preach." There is no need of doing any great work to come at this rest; the way is plain to it; it is but going to it, it is but sitting down under Christ's shadow. Christ requires no money to purchase rest of him, he calls to us to come freely, and for nothing. If we are poor and have no money, we may come. Christ sent out his servants to invite the poor, the maimed, the halt, and the blind. Christ does not want to be hired to accept of you, and to give you rest. It is his work as Mediator to give rest to the weary, it is the work that he was anointed for, and in which he delights. "The Spirit of the Lord God is upon me; because the Lord hath anointed me to preach good tidings unto the meek; he hath sent me to bind up the broken-hearted, to proclaim liberty to the captives, and the opening of the prison to them that are bound."

Sit down

His Job

3d. Christ is not only a remedy for your weariness and trouble, but he will give you an abundance of the contrary, joy and delight. They who come to Christ, do not only come to a resting-place after they have been wandering in a wilderness, but they come to a banqueting-house where they may rest, and where they may feast. They may cease from their former troubles and toils, and they may enter upon a course of delights and spiritual joys.

Joy

Christ not only delivers from fears of hell and of wrath, but he gives hopes of heaven, and the enjoyment of God's love. He delivers from inward tumults and inward pain, from that guilt of conscience which is as a worm gnawing within, and he gives delight and inward glory. He brings us out of a wilderness of pits, and drought, and fiery flying spirits; and he brings us into a

M

pleasant land, a land flowing with milk and honey. He delivers us out of prison, and lifts us off from the dunghill, and he sets us among princes, and causes us to inherit the throne of glory. Wherefore, if any one is weary, if any is in prison, if any one is in captivity, if any one is in the wilderness, let him come to the blessed Jesus, who is as the shadow of a great rock in a weary land. Delay not, arise and come away.

2. There are quiet rest and sweet refreshment in Christ for God's people that are weary.

The saints themselves, while they remain in this imperfect state, and have so much remains of sin in their hearts, are liable still to many troubles and sorrows, and much weariness, and have often need to resort anew unto Jesus Christ for rest. I shall mention three cases wherein Christ is a sufficient remedy.

First. There is rest and sweet refreshment in Christ for those that are wearied with persecutions. It has been the lot of God's church in this world for the most part to be persecuted. It has had now and then some lucid intervals of peace and outward prosperity, but generally it has been otherwise. This has accorded with the first prophecy concerning Christ; "I will put enmity between thee and the woman, and between thy seed and her seed." Those two seeds have been at enmity ever since the time of Abel. Satan has borne great malice against the church of God, and so have those that are his seed. And oftentimes God's people have been persecuted to an extreme degree, have been put to the most exquisite torments that wit or art could devise, and thousands of them have been tormented to death.

But even in such a case there are rest and refreshment to be found in Christ Jesus. When their cruel enemies have given them no rest in this world; when, as oftentimes has been the case, they could not flee, nor in any way avoid the rage of their adversaries, but many of them have been tormented gradually from day to day, that their torments might be lengthened; still rest has been found even then in Christ. It has been often found by experience; the martyrs have often showed plainly that the peace and calm of their minds were undisturbed in the midst of the greatest bodily torment, and have sometimes rejoiced and sung praises upon the rack and in the fire. If Christ is pleased to send forth his Spirit to manifest his love, and speaks friendly to the soul, it will support it even in the greatest outward torment that man can inflict. Christ is the joy of the soul, and if the soul be but rejoiced and filled with divine light, such joy no man can take away; whatever outward misery there be, the spirit will sustain it.

Secondly. There is in Christ rest for God's people, when exercised with afflictions. If a person labour under great bodily weakness, or under some disease that causes frequent and strong pains, such things will tire out so feeble a creature as man. It may to such an one be a comfort and an effectual support to think that he has a Mediator who knows by experience what pain is; who by his pain has purchased eternal ease and pleasure for him; and who will make his brief sufferings to work out a far more exceeding delight, to be bestowed when he shall rest from his labours and sorrows.

If a person be brought into great straits as to outward subsistence, and poverty brings abundance of difficulties and extremities; yet it may be a supporting, refreshing consideration to such an one to think, that he has a compassionate Saviour, who when upon earth, was so poor that he had not where to lay his head, and who became poor to make him rich, and purchased for him durable riches, and will make his poverty work out an exceeding and eternal weight of glory.

If God in his providence calls his people to mourn over lost relations, and if he repeats his stroke and takes away one after another of those that were dear to him; it is a supporting, refreshing consideration to think, that Christ has declared that he will be in stead of all relations unto those who trust in him. They are as his mother, and sister, and brother; he has taken them into a very near relation to himself: and in every other afflictive providence, it is a great comfort to a believing soul to think that he has an intercessor with God, that by him he can have access with confidence to the throne of grace, and that in Christ we have so many great and precious promises, that all things shall work together for good, and shall issue in eternal blessedness. God's people, whenever they are scorched by afflictions as by hot sunbeams, may resort to him, who is as a shadow of a great rock, and be effectually sheltered, and sweetly refreshed.

Thirdly. There is in Christ quiet rest and sweet refreshment for God's people, when wearied with the buffetings of Satan. The devil, that malicious enemy of God and man, does whatever lies in his power to darken and hinder, and tempt God's people, and render their lives uncomfortable. Often he raises needless and groundless scruples, and casts in doubts, and fills the mind with such fear as is tormenting, and tends to hinder them exceedingly in the christian course; and he often raises mists and clouds of darkness, and stirs up corruption, and thereby fills the mind with concern and anguish, and sometimes wearies out the soul. So that they may say as the psalmist; "Many bulls have compassed me: strong bulls of Bashan have beset me round. They gaped upon me with their mouths, as a ravening and a roaring lion."

In such a case if the soul flies to Jesus Christ, they may find rest in him, for he came into the world to destroy Satan, and to rescue souls out of his hands. And he has all things put under his feet, whether they be things in heaven, or things on earth, or things in hell, and therefore he can restrain Satan when he pleases. And that he is doubtless ready enough to pity us under such temptations, we may be assured, for he has been tempted and buffeted by Satan as well as we. He is able to succour those that are tempted, and he has promised that he will subdue Satan under his people's feet. Let God's people therefore, when they are exercised with any of those kinds of weariness, make their resort unto Jesus Christ for refuge and rest.

REFLECTIONS

1. We may here see great reason to admire the goodness and grace of God to us in our low estate, that he has so provided for our help and relief. We are by our own sin against God plunged into all sorts of evil, and God has provided a remedy for us against every sort of evil, he has left us helpless in no calamity. We by our sin have exposed ourselves to wrath, to a vindictive justice; but God has done very great things that we might be saved from that wrath; he has been at infinite cost that the law might be answered without our suffering. We by our sins have exposed ourselves to terror of conscience, in expectation of the dreadful storm of God's wrath; but God has provided for us a hiding-place from the storm, he bids us enter into his chambers, and hide ourselves from indignation. We by sin have made ourselves poor, needy creatures; but God has provided for us gold tried in the

fire. We by sin have made ourselves naked; and when he passed by, he took notice of our want, and has provided us white raiment that we may be clothed. We have made ourselves blind, and God in mercy to us has provided eye-salve, that we may see. We have deprived ourselves of all spiritual food; we are like the prodigal son that perished with hunger, and would gladly have filled his belly with husks. God has taken notice of this our condition, and has provided for us a feast of fat things, and has sent forth his servants to invite the poor, the maimed, the halt, and the blind. We by sin have brought ourselves into a dry and thirsty wilderness; but God was merciful, and took notice of our condition, and has provided for us rivers of water, water out of the rock. We by sin have brought upon ourselves a miserable slavery and bondage; God has made provision for our liberty. We have exposed ourselves to weariness; God has provided a resting-place for us. We by sin have exposed ourselves to many outward troubles and afflictions; God has pitied us, and in Christ has provided true comfort for us. We have exposed ourselves to our grand enemy, even Satan, to be tempted and buffeted by him; God has pitied, and has provided for us a Saviour and Captain of salvation, who has overcome Satan, and is able to deliver us. Thus God has in Christ provided sufficiently for our help in all kinds of evils.

How ought we to bless God for this abundant provision he has made for us, poor and sinful as we were, who were so undeserving and so ungrateful. He made no such provision for the fallen angels, who are left without remedy in all the woes and miseries into which they are plunged.

2. We should admire the love of Christ to men, that he has thus given himself to be the remedy for all their evil, and a fountain of all good. Christ has given himself to us, to be all things to us that we need. We want clothing, and Christ does not only give us clothing, but he gives himself to be our clothing, that we might put him on. Gal. iii. 27. "For as many of you as have been baptized into Christ have put on Christ." Rom. xiii. 14. "But put ye on the Lord Jesus Christ, and make not provision for the flesh, to fulfil the lusts thereof."

We want food, and Christ has given himself to be our food; he has given his own flesh to be our meat, and his blood to be our drink, to nourish our soul. Thus Christ tells us that he is the bread which came down from heaven, and the bread of life. "I am that bread of life. Your fathers did eat manna in the wilderness, and are dead. This is the bread which cometh down from heaven, that a man may eat thereof, and not die. I am the living bread which came down from heaven: if any man eat of this bread, he shall live for ever; and the bread that I will give is my flesh, which I will give for the life of the world." In order to our eating of his flesh, it was necessary that he should be slain, as the sacrifices must be slain before they could be eaten; and such was Christ's love to us, that he consented to be slain, he went as a sheep to the slaughter, that he might give us his flesh to be food for our poor, famishing souls.

We are in need of a habitation; we by sin have, as it were, turned ourselves out of house and home; Christ has given himself to be the habitation of his people. Ps. xc. 1. "Lord, thou hast been our dwelling-place in all generations." It is promised to God's people that they should dwell in the temple of God for ever, and should go no more out; and we are told that Christ is the temple of the new Jerusalem.

Christ gives himself to his people to be all things to them that they need, and all things that make for their happiness. Col. iii. 11. "Where there is neither Greek nor Jew, circumcision nor uncircumcision, barbarian, Scythian, bond, nor free; but Christ is all, and in all." And that he might be so, he has refused nothing that is needful to prepare him to be so. When it was needful that he should be incarnate, he refused it not, but became man, and appeared in the form of a servant. When it was needful that he should be slain, he refused it not, but gave himself for us, and gave himself to us upon the cross.

Here is love for us to admire, for us to praise, and for us to rejoice in, with joy that is full of glory for ever.

Sermon VII*

SINNERS IN THE HANDS OF AN ANGRY GOD

Deut. xxxii. 35

—Their foot shall slide in due time:—

In this verse is threatened the vengeance of God on the wicked unbelieving Israelites, who were God's visible people, and who lived under the means of grace; but who, notwithstanding all God's wonderful works towards them, remained (as ver. 28) void of counsel, having no understanding in them. Under all the cultivations of Heaven, they brought forth bitter and poisonous fruit; as in the two verses next preceding the text.—The expression I have chosen for my text, *Their foot shall slide in due time*, seems to imply the following things, relating to the punishment and destruction to which these wicked Israelites were exposed.

1. That they were always exposed to *destruction*; as one that stands or walks in slippery places is always exposed to fall. This is implied in the manner of their destruction coming upon them, being represented by their foot sliding. The same is expressed, Psalm lxxiii. 18. " Surely thou didst set them in slippery places; thou castedst them down into destruction."

2. It implies, that they were always exposed to sudden unexpected destruction. As he that walks in slippery places is every moment liable to fall, he cannot foresee one moment whether he shall stand or fall the next; and when he does fall, he falls at once without warning: which is also expressed in Psalm lxxiii. 18, 19. " Surely thou didst set them in slippery places, thou castedst them down into destruction: how are they brought into desolation as in a moment?"

* Preached at Enfield, July 8th, 1741, at a time of great awakenings; and attended with remarkable impressions on many of the hearers.

3. Another thing implied is, that they are liable to fall *of themselves*, without being thrown down by the hand of another; as he that stands or walks on slippery ground needs nothing but his own weight to throw him down.

4. That the reason why they are not fallen already, and do not fall now, is only that God's appointed time is not come. For it is said that when that due time, or appointed time, comes, *their foot shall slide*. Then they shall be left to fall, as they are inclined by their own weight. God will not hold them up in these slippery places any longer, but will let them go; and then, at that very instant, they shall fall into destruction; as he that stands in such slippery declining ground, on the edge of a pit, he cannot stand alone, when he is let go he immediately falls and is lost.

The observation from the words that I would now insist upon is this.—"There is nothing that keeps wicked men at any one moment out of hell, but the mere pleasure of God."—By the *mere* pleasure of God, I mean his *sovereign* pleasure, his arbitrary will, restrained by no obligation, hindered by no manner of difficulty, any more than if nothing else but God's mere will had in the least degree, or in any respect whatsoever, any hand in the preservation of wicked men one moment.—The truth of this observation may appear by the following considerations.

1. There is no want of *power* in God to cast wicked men into hell at any moment. Men's hands cannot be strong when God rises up: the strongest have no power to resist him, nor can any deliver out of his hands.—He is not only able to cast wicked men into hell, but he can most easily do it. Sometimes an earthly prince meets with a great deal of difficulty to subdue a rebel, who has found means to fortify himself, and has made himself strong by the numbers of his followers. But it is not so with God. There is no fortress that is any defence from the power of God. Though hand join in hand, and vast multitudes of God's enemies combine and associate themselves, they are easily broken in pieces. They are as great heaps of light chaff before the whirlwind; or large quantities of dry stubble before devouring flames. We find it easy to tread on and crush a worm that we see crawling on the earth; so it is easy for us to cut or singe a slender thread that any thing hangs by: thus easy is it for God, when he pleases, to cast his enemies down to hell. What are we, that we

should think to stand before him, at whose rebuke the earth trembles, and before whom the rocks are thrown down?

2. They *deserve* to be cast into hell; so that divine justice never stands in the way, it makes no objection against God's using his power at any moment to destroy them. Yea, on the contrary, justice calls aloud for an infinite punishment of their sins. Divine justice says of the tree that brings forth such grapes of Sodom, "Cut it down, why cumbereth it the ground?" Luke xiii. 7. The sword of divine justice is every moment brandished over their heads, and it is nothing but the hand of arbitrary mercy, and God's mere will, that holds it back.

3. They are already under a sentence of *condemnation* to hell. They do not only justly deserve to be cast down thither, but the sentence of the law of God, that eternal and immutable rule of righteousness that God has fixed between him and mankind, is gone out against them, and stands against them; so that they are bound over already to hell. John iii. 18. "He that believeth not is condemned already." So that every unconverted man properly belongs to hell: that is his place; from thence he is, John viii. 23. "Ye are from beneath," and thither he is bound; it is the place that justice, and God's word, and the sentence of his unchangeable law, assign to him.

4. They are now the objects of that very same *anger* and wrath of God, that is expressed in the torments of hell. And the reason why they do not go down to hell at each moment is not because God, in whose power they are, is not then very angry with them, as he is with many miserable creatures now tormented in hell, and who there feel and bear the fierceness of his wrath. Yea, God is a great deal more angry with great numbers that are now on earth; yea, doubtless with many that are now in this congregation, who it may be are at ease, than he is with many of those who are now in the flames of hell.—So that it is not because God is unmindful of their wickedness, and does not resent it, that he does not let loose his hand and cut them off. God is not altogether such a one as themselves, though they imagine him to be so. The wrath of God burns against them, their damnation does not slumber; the pit is prepared, the fire is made ready, the furnace is now hot, ready to receive them; the flames do now rage and glow. The glittering sword is whet, and held over them, and the pit hath opened its mouth under them.

5. The *devil* stands ready to fall upon them, and seize them as his own, at what moment God shall permit him. They belong to him; he has their souls in his possession, and under his dominion. The Scripture represents them as his goods, Luke xi. 12. The devils watch them; they are ever by them, at their right hand; they stand waiting for them, like greedy hungry lions that see their prey, and expect to have it, but are for the present kept back. If God should withdraw his hand, by which they are restrained, they would in one moment fly upon their poor souls. The old serpent is gaping for them; hell opens its mouth wide to receive them; and if God should permit it, they would be hastily swallowed up and lost.

6. There are in the souls of wicked men those hellish *principles* reigning, that would presently kindle and flame out into hell-fire, if it were not for God's restraints. There is laid in the very nature of carnal men, a foundation for the torments of hell. There are those corrupt principles, in reigning power in them, and in full possession of them, that are seeds of hell-fire. These principles are active and powerful, exceeding violent in their nature, and if it were not for the restraining hand of God upon them, they would soon break out, they would flame out after the same manner as the same corruptions, the same enmity, does in the hearts of damned souls, and would beget the same torments as they do in them. The souls of the wicked are in Scripture compared to the troubled sea, Isaiah lvii. 20. For the present, God restrains their wickedness by his mighty power, as he does the raging waves of the troubled sea, saying, "Hitherto shalt thou come, and no further;" but if God should withdraw that restraining power, it would soon carry all before it. Sin is the ruin and misery of the soul; it is destructive in its nature; and if God should leave it without restraint, there would need nothing else to make the soul perfectly miserable. The corruption of the heart of man is immoderate and boundless in its fury; and while wicked men live here, it is like fire pent up by God's restraints, whereas if it were let loose, it would set on fire the course of nature; and as the heart is now a sink of sin, so, if sin was not restrained, it would immediately turn the soul into a fiery oven, or a furnace of fire and brimstone.

7. It is no security to wicked men for one moment, that there are no visible means of death at hand. It is no security to a

natural man, that he is now in health, and that he does not see which way he should now immediately go out of the world by any accident, and that there is no visible danger in any respect in his circumstances. The manifold and continual experience of the world in all ages shows this is no evidence that a man is not on the very brink of eternity, and that the next step will not be into another world. The unseen, unthought of ways and means of persons going suddenly out of the world are innumerable and inconceivable. Unconverted men walk over the pit of hell on a rotten covering, and there are innumerable places in this covering so weak that they will not bear their weight, and these places are not seen. The arrows of death fly unseen at noon-day; the sharpest sight cannot discern them. God has so many different unsearchable ways of taking wicked men out of the world and sending them to hell, that there is nothing to make it appear that God had need to be at the expense of a miracle, or go out of the ordinary course of his providence, to destroy any wicked man at any moment. All the means that there are of sinners going out of the world, are so in God's hands, and so universally and absolutely subject to his power and determination, that it does not depend at all the less on the mere will of God, whether sinners shall at any moment go to hell, than if means were never made use of, or at all concerned in the case.

8. Natural men's prudence and care to preserve their own lives, or the care of others to preserve them, do not secure them a moment. To this, divine providence and universal experience does also bear testimony. There is this clear evidence that men's own wisdom is no security to them from death; that if it were otherwise we should see some difference between the wise and politic men of the world, and others, with regard to their liableness to early and unexpected death: but how is it in fact? Eccl. ii. 16. "How dieth the wise man? even as the fool."

9. All wicked men's pains and *contrivance* which they use to escape hell, while they continue to reject Christ, and so remain wicked men, do not secure them from hell one moment. Almost every natural man that hears of hell, flatters himself that he shall escape it; he depends upon himself for his own security; he flatters himself in what he has done, in what he is now doing, or what he intends to do. Every one lays out matters in his own mind how he shall avoid damnation, and flatters himself that he

contrives well for himself, and that his schemes will not fail. They hear indeed that there are but few saved, and that the greater part of men that have died heretofore are gone to hell; but each one imagines that he lays out matters better for his own escape than others have done. He does not intend to come to that place of torment; he says within himself, that he intends to take effectual care, and to order matters so for himself as not to fail.

But the foolish children of men miserably delude themselves in their own schemes, and in confidence in their own strength and wisdom; they trust to nothing but a shadow. The greater part of those who heretofore have lived under the same means of grace, and are now dead, are undoubtedly gone to hell; and it was not because they were not as wise as those who are now alive; it was not because they did not lay out matters as well for themselves to secure their own escape. If we could speak with them, and inquire of them, one by one, whether they expected, when alive, and when they used to hear about hell, ever to be the subjects of that misery, we, doubtless, should hear one and another reply, " No, I never intended to come here: I had laid out matters otherwise in my mind; I thought I should contrive well for myself: I thought my scheme good. I intended to take effectual care; but it came upon me unexpected: I did not look for it at that time, and in that manner; it came as a thief: Death outwitted me: God's wrath was too quick for me. O my cursed foolishness! I was flattering myself, and pleasing myself with vain dreams of what I would do hereafter; and when I was saying, Peace and safety, then sudden destruction came upon me."

10. God has laid himself under *no obligation*, by any promise, to keep any natural man out of hell one moment. God certainly has made no promises either of eternal life, or of any deliverance or preservation from eternal death, but what are contained in the covenant of grace, the promises that are given in Christ, in whom all the promises are yea and amen. But surely they have no interest in the promises of the covenant of grace who are not the children of the covenant, who do not believe in any of the promises, and have no interest in the Mediator of the covenant.

So that, whatever some have imagined and pretended about promises made to natural men's earnest seeking and knocking, it is plain and manifest, that whatever pains a natural man takes in religion, whatever prayers he makes, till he believes in Christ, God is under no manner of obligation to keep him a moment from eternal destruction.

So that thus it is that natural men are held in the hand of God over the pit of hell; they have deserved the fiery pit, and are already sentenced to it; and God is dreadfully provoked, his anger is as great towards them as to those that are actually suffering the executions of the fierceness of his wrath in hell, and they have done nothing in the least to appease or abate that anger, neither is God in the least bound by any promise to hold them up one moment: the devil is waiting for them, hell is gaping for them, the flames gather and flash about them, and would fain lay hold on them, and swallow them up; the fire pent up in their own hearts is struggling to break out; and they have no interest in any Mediator, there are no means within reach that can be any security to them. In short, they have no refuge, nothing to take hold of; all that preserves them every moment is the mere arbitrary will, and uncovenanted, unobliged forbearance, of an incensed God.

APPLICATION

The use of this awful subject may be for awakening unconverted persons in this congregation. This that you have heard is the case of every one of you that are out of Christ.—That world of misery, that lake of burning brimstone, is extended abroad under you. There is the dreadful pit of the glowing flames of the wrath of God; there is hell's wide gaping mouth open; and you have nothing to stand upon, nor any thing to take hold of; there is nothing between you and hell but the air; it is only the power and mere pleasure of God that holds you up.

You probably are not sensible of this; you find you are kept out of hell, but do not see the hand of God in it; but look at other things, as the good state of your bodily constitution, your care of your own life, and the means you use for your own preservation. But indeed these things are nothing; if God should withdraw his hand, they would avail no more to keep you from falling, than the thin air to hold up a person that is suspended in it.

Your wickedness makes you as it were heavy as lead, and to tend downwards with great weight and pressure towards hell;

and if God should let you go, you would immediately sink and swiftly descend and plunge into the bottomless gulf; and your healthy constitution, and your own care and prudence, and best contrivance, and all your righteousness, would have no more influence to uphold you and keep you out of hell, than a spider's web would have to stop a falling rock. Were it not for the sovereign pleasure of God, the earth would not bear you one moment; for you are a burden to it: the creation groans with you; the creature is made subject to the bondage of your corruption, not willingly; the sun does not willingly shine upon you to give you light to serve sin and Satan; the earth does not willingly yield her increase to satisfy your lusts; nor is it willingly a stage for your wickedness to be acted upon; the air does not willingly serve you for breath to maintain the flame of life in your vitals, while you spend your life in the service of God's enemies. God's creatures are good, and were made for men to serve God with, and do not willingly subserve to any other purpose, and groan when they are abused to purposes so directly contrary to their nature and end. And the world would spew you out, were it not for the sovereign hand of him who hath subjected it in hope. There are the black clouds of God's wrath now hanging directly over your heads, full of the dreadful storm, and big with thunder; and were it not for the restraining hand of God, it would immediately burst forth upon you. The sovereign pleasure of God, for the present, stays his rough wind; otherwise it would come with fury, and your destruction would come like a whirlwind, and you would be like the chaff of the summer threshing-floor.

The wrath of God is like great waters that are dammed for the present; they increase more and more, and rise higher and higher, till an outlet is given; and the longer the stream is stopped, the more rapid and mighty is its course, when once it is let loose. It is true, that judgment against your evil works has not been executed hitherto; the floods of God's vengeance have been withheld; but your guilt in the mean time is constantly increasing, and you are every day treasuring up more wrath; the waters are constantly rising, and waxing more and more mighty; and there is nothing but the mere pleasure of God that holds the waters back, that are unwilling to be stopped, and press hard to go forward. If God should only withdraw his hand from the flood-gate, it would immediately fly open, and the fiery floods of the fierceness and wrath of God would rush forth with inconceivable fury, and would come upon you with omnipotent power; and if your strength were ten thousand times greater than it is, yea, ten thousand times greater than the strength of the stoutest, sturdiest devil in hell, it would be nothing to withstand or endure it.

The bow of God's wrath is bent, and the arrow made ready on the string, and justice bends the arrow at your heart, and strains the bow, and it is nothing but the mere pleasure of God, and that of an angry God, without any promise or obligation at all, that keeps the arrow one moment from being made drunk with your blood. Thus all you that never passed under a great change of heart, by the mighty power of the Spirit of God upon your souls; all you that were never born again, and made new creatures, and raised from being dead in sin, to a state of new, and before altogether unexperienced, light and life, are in the hands of an angry God. However you may have reformed your life in many things, and may have had religious affections, and may keep up a form of religion in your families and closets, and in the house of God, it is nothing but his mere pleasure that keeps you from being this moment swallowed up in everlasting destruction. However unconvinced you may now be of the truth of what you hear, by and by you will be fully convinced of it. Those that are gone from being in the like circumstances with you, see that it was so with them; for destruction came suddenly upon most of them; when they expected nothing of it, and while they were saying, Peace and safety: now they see, that those things on which they depended for peace and safety, were nothing but thin air and empty shadows.

The God that holds you over the pit of hell, much as one holds a spider, or some loathsome insect, over the fire, abhors you, and is dreadfully provoked: his wrath towards you burns like fire; he looks upon you as worthy of nothing else, but to be cast into the fire; he is of purer eyes than to bear to have you in his sight; you are ten thousand times more abominable in his eyes, than the most hateful venomous serpent is in ours. You have offended him infinitely more than ever a stubborn rebel did his prince: and yet, it is nothing but his hand that holds you from falling into the fire every moment. It is to be ascribed to nothing else, that you did not go to hell the last night; that you were suffered to awake again in this world, after you closed your eyes to sleep. And there is no other reason to be given, why you have not dropped into hell since you arose in the morning, but that God's hand has held you up. There is no other reason to be given why you have not gone to hell, since you have sat here in the house of God, provoking his pure eyes by your sinful wicked manner of attending his solemn worship. Yea, there is nothing else that is to be given as a reason why you do not this very moment drop down into hell.

O sinner! consider the fearful danger you are in: it is a great furnace of wrath, a wide and bottomless pit, full of the fire of wrath, that you are held over in the hand of that God, whose wrath is provoked and incensed as much against you, as against many of the damned in hell. You hang by a slender thread, with the flames of divine wrath flashing about it, and ready every moment to singe it, and burn it asunder; and you have no interest in any Mediator, and nothing to lay hold of to save yourself, nothing to keep off the flames of wrath, nothing of your own, nothing that you ever have done, nothing that you can do, to induce God to spare you one moment.—And consider here more particularly,

1. *Whose* wrath it is: it is the wrath of the infinite God. If it were only the wrath of man, though it were of the most potent prince, it would be comparatively little to be regarded. The wrath of kings is very much dreaded, especially of absolute monarchs, who have the possessions and lives of their subjects wholly in their power, to be disposed of at their mere will. Prov. xx. 2. " The fear of a king is as the roaring of a lion: whoso provoketh him to anger, sinneth against his own soul." The subject that very much enrages an arbitrary prince, is liable to suffer the most extreme torments that human art can invent, or human power can inflict. But the greatest earthly potentates, in their greatest majesty and strength, and when clothed in their greatest terrors, are but feeble, despicable worms of the dust, in comparison of the great and almighty Creator and King of heaven and earth. It is but little that they can do, when most enraged, and when they have exerted the utmost of their fury. All the kings of the earth, before God, are as grasshoppers; they are nothing, and less than nothing; both their love and their hatred is to be despised. The wrath of the great King of kings,

is as much more terrible than theirs, as his majesty is greater.
Luke xii. 4, 5. "And I say unto you, my friends, Be not afraid
of them that kill the body, and after that have no more that they
can do. But I will forewarn you whom ye shall fear: Fear him,
which after he hath killed, hath power to cast into hell; yea, I
say unto you, Fear him."

2. It is the *fierceness* of his wrath that you are exposed to. We
often read of the fury of God; as in Isa. lix. 18. "According to
their deeds, accordingly he will repay fury to his adversaries."
So Isa. lxvi. 15. "For behold, the Lord will come with fire, and
with his chariots like a whirlwind, to render his anger with fury,
and his rebuke with flames of fire." And in many other places.
So, Rev. xix. 15. we read of "the wine-press of the fierceness and
wrath of Almighty God." The words are exceeding terrible. If
it had only been said, "the wrath of God," the words would have
implied that which is infinitely dreadful: but it is the "fierceness
and wrath of God." The fury of God! the fierceness of Jehovah!
O how dreadful must that be! Who can utter or conceive what
such expressions carry in them? But it is also "the fierceness and
wrath of *Almighty* God." As though there would be a very great
manifestation of his almighty power in what the fierceness of his
wrath should inflict; as though omnipotence should be as it were
enraged, and exerted, as men are wont to exert their strength in
the fierceness of their wrath. Oh! then, what will be the consequence! What will become of the poor worm that shall suffer it!
Whose hands can be strong? and whose heart can endure? To
what a dreadful, inexpressible, inconceivable depth of misery
must the poor creature be sunk who shall be the subject of
this!

Consider this, you that are here present, that yet remain in an
unregenerate state. That God will execute the fierceness of his
anger, implies, that he will inflict wrath without any pity. When
God beholds the ineffable extremity of your case, and sees your
torment to be so vastly disproportioned to your strength, and
sees how your poor soul is crushed, and sinks down, as it were,
into an infinite gloom; he will have no compassion upon you, he
will not forbear the executions of his wrath, or in the least lighten
his hand; there shall be no moderation or mercy, nor will God
then at all stay his rough wind; he will have no regard to your
welfare, nor be at all careful lest you should suffer too much in

N

any other sense, than only that you shall *not suffer beyond what strict justice requires*. Nothing shall be withheld, because it is so hard for you to bear. Ezek. viii. 18. "Therefore will I also deal in fury; mine eye shall not spare, neither will I have pity; and though they cry in mine ears with a loud voice, yet I will not hear them." Now God stands ready to pity you; this is a day of mercy; you may cry now with some encouragement of obtaining mercy. But when once the day of mercy is past, your most lamentable and dolorous cries and shrieks will be in vain; you will be wholly lost and thrown away of God, as to any regard to your welfare. God will have no other use to put you to, but to suffer misery; you shall be continued in being to no other end; for you will be a vessel of wrath fitted to destruction; and there will be no other use of this vessel, but to be filled full of wrath. God will be so far from pitying you when you cry to him, that it is said he will only "laugh and mock," Prov. i. 25, 26, etc.

How awful are those words, Isa. lxiii. 3. which are the words of the great God, "I will tread them in mine anger, and will trample them in my fury, and their blood shall be sprinkled upon my garments, and I will stain all my raiment." It is perhaps impossible to conceive of words that carry in them greater manifestations of these three things, *viz.* contempt, and hatred, and fierceness of indignation. If you cry to God to pity you, he will be so far from pitying you in your doleful case, or showing you the least regard or favour, that, instead of that, he will only tread you under foot. And though he will know that you cannot bear the weight of omnipotence treading upon you, yet he will not regard that, but he will crush you under his feet without mercy; he will crush out your blood, and make it fly, and it shall be sprinkled on his garments, so as to stain all his raiment. He will not only hate you, but he will have you in the utmost contempt; no place shall be thought fit for you, but under his feet, to be trodden down as the mire of the streets.

3. The misery you are exposed to is that which God will inflict to that end, that he might show what that wrath of Jehovah is. God hath had it on his heart to show to angels and men, both how excellent his love is, and also how terrible his wrath is. Sometimes earthly kings have a mind to show how terrible their wrath is, by the extreme punishments they would execute on

those that would provoke them. Nebuchadnezzar, that mighty and haughty monarch of the Chaldean empire, was willing to show his wrath when enraged with Shadrach, Meshech, and Abednego; and accordingly gave order that the burning fiery furnace should be heated seven times hotter than it was before: doubtless, it was raised to the utmost degree of fierceness that human art could raise it. But the great God is also willing to show his wrath, and magnify his awful majesty and mighty power, in the extreme sufferings of his enemies. Rom. ix. 22. "What if God, willing to show his wrath, and to make his power known, endured with much long-suffering the vessels of wrath fitted to destruction?" And seeing this is his design, and what he has determined, even to show how terrible the unrestrained wrath, the fury and fierceness, of Jehovah is, he will do it to effect. There will be something accomplished and brought to pass that will be dreadful with a witness. When the great and angry God hath risen up and executed his awful vengeance on the poor sinner, and the wretch is actually suffering the infinite weight and power of his indignation, then will God call upon the whole universe to behold that awful majesty and mighty power that is to be seen in it. Isaiah xxxiii. 12-14. "And the people shall be as the burnings of lime, as thorns cut up shall they be burnt in the fire. Hear, ye that are afar off, what I have done; and ye that are near, acknowledge my might. The sinners in Zion are afraid; fearfulness hath surprised the hypocrites," etc.

Thus it will be with you that are in an unconverted state, if you continue in it; the infinite might, and majesty, and terribleness of the omnipotent God shall be magnified upon you, in the ineffable strength of your torments. You shall be tormented in the presence of the holy angels, and in the presence of the Lamb; and when you shall be in this state of suffering, the glorious inhabitants of heaven shall go forth and look on the awful spectacle, that they may see what the wrath and fierceness of the Almighty is; and when they have seen it, they will fall down and adore that great power and majesty. Isaiah lxvi. 23, 24. "And it shall come to pass, that from one new moon to another, and from one sabbath to another, shall all flesh come to worship before me, saith the Lord. And they shall go forth and look upon the carcasses of the men that have transgressed against me; for their worm shall not die; neither shall their fire be quenched, and they shall be an abhorring unto all flesh."

4. It is *everlasting* wrath. It would be dreadful to suffer this fierceness and wrath of Almighty God one moment; but you must suffer it to all eternity. There will be no end to this exquisite horrible misery. When you look forward, you shall see a long forever, a boundless duration before you, which will swallow up your thoughts, and amaze your soul; and you will absolutely despair of ever having any deliverance, any end, any mitigation, any rest at all. You will know certainly that you must wear out long ages, millions of millions of ages in wrestling and conflicting with this almighty merciless vengeance; and then when you have so done, when so many ages have actually been spent by you in this manner, you will know that all is but a point to what remains. So that your punishment will indeed be infinite. Oh who can express what the state of a soul in such circumstances is! All that we can possibly say about it, gives but a very feeble, faint representation of it; it is inexpressible and inconceivable: for " who knows the power of God's anger?"

How dreadful is the state of those that are daily and hourly in danger of this great wrath and infinite misery! But this is the dismal case of every soul in this congregation that has not been born again, however moral and strict, sober and religious, they may otherwise be. Oh that you would consider it, whether you be young or old! There is reason to think, that there are many in this congregation now hearing this discourse, that will actually be the subjects of this very misery to all eternity. We know not who they are, or in what seats they sit, or what thoughts they now have. It may be they are now at ease, and hear all these things without much disturbance, and are now flattering themselves that they are not the persons, promising themselves that they shall escape. If we knew that there was one person, and but one, in the whole congregation, that was to be the subject of this misery, what an awful thing would it be to think of! If we knew who it was, what an awful sight would it be to see such a person! How might all the rest of the congregation lift up a lamentable and bitter cry over him! But, alas! instead of one, how many is it likely will remember this discourse in hell! And it would be a wonder, if some that are now present should not be in hell in a very short time, even before this year is out. And it would be no wonder if some persons, that now sit here, in some seats of this meeting-house, in health, quiet and secure, should be there before to-morrow morning. Those of you that finally continue in a natural condition, that shall keep out of hell longest, will be there in a little time! your damnation does not slumber; it will come swiftly, and, in all probability, very suddenly, upon many of you. You have reason to wonder that you are not already in hell. It is doubtless the case of some whom you have seen and known, that never deserved hell more than you, and that heretofore appeared as likely to have been now alive as you. Their case is past all hope; they are crying in extreme misery and perfect despair; but here you are in the land of the living, and in the house of God, and have an opportunity to obtain salvation. What would not those poor damned, hopeless souls give for one day's opportunity such as you now enjoy!

And now you have an extraordinary opportunity, a day wherein Christ has thrown the door of mercy wide open, and stands calling, and crying with a loud voice to poor sinners; a day wherein many are flocking to him, and pressing into the kingdom of God. Many are daily coming from the east, west, north, and south; many that were very lately in the same miserable condition that you are in, are now in a happy state, with their hearts filled with love to him who has loved them, and washed them from their sins in his own blood, and rejoicing in hope of the glory of God. How awful it is to be left behind at such a day! To see so many others feasting, while you are pining and perishing! To see so many rejoicing and singing for joy of heart, while you have cause to mourn for sorrow of heart, and howl for vexation of spirit! How can you rest one moment in such a condition? Are not your souls as precious as the souls of the people at Suffield,* where they are flocking from day to day to Christ?

Are there not many here who have lived long in the world, and are not to this day born again? and so are aliens from the commonweath of Israel, and have done nothing ever since they have lived, but treasure up wrath against the day of wrath? Oh, Sirs, your case, in an especial manner, is extremely dangerous. Your guilt and hardness of heart is extremely great. Do not you see how generally persons of your years are passed over and left,

* A town in the neighbourhood.

in the present remarkable and wonderful dispensation of God's mercy? You had need to consider yourselves, and awake thoroughly out of sleep. You cannot bear the fierceness and wrath of the infinite God.—And you, young men and young women, will you neglect this precious season which you now enjoy, when so many others of your age are renouncing all youthful vanities, and flocking to Christ? You especially have now an extraordinary opportunity; but if you neglect it, it will soon be with you as with those persons who spent all the precious days of youth in sin, and are now come to such a dreadful pass in blindness and hardness.—And you, children, who are unconverted, do not you know that you are going down to hell, to bear the dreadful wrath of that God, who is now angry with you every day and every night? Will you be content to be the children of the devil, when so many other children in the land are converted, and are become the holy and happy children of the King of kings?

And let every one that is yet out of Christ, and hanging over the pit of hell, whether they be old men and women, or middle aged, or young people, or little children, now hearken to the loud calls of God's word and providence. This acceptable year of the Lord, a day of such great favour to some, will doubtless be a day of as remarkable vengeance to others. Men's hearts harden, and their guilt increases apace, at such a day as this, if they neglect their souls; and never was there so great danger of such persons being given up to hardness of heart and blindness of mind. God seems now to be hastily gathering in his elect in all parts of the land; and probably the greater part of adult persons that ever shall be saved, will be brought in now in a little time, and that it will be as it was on the great out-pouring of the Spirit upon the Jews in the apostles' days, the election will obtain, and the rest will be blinded. If this should be the case with you, you will eternally curse this day, and will curse the day that ever you were born, to see such a season of the pouring out of God's Spirit, and will wish that you had died and gone to hell before you had seen it. Now undoubtedly it is, as it was in the days of John the Baptist, the axe is in an extraordinary manner laid at the roots of the trees, that every tree which brings not forth good fruit, may be hewn down, and cast into the fire.

Therefore, let every one that is out of Christ, now awake and fly from the wrath to come. The wrath of Almighty God is now undoubtedly hanging over a great part of this congregation. Let every one fly out of Sodom: "Haste and escape for your lives, look not behind you. escape to the mountain, lest you be consumed."

Sermon VIII

CHRISTIANS A CHOSEN GENERATION, A ROYAL PRIESTHOOD, A HOLY NATION, A PECULIAR PEOPLE

1 Peter ii. 9

But ye are a chosen generation, a royal priesthood, an holy nation, a peculiar people; that ye should show forth the praises of him who hath called you out of darkness into his marvellous light.

THE apostle in the preceding verses speaks of the great difference between Christians and unbelievers, on account of their diverse and opposite relations to Jesus Christ. The former have Christ for their foundation, they come to him as a living stone, a stone chosen of God, and precious; and they also as living stones are built up a spiritual house. The christian church is the temple of God, and particular believers are the stones of which that temple is built. The stones of Solomon's temple, which were so curiously polished and well fitted for their places in that building, were a type of believers. And Christ is the foundation of this building, or the chief corner stone. On the contrary, to the latter, to unbelievers, Christ, instead of being a foundation on which they rest and depend, is a stone of stumbling, and a rock of offence; instead of being a foundation to support them and keep them from falling, he is an occasion of their stumbling and falling.

And again, to believers Christ is a precious stone: "Unto you therefore which believe, he is precious." But to unbelievers he is a stone that is disallowed, and rejected, and set at nought. They set light by him, as by the stones of the street; they make no account of him, they disallow him; when they come to build, they cast this stone away as being of no use, not fit for a foundation, not fit for a place in their building. In the eighth verse the

apostle tells the Christians to whom he writes, that those unbelievers who thus reject Christ, and to whom he is a stone of
stumbling, and rock of offence, were appointed to this. "And
a stone of stumbling, and a rock of offence, even to them which
stumble at the word, being disobedient, whereunto also they
were appointed." It was appointed that they should stumble at
the word that Christ should be an occasion not of their salvation,
but of their deeper damnation. And then in our text, he puts
the Christians in mind how far otherwise God had dealt with
them, than with those reprobates. They were a chosen generation. God had rejected the others in his eternal counsels;
but themselves he had chosen from eternity. They were a
chosen generation, a royal priesthood, a holy nation, a peculiar
people.

As God distinguished the people of Israel of old from all other
nations, so he distinguishes true Christians. It is probable the
apostle had in his mind some expressions that are used in the
Old Testament, concerning the people of Israel. Christians are
said here to be a chosen generation, according to what was said
of Israel of old. Deut. x. 15. "Only the Lord thy God had a
delight in thy fathers to love them, and he chose their seed after
them, even you above all people, as it is this day." Christians are
here said to be a royal priesthood, a holy nation, a peculiar people,
agreeable to what was said of old of Israel. Exod. xix. 5, 6.
"Now, therefore, if ye will obey my voice indeed, and keep my
covenant, then ye shall be a peculiar treasure unto me above all
people: for all the earth is mine. And ye shall be unto me a
kingdom of priests, and an holy nation. These are the words
which thou shalt speak unto the children of Israel."

But there is something further said here of Christians than
there of Israel. There, it is promised to Israel that, if they obey,
they shall be *a kingdom of priests;* but here, Christians are said
to be *a priesthood of kings,* or a royal priesthood. They are a
priesthood, and they are also kings.

I propose to insist distinctly upon the several propositions contained in the words of the text.

I. True Christians are *a chosen generation.* Two things are
here implied.

1. That true Christians are chosen by God from the rest of the
world, to be his.

2. That God's people are of a peculiar descent and pedigree, different from all the world besides.

1. True Christians are chosen by God from the rest of the world.

God does not utterly cast off the world of mankind. Though they are fallen and corrupted, and there is a curse brought upon the world, yet God entertained a design of appropriating a certain number to himself. Indeed all men and all creatures are his, as well since as before the fall; whether they are elected or not, they are his. God does not lose his right to them by the fall, neither does he lose his power to dispose of them; they are still in his hands. Neither does he lose his end in creating them. God hath made all things for himself, even the wicked for the day of evil. It possibly was Satan's design, in endeavouring the fall of man, to cause that God should lose the creature that he had made, by getting him away from God into his own possession, and to frustrate God of his end in creating man; but this Satan has not obtained.

But yet in a sense the wicked may be said not to belong to God. God doth not own them; he hath rejected them and cast them away; they are not God's portion, they are Satan's portion; God hath left them, and they are lost. When man fell, God left and cast off the bulk of mankind; but he was pleased, notwithstanding the universal fall, to choose out a number of them to be his, whom he would still appropriate to himself. Though the world is a fallen world, yet it was the will of God still to have a portion in it, and therefore he chose out some and set them apart for himself. Psal. iv. 3. " But know that the Lord hath set apart him that is godly for himself: the Lord will hear when I call unto him." God's portion is his people, and Jacob is the lot of his inheritance. Deut. xxxii. 9. Those who are God's enemies, and to whom he is an enemy, are still his. But those who are his friends, his children, his jewels, that compose his treasure, are his in a very different manner. God has chosen the godly out of the rest of the world to be nearly related to him, to stand in the relation of children, to have a property in him, that they might not only be his people, but that he might be their God; he has chosen these to bestow himself upon them. He hath chosen them from among others to be gracious to them, to show them his favour; he has chosen them to enjoy him, to see his glory, and to dwell with him for ever.   He hath chosen them as his treasure, as a man chooses out gems from a heap of stones, with this difference, the man finds gems very different from other stones, and therefore chooses.   But God chooses them, and therefore they become gems, and very different from others.   Mal. iii. 17.   "And they shall be mine, saith the Lord of hosts, in that day when I make up my jewels; and I will spare them as a man spareth his own son that serveth him." Psal. cxxxv. 4 " For the Lord hath chosen Jacob unto himself, and Israel for his peculiar treasure."   God hath chosen them for a most noble and excellent use, and therefore they are called vessels unto honour, and elect vessels.   God has different uses for different men.   Some are destined to a baser use, and are vessels unto dishonour; others are chosen for the most noble use, for serving and glorifying God, and that God may show the glory of divine grace upon them.

Several things may here be observed concerning this election of God, whereby he chooses truly godly persons.

First. This election supposes that the persons chosen are found among others. The word election denotes this, it signifies *a choosing out.*   The elect are favoured by electing grace among the rest of mankind, with whom they are found mixed together as the tares and the wheat.   They are found among them in the same sinfulness, and in the same misery, and are alike partakers of original corruption.   They are among them in being destitute of any thing in them that is good, in enmity against God, in being in bondage to Satan, in condemnation to eternal destruction, and in being without righteousness.   So that there is no distinction between them prior to that which the election makes, there is no respect wherein the elect are not among the common multitude of mankind.   1 Cor. iv. 7. " For who maketh thee to differ from another? and what hast thou that thou didst not receive? now, if thou didst receive it, why dost thou glory as if thou hadst not received it?" 1 Cor. vi. 11. "And such were some of you; but ye are washed, but ye are sanctified, but ye are justified, in the name of the Lord Jesus, and by the Spirit of our God."   And therefore,

Secondly. No foreseen excellency in the elected is the motive that influences God to choose them. Election is only from his good pleasure.   God's election being the first thing that causes any distinction, there can be no distinction already existing, the foresight of which influences God to choose them. It is not the seeing of any amiableness in them above others, that causes God to choose them rather than the rest. God does not choose men, because they are excellent; but he makes them excellent, and because he has chosen them. It is not because God considers them as holy that he chooses them; but he chooses them that they might be holy. Eph. i. 4, 5. "According as he hath chosen us in him before the foundation of the world, that we should be holy, and without blame before him in love; having predestinated us unto the adoption of children by Jesus Christ to himself, according to the good pleasure of his will." God does not choose them from the foresight of any respect they will have towards him more than others. God does not choose men and set his care upon them because they love him, for he hath first loved us. 1 John iv. 10. "Herein is love, not that we loved God, but that he loved us, and sent his Son to be the propitiation for our sins;" ver. 19. "We love him, because he first loved us."

It is not from any foresight of good works that men do before or after conversion; but on the contrary, men do good works because God hath chosen them. John xv. 16. "Ye have not chosen me, but I have chosen you, and ordained you, that ye should go and bring forth fruit, and that your fruit should remain; that whatsoever ye shall ask of the Father in my name, he may give it you." Nor did God choose men, because he foresaw that they would believe and come to Christ. Faith is the consequence of election, and not the cause of it. Acts xiii. 48. "And when the Gentiles heard this they were glad, and glorified the word of the Lord: and as many as were ordained to eternal life, believed." It is because God hath chosen men, that he calls them to Christ, and causes them to come to him. To suppose that election is from the foresight of faith, is to place calling before election, which is contrary to the order in which the Scripture represents things. Rom. viii. 30. "Moreover, whom he did predestinate, them he also called; and whom he called, them he also justified; and whom he justified, them he also glorified." It is not from the foresight of any, either moral or natural qualifications, that God chooses men, nor because he sees that some men are of a more amiable make, and better natural temper, or genius, nor because he foresees that some men will have better abilities, and will have more wisdom than others, and so will be able to do more service for God than others; nor because he foresees that they will be great and rich, and so possessed of greater advantages to serve him. 1 Cor. i. 27, 28. "But God hath chosen the foolish things of the world, to confound the wise; and God hath chosen the weak things of the world, to confound the things which are mighty; and the base things of the world, and things despised, hath God chosen, yea, and things which are not, to bring to nought things that are." Nor is it from any foresight of men's endeavours after conversion, because he sees that some whom he chooses will do much more than others to obtain heaven; but God chooses them, and therefore awakens them, and prompts them to strive for conversion. Rom. ix. 16. " So then it is not of him that willeth, nor of him that runneth, but of God that showeth mercy." Election in Scripture is every where referred to God's own good pleasure. Matt. xi. 26. "Even so, Father; for so it seemed good in thy sight." 2 Tim. i. 9. "Who hath saved us, and called us with an holy calling, not according to our works, but according to his own purpose and grace, which was given us in Christ Jesus before the world began."

Thirdly. True Christians are chosen of God from all eternity; not only before they were born, but before the world was created. They were foreknown of God, and chosen by him out of the world. Eph. i. 4. "According as he hath chosen us in him before the foundation of the world, that we should be holy, and without blame before him in love." 2 Tim. i. 9. "According to his own purpose and grace, which was given us in Christ Jesus, before the world began."

Fourthly. God in election set his love upon those whom he elected. Rom. ix. 13. "Jacob have I loved, but Esau have I hated." Jer. xxxi. 3. "The Lord hath appeared of old unto me, saying, Yea, I have loved thee with an everlasting love; therefore with loving-kindness have I drawn thee." 1 John iv. 19. "We love him because he first loved us." A God of infinite goodness and benevolence loves those that have no excellency to move or attract it: the love of men is consequent upon some loveliness in the object, but the love of God is antecedent to, and the cause of it. Believers were from all eternity beloved both by the Father and the Son. The eternal love of the Father appears in that he from all eternity contrived a way for their salvation, and chose Jesus Christ to be their Redeemer, and laid help upon him. It

is a fruit of this electing love that God sent his Son into the
world to die, it was to redeem those whom he so loved. 1 John
iv. 10. "Herein is love, not that we loved God, but that he loved
us, and sent his Son to be the propitiation for our sins." It is a
fruit of the eternal, electing love of Jesus Christ, that he was willing to come into the world, and die for sinners, and that he
actually came and died. Gal. ii. 20. "I am crucified with Christ:
nevertheless, I live; yet not I, but Christ liveth in me: and the
life which I now live in the flesh, I live by the faith of the Son of
God, who loved me, and gave himself for me." And so conversion, and glorification, and all that is done for a believer from the
first to the last, is a fruit of electing love.

Fifthly. This electing love of God is singly of every particular
person. Some deny a particular election, and say that there is no
other election than a general determination, that all that believe
and obey shall be saved. Some also own no more than an absolute election of nations. But God did from all eternity singly and
distinctly choose, and set his love upon, every particular person
that ever believes, as is evident by Gal. ii. 20. "Who loved me
and gave himself for me." God set his love from eternity upon
this and that person, as particularly as if there were no other
chosen than he; and therefore it is represented as though they
were mentioned by name, that their names are written in the
book of life. Luke x. 20. "Notwithstanding, in this rejoice not,
that the spirits are subject unto you; but rather rejoice, because
your names are written in heaven." Rev. xiii. 8. "And all that
dwell upon the earth shall worship him, whose names are not
written in the book of life of the Lamb slain from the foundation
of the world."

Sixthly. In election, believers were from all eternity given to
Jesus Christ. As believers were chosen from all eternity, so Christ
was from eternity chosen and appointed to be their Redeemer,
and he undertook the work of redeeming them. There was a
covenant respecting it between the Father and Son. Christ, as
we have already observed, loved them before the creation of the
world; and then he had their names, as it were, written in a book,
and therefore the book of life is called the Lamb's book. Rev.
xxi. 27. "And there shall in no wise enter into it any thing that
defileth, neither whatsoever worketh abomination, or maketh a
lie: but they which are written in the Lamb's book of life." And

he bears their names upon his heart, as the high priest of old did the names of the tribes of the children of Israel on his breast-plate. Christ often calls the elect those whom God had given him. John xvii. 2. " As thou hast given him power over all flesh, that he should give eternal life to as many as thou hast given him." In the 9th verse, "I pray for them; I pray not for the world, but for them which thou hast given me; for they are thine." In the 11th verse, "And now I am no more in the world, but these are in the world, and I come to thee. Holy Father, keep through thine own name those whom thou hast given me, that they may be one, as we are."

This part of the subject may suggest to us the following re-flections.

First. God's thus electing a certain definite number from among fallen men from all eternity, is a manifestation of his glory. It shows the glory of the divine sovereignty. God hereby declares himself the absolute disposer of the creature; he shows us how far his sovereignty and dominion extend, in eternally choosing some and passing by others, and leaving them to perish. God here appears in a majesty that is unparalleled. Those who can see no glory of dominion in this act, have not attained to right apprehensions of God, and never have been made sensible of his glorious greatness. And here is especially shown the glory of divine grace, in God's having chosen his people to blessedness and glory long before they are born; in his choosing them out of the mass of mankind, from whom they were not distinguished, and in his love to them being prior to all that they have or do, being uninfluenced by any excellency of theirs, by the light of any labours or endeavours of theirs, or any respect of theirs towards him.

The doctrine of election shows, that if those who are converted have earnestly sought grace and holiness, and in that way have obtained it, their obtaining it is not owing to their endeavours, but that it was the grace and mercy of God that caused them earnestly to seek conversion, that they might obtain it. It shows also that faith itself is the gift of God, and that the saints per-severing in a way of holiness unto glory, is also the fruit of elect-ing love. Believers' love to God is the fruit of God's love to them, and the giving of Christ, the preaching of the gospel, the appoint-ing of ordinances, are all fruits of the grace of election. All the grace that is shown to any of mankind, either in this world, or in the world to come, is comprised in the electing love of God.

Secondly. If believers are the chosen of God, here is a great argument for their love and gratitude towards him. The consideration of the miserable condition in which God found you, and in which he left others, should move your hearts. How wonderful that God should take such thought of a poor worm from all eternity! God might have left you as well as many others, but it pleased the Lord to set his love upon you. What cause have you for love and thankfulness, that God should make choice of you, and set you apart for himself, rather than so many thousands of others!

God hath chosen you not merely to be his subjects and servants, but to be his children, to be his particular treasure; he has chosen you to be blessed for ever in the enjoyment of himself, and to dwell with him in his glory. He has given you from all eternity to his Son, to be united unto him, to become the spouse of Christ. He has chosen you that you might be holy and without blame, that you might have your filth taken away, and that you might have the image of God put upon you, and that your soul might be adorned, to be the bride of his glorious and dear Son. What cause for love is here!

Thirdly. If believers are a chosen generation, let all labour earnestly to make their election sure. If true Christians are chosen of God, this should induce all earnestly to inquire whether they are true Christians. 2 Peter i. 5, 6, 7. " And besides this, giving all diligence, add to your faith, virtue; and to virtue, knowledge; and to knowledge, temperance; and to temperance, patience; and to patience, godliness; and to godliness, brotherly kindness; and to brotherly kindness, charity."

2. True Christians are a distinct race of men; they are of a peculiar descent or pedigree, different from the rest of the world. This is implied in their being called a generation. There are three significations of the word generation in the Scriptures. Sometimes it means, as is its meaning in common use, *a class of persons among a people, or in the world, that are born together, or so nearly together, that the time of their being in the different stages of the age of man is the same.* They shall be young persons, middle aged, and old together; or they shall be together

upon the stage of action. All that are together upon the face of the earth, or the stage of action, are very often accounted as one generation. Thus when God threatened that not one of the Israelites of that generation should see the good land, it is meant, all from twenty years old and upwards.

A second meaning is, *those who are born of a common progenitor.*

A third meaning of the word in Scripture, is, *a certain race of mankind, whose generation and birth agree, not as to time,* but *as to descent and pedigree,* or *as to those persons from whom they originally proceeded.* So it is to be understood, Matt. i. 1. "This is the book of the generation of Jesus Christ, the Son of David, the son of Abraham;" that is, this is the book that gives an account of his pedigree. And this meaning, *viz.* those who are of the same race and descent, must be given to the word in the text. The righteous are often spoken of in Scripture as being a distinct generation. Psal. xiv. 5. "There were they in great fear: for God is in the generation of the righteous." Psal. xxiv. 6. "This is the generation of them that seek him, that seek thy face, O Jacob." Psal. lxxiii. 15. "If I say, I will speak thus: behold, I should offend against the generation of thy children."

That the godly are a distinct race appears evident, since they are descended from God, they are a heavenly race, they are derived from above. The heathen were wont to feign that their heroes and great men were descended from the gods, but God's people are descended from the true and living God, without any fiction. Psal. xxii. 30. "A seed shall serve him; it shall be accounted to the Lord for a generation." That is, a seed, a posterity, shall serve him, and it shall be accounted to the Lord for his posterity or offspring.

Now the people of God may be considered as descending from God, and as being his posterity, either remotely or immediately.

First. They are *remotely* descended from God. The church is a distinct race, that originally came from God. Other men are of the earth, they are of earthly derivation, they are the posterity of men; but the church is the posterity of God. Thus it is said, Gen. vi. 2. "That the sons of God saw the daughters of men, that they were fair; and they took them wives of all which they chose." The sons of God were the children of the church, of the posterity of Seth; the daughters of men were those that were born

o

out of the church, and of the posterity of Cain, and those that adhered to him.

It was God that set up the church in the world, and those, who were the first founders of the church, were of God, and were called specially *the sons of God*. Seth was the seed that God appointed. Gen. iv. 25. "And Adam knew his wife again; and she bare a son, and called his name Seth. For God, said she, hath appointed me another seed instead of Abel, whom Cain slew." Adam, in Luke's genealogy of Christ, (Luke iii. 38. "Which was the son of Enos, which was the son of Seth, which was the son of Adam, which was the son of God,") is called the son of God; possibly, not only because he was immediately created by God, but also because he was from God, and was begotten by him. As he was a good man, and was the founder of the church, of which Christ himself became a son, he was the first in line of the church, and as such he was from God. When the church was almost extinct God called Abraham out of Ur of the Chaldees, and afterwards out of Haran. Abraham was one immediately from God, and all God's people in all succeeding ages are accounted as the children of Abraham. God promised Abraham that his seed should be as the stars of heaven, and as the sand on the sea-shore, meaning primarily not his posterity according to the flesh. John the Baptist said, God is able of the stones to raise up children unto Abraham. Those are the seed of Abraham, as we are taught in the New Testament, that are of the faith of Abraham; Christians, as well as Jews, are the seed of Abraham. Gal. iii. 29. "And if ye be Christ's, then are ye Abraham's seed, and heirs according to the promise." So the church is the seed of Jacob, who is called God's son. Hosea xi. 1. "When Israel was a child, then I loved him, and called *my son* out of Egypt." All God's people are called Israel; not only his posterity according to the flesh, but proselytes of old, and Gentile Christians now under the gospel. The sincerely godly, and they only, are the true Israel.

So the people of God are descended from God the Father originally, as they are descended from Christ the Son of God. Christians are called *the seed of Christ*. Gal. iii. 29. "And if ye be Christ's," etc. They are, as it were, his *posterity;* Christ calls them his *children*. Heb. ii. 13. "Behold I and the children which thou hast given me." So that if we trace the pedigree of God's people up to their original, they will be found to be descended from God: they are of heaven, they are not of this world. Other men are of the earth, and are earthly, but these are heavenly, and are of heaven. The wicked are called the men of this world. Psal. xvii. 14. "From men which are thy hand, O Lord, from men of the world which have their portion in this life, and whose belly thou fillest with thy hid treasure: they are full of children, and leave the rest of their substance to their babes." The first beginnings of the church were from God, the great founder of the church. Jesus Christ is the Son of God, and those men, who under him have been founders, were of God, were of him. God chose them, called them, and created them for this purpose. Since which, God's people are descended one from another; the church is continued and propagated, as it were, by generation. If there were no ordinary and stated means made use of for the continuing and propagating the church, it would not be so; but God's people are made the instruments of one another's conversion, by begetting one another's souls. The church is continued by itself instrumentally through all generations, the people of God are begotten through the education, instruction, and endeavours of those who were God's people before. Therefore the church is represented in Scripture as being the mother of its members. Gal. iv. 26. "But Jerusalem which is above is free, which is the mother of us all." Believers are the children of the church, as they are often called. Isa. xlix. 20. "The children which thou shalt have, after thou hast lost the other, shall say again in thine ears, the place is too strait for me; give place to me, that I may dwell." Isa. liv. 1. "Sing, O barren, thou that didst not bear; break forth into singing, and cry aloud, thou that didst not travail with child: for more are the children of the desolate than the children of the married wife, saith the Lord." And many other places.

God's people are often, through their education and instruction, the spiritual parents of those of whom they are the natural parents. The ministers of the word and ordinances are spiritual fathers. The apostle tells the christian Corinthians, that he had begotten them through the gospel.

Secondly. God's people are immediately begotten of God. When they become saints, they are *born again*, they have a new nature given them, they have a new life begun, they are renewed in the whole man by a new generation and birth wherein they are born of God. John i. 12, 13. "But as many as received him, to them gave he power to become the sons of God, even to them that believe on his name: which were *born*, not of blood, nor of the will of the flesh, nor of the will of man, but *of God*." They are born of the Spirit of God. John iii. 8. "The wind bloweth where it listeth, and thou hearest the sound thereof, but canst not tell whence it cometh nor whither it goeth: so is every one that is *born of the Spirit*." God is said to have formed the church from the womb. Isa. xliv. 2. "Thus saith the Lord that made thee, and formed thee from the womb, which will help thee: Fear not, O Jacob my servant; and thou, Jeshurun, whom I have chosen."

This truth also may suggest to us a few profitable reflections.

First. Christians ought to bear with one another. It appears from what has been said, that they are all of one kindred, that they have a relation to other Christians which they have not to the rest of the world; being of a distinct race from them, but of the same race one with another. They are descended all along from the same progenitors; they are the children of the same universal church of God; they are all the children of Abraham; they are the seed of Jesus Christ; they are the offspring of God. And they are yet much more alike, than their being of the same race originally argues them to be: they are also immediately the children of the same Father. God hath begotten all by the same word and Spirit; they are all of one family, and should therefore love as brethren. 1 Peter iii. 8. "Finally, be ye all of one mind, having compassion one of another; love as brethren, be pitiful, be courteous."

It is very unbecoming those who are God's offspring, to entertain a spirit of hatred and ill will one towards another. It is very unbecoming to be backward in helping and assisting one another, and supplying each other's wants; much more, to contrive and seek one another's hurt, to be revengeful one towards another.

Secondly. Let Christians take heed so to walk, that they may not dishonour their pedigree. You are of a very honourable race, more honourable by far than if you were the offspring of kings, and had royal blood in your veins; you are a heavenly offspring, the seed of Jesus Christ, the children of God. They that are of noble race are wont to value themselves highly upon the honour of their families, to dwell on their titles, their coats of arms, and their ensigns of honour, and to recount the exploits of their illustrious forefathers. How much more careful should you be of the honour of your descent, that you in nothing behave yourself unworthy of the great God, the eternal and omnipotent King of heaven and earth, whose offspring you are!

There are many things that are very base, and too mean for such as you; such are a giving way to earthly-mindedness, a grovelling like moles in the earth, a suffering your soul to cleave to those earthly things, which ought to be neglected and despised by those who are of heavenly descent; an indulgence of the lusts of the flesh, suffering the soul to be immersed in filth, being taken up with mean and unworthy delights common to the beasts, being intemperate in the gratification of any carnal appetite whatsoever, or a being much concerned about earthly honour. It is surely a disgrace to them, who are accounted to God for a generation, much to care whether they are accounted great upon this dunghill. So it is unworthy of your noble descent to be governed by your passions : you should be guided by higher principles of reason and virtue, and an universal respect to the glory and honour of God.

But Christians should seek after those things which will be to the honour of their birth, after spiritual wisdom, and knowledge of the most worthy and noble truths. They should seek more and more an acquaintance with God, and to be assimilated to him, their great progenitor, and their immediate Father, that they may have the image of his excellent and divine perfections. They should endeavour to act like God, wherein they are capable of imitation of him. They should seek heavenly-mindedness, those noble appetites after heavenly and spiritual enjoyments, a noble ambition after heavenly glory, a contempt of the trifles and mean things of this world. They should seek after those delights and satisfactions that can be enjoyed by none but heavenly minds. They should exercise a spirit of true, universal, and disinterested love and confidence, and christian charity. They should be much in devotion, and divine contemplation.

Thirdly. We see here a reason why Christians are of so different a nature and temper from the rest of the world. The truly godly are very different in their disposition from others. They hate those things that the rest of the world love, and love those things for which the rest of the world have no relish; insomuch that others are ready to wonder that they should place any happiness in a strict observance of the self-denying duties of religion; they wonder what delight they can take in spending so much time in meditation and prayer, and that they do not place happiness in those things which themselves do. 1 Peter iv. 4. " Wherein they think it strange that ye run not with them to the same excess of riot; speaking evil of you." But the reason is, they are of a different race, and so derive different dispositions.

It is ordinary to see those who are of different families, of a different temper. The natural temper of parents is commonly in some degree transmitted to their posterity. Indeed, all agree in many things, for all are of the same blood originally; all are descended from the same Adam, and the same Noah. But Christians are born again of another stock, different from all the rest of the world; and therefore they are of a temper by themselves, wherein none of the rest of the world agree with them. Rev. i. 6. " And hath made us kings and priests unto God, and his Father: to him be glory and dominion, for ever and ever."

II. True Christians are a royal priesthood.

The two offices of king and priest were accounted very honourable both among Jews and heathens; but it was a thing not known under the law of Moses, that the same person should sustain both these offices in a stated manner; and while Moses himself is said to have been king in Jeshurun, yet his brother Aaron was the high priest. Those who were kings by divine appointment in Israel were of another tribe from the priesthood, viz. the tribe of Judah. Before the giving the law we have an instance of one who was both king and priest, viz. Melchizedek. Gen. xiv. 18. "And Melchizedek, king of Salem, brought forth bread and wine; and he was the priest of the most high God."

Therefore, in some of the prophecies of Christ, it is spoken of as a remarkable thing of him, that he should be a priest after the order of Melchizedek. Psal. cx. 4. "The Lord hath sworn and will not repent; thou art a priest for ever, after the order of Melchizedek." The same again is prophesied of as a wonderful thing by Zechariah, that he should be a priest upon a throne. Zech. vi. 13. " Even he shall build the temple of the Lord; and he shall bear the glory, and shall sit and rule upon his throne; and he shall be a priest upon his throne; and the counsel of peace shall be between them both." In this respect the gospel dispensation differs from the legal, that it reveals the compatibleness of the two offices. One person, Jesus Christ, is antitype of both kings and priests, under the law; and as it is the will of Christ, who became in all things like unto us, that his disciples should in many things become like unto him, so it is in this among others. As Christ is the Son of God, so those that are Christ's are the children of God; as Christ is the heir of God, so, as Christ liveth, it is his will that they should live also. As Christ rose from the dead, so it is the will of Christ that his saints should rise also. As Christ is in heaven in glory, so it is the will of Christ that they should be with him where he is. So, as Christ is both King and Priest, so shall believers be made kings and priests. What is said in the text is either with respect to what they now are, or what they shall be hereafter. The apostle says, "ye are a royal priesthood;" that is, ye have those honours in reversion. Christians are kings here, as a king who is in his minority; who, though the crown is his right, has not yet come actually to reign. They are indeed in an exalted state while here, but not as they will be hereafter. Christians while here are indeed priests, but not as they will be. Christians are called kings and priests here, in this world. Rev. i. 6. "And hath made us kings and priests unto God and his Father." But in Rev. v. the saints in heaven speak of this as the consequence of their glory and exaltation. Rev. v. 9, 10. "And they sung a new song, saying, Thou art worthy to take the book, and to open the seals thereof; for thou wast slain, and hast redeemed us to God by thy blood out of every kindred, and tongue, and people, and nation; and hast made us unto our God kings and priests; that we should reign on the earth."

1. Christians are kings.

When Christians are called kings, the Scriptures include both what they actually have in this world, and what they have in a future state. The reward which our Lord Jesus promised to his disciples was a kingdom. Luke xxii. 29. "And I appoint unto you a kingdom, as my Father hath appointed unto me." Christians, having this promise, are therefore heirs of a kingdom here, which they are hereafter to receive. James ii. 5. "Hearken, my beloved brethren; hath not God chosen the poor of this world rich in faith, and heirs of the kingdom which he hath promised to them that love him?"

The reward of the saints is represented as a kingdom, because the possession of a kingdom is the height of human advancement in this world, and as it is the common opinion that those who have a kingdom have the greatest possible happiness. The happiness of a kingdom, or royal state, for which it is so much admired by mankind, consists in these things:

First. The honour of a kingdom.

Secondly. The possessions of kings.

Thirdly. The government or authority of kings.

Now with respect to each of these, the happiness of the saints is far greater than that of the kings and greatest potentates in the world.

First. True Christians will be advanced to honours far above those of earthly kings, they will have a vastly higher dignity than any princes. If these are nobly descended, it is not so great an honour as to be the sons of God; if they are nobly educated, and have their minds formed for government, and have princely qualifications, these qualifications are not so honourable as those with which God endows his saints, whose minds he fills with divine knowledge, and gives them true and perfect holiness. Princes appear honourable from their outward enjoyment of honour and dignity, their royal robes, their stately palaces, and their splendid equipage. But these are not so honourable as those white robes, those inherent ornaments, with which the saints shall appear in heaven, with which they " shall shine forth as the sun in the kingdom of their Father." What is a king's palace to those mansions in heaven, that Christ prepares for his saints? The honour of the creature consists in likeness and nearness to the Creator in heaven. The saints shall be like him, for they shall see him as he is; they shall be most near to him, shall be admitted to a most intimate fellowship.

Secondly. The saints shall have greater and more extensive possessions than any earthly monarch. One reason for which the state of kings is admired is their wealth; they have the most precious things laid up in their treasures. We read of the peculiar treasure of kings. Eccles. ii. 8. "I gathered me also silver and gold, and the peculiar treasure of kings and of the provinces: I gat me men singers and women singers, and the delights of the sons of men, as musical instruments, and that of all sorts;" that is, the peculiar treasure of other kings. David conquered and subdued many kings, and spoiled their peculiar treasure, which fell to his son Solomon.

But the precious treasures of kings are not to be compared to those precious things which Christ will give his saints in another world; the gold tried in the fire that Christ has purchased with his own blood, those precious jewels, those graces and joys of his Spirit, and that beauty of mind with which he will endow them. King's possessions are very extensive; especially were they thus, when kings were generally absolute, and their whole dominions, their subjects and their fortunes, were looked upon as their possessions. But these fall short of the extensive possessions of the saints, who possess all things; they are the heirs of God, and all that is God's is theirs so far as it can contribute to their happiness. Rev. xxi. 7. "He that overcometh shall inherit all things; and I will be his God, and he shall be my son." 1 Cor. iii. 21, 22. "Therefore let no man glory in men, for all things are yours; whether Paul, or Apollos, or Cephas, or the world, or life, or death, or things present, or things to come; all are yours."

Thirdly. The saints shall also be advanced to the authority of kings. Christ has appointed to them a kingdom, and in that kingdom they shall reign. It is promised concerning the saints, that they shall reign. Rev. v. 10. "And hath made us unto our God kings and priests: and we shall reign on the earth." Rev. xxii. 5. "And there shall be no night there: and they need no candle, neither light of the sun, for the Lord God giveth them light: and they shall reign for ever and ever." It is evident that they shall have a kingdom with respect to rule and government, as appears, Rev. ii. 26, 27. "And he that overcometh, and keepeth my works unto the end, to him will I give power over all nations: and he shall rule them with a rod of iron; as the vessels of a potter shall they be broken to shivers: even as I received of my Father." But we must see that we rightly understand this. They shall not be appointed by God as sovereigns of the world, without any superior to direct them; neither shall they be properly deputies or viceroys, as king Agrippa and some other kings were the deputies of the Roman emperors; but they shall reign in fellowship with Christ as joint heirs; they shall reign in the same kingdom with him, and shall have the happiness of having things done according to their will as much as if their own wills were paramount. Christ wills their will. All things will be disposed in the best manner for them, and to promote their happiness. "To him that overcometh will I grant to sit with me in my throne; even as I also overcame, and am set down with my Father in his throne."

The reigning of the saints will consist partly in *judging;* for the saints shall judge the world, angels and men with Christ. Matt. xix. 28. "And Jesus said unto them, Verily I say unto you, That ye which have followed me, in the regeneration when the Son of man shall sit on the throne of his glory, ye also shall sit upon twelve thrones, judging the twelve tribes of Israel." 1 Cor. vi. 2, 3. "Do ye not know that the saints shall judge the world? And if the world shall be judged by you, are ye unworthy to judge the smallest matters? Know ye not that we shall judge angels? how much more things that pertain to this life!" How earnestly do men seek a kingdom! What fatigues, what dangers, what bloodshed, will they not encounter! In seeking conversion, you seek a kingdom. You who are poor, you who are children, have opportunity to obtain a kingdom, to advance yourselves to higher dignity, to more substantial honours, to greater possessions, to more precious treasures, to be clothed in robes of richer splendour, and to fill a loftier throne, than those enjoyed by the greatest earthly monarchs. It is a crown that you are to run for, an incorruptible crown, to be given you by the Great King of heaven, and to be worn by you as long as his throne shall endure. What encouragement is here afforded to the saints under afflictions and reproaches; what are they, to the worth and honour of a heavenly kingdom? When you shall have a crown of glory placed on your head, and be seated on Christ's throne, and shine forth as the light, and are seated at his royal banquet, then you will suffer no more for ever; all trouble, all reproach, shall be driven away; you will be too high to be reached by the malice of men and devils, and shall soon forget all your sorrows.

2. True Christians are priests of God. The priesthood under the law was a very honourable and sacred office. Heb. v. 4. "And no man taketh this honour unto himself, but he that is called of God, as was Aaron." It was on account of this honour that those proud men, Korah and his company, envied Aaron; and God asserted and vindicated Aaron's right to it, by causing his rod to bud.

It was an honour which, before the giving of the law, when

every particular family was wont to offer sacrifices for themselves, the first-born used to claim, and therefore the birthright was so much esteemed and valued. Therefore Jacob had
such a desire of having the birthright of his brother Esau, and
Esau's despising of it is spoken of as a great instance of his profaneness. A priest is said to be a chief man among his people.
Lev. xxi. 4. " But he shall not defile himself, being a chief man
among his people, to profane himself." Because the office of the
priesthood was so honourable, it is noticed as a wicked contempt
of it in several wicked kings, that they made of the meanest of
the people priests. The office was so honourable, that a king,
Uzziah, coveted the honour of it, and it is mentioned as an
instance of his pride that he did so. 2 Chron. xxvi. 16. "But
when he was strong, his heart was lifted up to his destruction:
for he transgressed against the Lord his God, and went into the
temple of the Lord to burn incense upon the altar of incense."
And it was a very sacred office, and that above all other offices;
and therefore those things were forbidden the priest that were
lawful for all others; such as to be defiled for the dead, or to take
to wife one that is put away from her husband; and the reason is
given, Levit. xxi. 6. "They shall be holy unto their God, and not
profane the name of their God, for the offerings of the Lord
made by fire, and the bread of their God, they do offer; therefore
they shall be holy. They shall not take a wife that is a whore,
or profane, neither shall they take a woman put away from her
husband; for he is holy unto his God. Thou shalt sanctify him
therefore, for he offereth the bread of thy God, he shall be holy
unto thee: for I, the Lord, which sanctify you, am holy."

Jesus Christ is the only proper priest that is to offer sacrifices,
and make atonement for sin, under the New Testament. He
was the priest of whom all the priests of old were typical. But
yet all believers are herein in a measure conformed to their head,
and assimilated to him. The priesthood now is no longer confined to one family, to Aaron and his sons, but all the true Israel
are priests. Every true Christian hath a work and office that is
as sacred as that of the priests was under the law, and every one
is advanced to a like honour, and indeed to a greater. But how
every true Christian is a priest of God will appear in the following
things.

First. Every true Christian is allowed as near an access to God,

and as free a use of the sacred things, as the priests were of old.
God under the law dwelt in the tabernacle and temple, that were
the symbol of his presence, and those places were holy.   The seed
of Aaron might go into the holy place to minister before the
Lord, but if any other came nigh, he was to be put to death.
Numb. iii. 10. "And thou shalt appoint Aaron and his sons, and
they shall wait on their priest's office: and the stranger that
cometh nigh, shall be put to death."

But now all are allowed to come nigh, we are all allowed a free
access to God, to come with boldness and confidence.   God's
people are not kept at such a distance now as they were under
the law.   The church then was in its minority, and the heir,
while a child, differs nothing from a servant.   The servant is not
allowed the free access of a child, he is kept more at a distance
with fear and dread.   Agreeably to the nature of that dispensation, there were not those special discoveries of the grace and love
of God that are now made, and which invite rather than forbid
near access.

When God was wont to appear to the children of Israel, it was
more with terror and manifestations of awful majesty, and not
so much with the discoveries of grace as now.   When God
appeared on mount Sinai, it was in flaming fire, and with thunder, and lightning, and earthquakes; but in how different a manner did he appear, when he appeared in the person of Christ,
with mildness, and gentleness, and love!   There is much the
same difference between us and them with respect of the liberty
of access to God, as there was between the liberty of access of the
children of Israel at mount Sinai, and the liberty which Christ's
disciples had of approach to him when he was upon earth.   At
mount Sinai, only Moses and Aaron, and Nadab and Abihu,
were allowed to come up into the mount, and none but Moses
was to approach nigh.   Exod. xxiv. 1. "And he said unto Moses,
Come up unto the Lord, thou and Aaron, Nadab and Abihu,
and seventy of the elders of Israel; and worship ye afar off."   But
if any other presumed to touch the mount, God would break
forth upon him.   But Christ's disciples used daily to converse
with him, as an intimate friend.   Heb. xii. 18. "For ye are
not come unto the mount that might be touched, and that
burned with fire, nor unto blackness, and darkness, and tempest."   Yea, Christians are now allowed as near an approach unto

God, as the high priest himself, who was allowed a much nearer approach than any of the other priests. God's dwelling-place was the temple, but more especially was it in the holy of holies, in the mercy-seat between the cherubim. There was a veil which separated that part of the temple from the rest, and no one might ever enter that veil but the high priest, and that but once a year; not oftener, upon pain of death. Lev. xvi. 2. "And the Lord said unto Moses, Speak unto Aaron thy brother, that he come not at all times into the holy place, within the veil before the mercy-seat, which is upon the ark, that he die not: for I will appear in the cloud upon the mercy-seat." The way into the holiest of all was not as yet made manifest, but now it is. Heb. ix. 7, 8. "But into the second went the high priest alone once every year, not without blood, which he offered for himself, and for the errors of the people. The Holy Ghost thus signifying, that the way into the holiest of all was not yet made manifest, while as yet the first tabernacle was standing."

But now we are all allowed as near an access to God as the high priest only was under the law, and with more freedom, for he might approach but once a year; but Christians may approach boldly at all times, through the blood of Christ, without any danger of dying. Heb. iv. 16. "Let us, therefore, come boldly unto the throne of grace, that we may obtain mercy, and find grace to help in time of need." The throne of grace and the mercy-seat are the same thing. "Having, therefore, brethren, boldness to enter into the holiest by the blood of Jesus, by a new and living way, which he hath consecrated for us through the veil, that is to say, his flesh; and having a high priest over the house of God; let us draw near with a true heart, in full assurance of faith, having our hearts sprinkled from an evil conscience, and our bodies washed with pure water." That access into the holiest of all was allowed to all under the gospel, and at any time: it is signified by the rending of the veil, upon the death of Christ, for then was that blood shed by which we have access. Matt. xxvii. 50, 51. "Jesus, when he had cried again with a loud voice, yielded up the ghost. And, behold, the veil of the temple was rent in twain from the top to the bottom; and the earth did quake, and the rocks rent."

But especially will the access of saints in another world be much more near and familiar than that of the high priest. They shall not only enter into the holy of holies, but shall dwell with God in it, for heaven is the holiest of all. They shall then dwell in God's presence, they shall see his face, which no man can see and live.

In this world, though there is greater liberty of access than there was of old, yet still Christians are kept at a great distance from God in comparison of what they will be in heaven, where they shall be admitted even to higher privileges than Moses in the mount, when he besought God to show him his glory. They shall then see with open face, and shall know as they are known.

Secondly. Christians are a priesthood with respect to their offerings to God. The principal part of the work of the priests of old was to offer sacrifice, and to burn incense. As the priests of old offered sacrifice, so the work of Christians is to offer up spiritual sacrifices to God. 1 Pet. ii. 5. "Ye also, as lively stones, are built up a spiritual house, an holy priesthood, to offer up spiritual sacrifices, acceptable to God by Jesus Christ." And here,

1st. Christians offer up their own hearts to God in sacrifice: they dedicate themselves to God. Rom. vi. 13. "Neither yield ye your members as instruments of unrighteousness unto sin: but yield yourselves unto God, as those that are alive from the dead, and your members as instruments of righteousness unto God." The Christian gives himself to God freely as of mere choice; he does it heartily; he desires to be God's, and to belong to no other; he gives all the faculties of his soul to God. He gives God his heart, and it is offered to God as a sacrifice in two ways.

Of these, the first is, when the heart is broken for sin. A sacrifice, before it can be offered, must be wounded and slain. The heart of a true Christian is first wounded by a sense of sin, of the great evil and danger of it, and is slain with godly sorrow and true repentance. When the heart truly repents, it dies unto sin. Repentance is compared unto a death in the word of God. Rom. vi. 6, 7, 8. "Knowing this, that our old man is crucified with him, that the body of sin might be destroyed, that henceforth we should not serve sin. For he that is dead is freed from sin. Now if we be dead with Christ, we believe that we shall also live with him. Likewise reckon ye also yourselves to be dead indeed unto sin, but alive unto God through Jesus Christ our Lord." Gal. ii. 20. "I am crucified with Christ: nevertheless I live; yet not I, but Christ liveth in me; and the life which I now live in the flesh,

I live by the faith of the Son of God, who loved me, and gave himself for me." As Christ, when he was offered, was offered broken upon the cross; so there is some likeness to this, when a soul is converted; the heart is offered to God slain and broken. Ps. li. 17. "The sacrifices of God are a broken spirit: a broken and a contrite heart, O God, thou wilt not despise."

The second way is, when a Christian offers his heart to God, flaming with love. The sacrifice of old was not only to be slain, but to be burnt upon the altar; it was to ascend in flame and smoke, and so to be a sweet savour to God.

That fire upon the altar was a type of two things; it was a type of the fire of the wrath of God, and it was also a type of the fire of the Spirit of God, or of divine love. The Holy Ghost is often compared to fire. With respect to the former, Christ alone is the sacrifice offered in the flame of God's wrath; but with regard to the latter, the hearts of the children of men are offered in the flame of divine love, and ascend up to God in that flame. This divine love is fire from heaven, as the fire upon the altar of old was. When a soul is drawn to God in true conversion, fire comes down from God out of heaven, in which the heart is offered in sacrifice, and the soul is baptized with the Holy Ghost and with fire.

In many of the sacrifices that were offered, only the fat about the inwards was burnt upon the altar; which fat of the inwards thus rising in flame, represented the offering of the soul. It is that which God looks at; it is that which must be offered in sacrifice to God. Especially hereafter, when the saints will be made priests in a more glorious manner than at present, will they offer up their hearts wholly to God in the flame of love. They shall, as it were, all be transformed into love, as burning oil is transformed into flame; and so, in that flame, shall they ascend up to God. Their souls will be as the angels, who are as a flame of fire not only for activity in God's service, but for love too. They shall be a flame ever burning, which shall burn longer than the fire upon the altar in Israel, that never went out, from the time that fire came down out of heaven in the wilderness, till the carrying away into Babylon.

2d. This spiritual priesthood offers to God the sacrifice of praise. Many of their sacrifices under the law were sacrifices of peace-offerings, which were mostly for thanksgiving and praise.

But the spiritual sacrifice of the hearty and sincere praises of a saint, are more acceptable to God than all the bulls, and rams, and he-goats that they offered. The heartfelt praises of one true Christian are of more account with God than all those two and twenty thousand oxen, and a hundred and twenty thousand sheep, which Solomon offered to God at the dedication of the temple, as a sacrifice of peace-offerings. Praise is called a sacrifice. Heb. xiii. 15. "By him, therefore, let us offer the sacrifice of praise to God continually, that is, the fruit of our lips, giving thanks to his name." Ps. i. 13, 14. "Will I eat the flesh of bulls, or drink the blood of goats? Offer unto God thanksgiving, and pay thy vows unto the Most High;" ver. 23. "Whoso offereth praise, glorifieth me; and to him that ordereth his conversation aright, will I show the salvation of God;" Ps. lxix. 30, 31. "I will praise the name of God with a song, and will magnify him with thanksgiving. This also shall please the Lord better than an ox or bullock that hath horns and hoofs." Praises are therefore in Hosea called *calves of our lips,* because they are like *calves offered in sacrifice;* Hosea xiv. 2. "Take with you words, and turn to the Lord : say unto him, Take away all iniquity, and receive us graciously; so will we render the calves of our lips." Only true Christians offer those sacrifices. However hypocrites pretend to praise God, and to offer thanksgiving to him, yet they, being insincere, offer not sacrifices with which God is well pleased; they offer not spiritual sacrifices, and therefore they are not of the spiritual priesthood. In heaven especially are the saints a holy priesthood upon this account; whose work it is for ever to offer these sacrifices to God, who cease not day nor night to praise God and sing forth their ardent joyful hallelujahs. They sing a new song, a song that never will end, and never will grow old.

3d. The next sacrifice which is offered by this spiritual priesthood, is obedience, sincere obedience. The sacrifices under the law did not only represent Christ's *satisfying for sin* by suffering, but they also represented Christ's *obeying* in suffering; for the sacrifices under the law were not only for propitiation, but they were for purchasing benefits, and so typified not only the satisfaction, but merit, which was by obedience. Ps. xl. 6, 7, 8. " Sacrifice and offering thou didst not desire: mine ears hast thou opened; burnt-offering and sin-offering hast thou not required. Then said I, Lo, I come: in the volume of the book it is written of me, I delight *to do thy will*, O my God; yea, *thy law* is within my heart." And though the obedience of saints has no merit, yet it is pleasing and acceptable to God; it is as a sweet-smelling savour, and is compared to sacrifices, and preferred before them. 1 Sam xv. 22. "And Samuel said, Hath the Lord as great delight in burnt-offerings and sacrifices as in obeying the voice of the Lord? Behold, to obey is better than sacrifice, and to hearken than the fat of rams." Christians, by offering obedience to God in their lives and conversation, do what the apostle calls offering their bodies to be a living sacrifice, holy and acceptable to God, as their reasonable service. They offer their bodies, that is, they dedicate their bodies, to holy uses and purposes; they yield their members as instruments of righteousness unto holiness. The soul, while here, acts externally by the body. And in this Christians serve God; they yield their eyes, their ears, their tongues, their hands, and feet, as servants to God, to be obedient to the dictates of his word, and of his Holy Spirit in the soul.

4th. Another sacrifice which we shall mention as offered by this spiritual priesthood is charity, or expressions of christian love in gifts to others. If the gift flows from a spirit of christian love although it be but a cup of cold water, it is an acceptable sacrifice to God. And indeed whatsoever is given for a pious use, if it be to promote religion, and uphold the public worship of God, or to benefit a particular person, if it be done from a good spirit, it is a christian sacrifice. Heb. xiii. 16. "But to do good, and to communicate, forget not; for with such sacrifices God is well pleased."

But sacrifices of this kind may principally be ranked under two heads; of which the first is,

Liberality to ministers of the gospel. The priests of old lived upon the sacrifices that were offered to God, and what is now offered to ministers for their comfortable and honourable support Christ looks upon as offered to himself. "He that receiveth you, receiveth me." Matt. x. 40. Thus Paul says of those things that were sent him by his hearers, that it was a sacrifice acceptable and well pleasing to God. Phil. iv. 14, etc. "Notwithstanding ye have well done that ye did communicate with my affliction. Now, ye Philippians, know also, that in the beginning of the gospel, when I departed from Macedonia, no church communicated with me as concerning giving and receiving, but ye

P

only. For even in Thessalonica ye sent once and again unto my necessity. Not because I desire a gift: but I desire fruit that may abound to your account. But I have all, and abound: I am full, having received of Epaphroditus the things which were sent from you, an odour of a sweet smell, a sacrifice acceptable, well pleasing to God."

The second is bounty to the poor. Christ accepts what is done to them as being done to himself. Matt. xxv. 40. "And the King shall answer, and say unto them, Verily I say unto you, Inasmuch as ye have done it unto one of the least of these my brethren, ye have done it unto me." This God prefers before the legal sacrifices. Hosea vi. 6. "I desire mercy, and not sacrifice; and the knowledge of God more than burnt-offerings."

5th. Another offering of this priesthood to God, is the prayer of faith. Though this is rather compared to *incense* in Scripture than to a *sacrifice*, yet it is equally an evidence of their priest-hood. Incense was that sweet confection which we read of. Exod. xxx. 34. "And the Lord said unto Moses, Take unto thee sweet spices, stacte, and onycha, and galbanum; these sweet spices, with pure frankincense; of each shall there be a like weight." These they were wont to burn upon the censer as they offered it, which made a most fragrant smell. That incense is a type of the merits of Jesus Christ, and seems also to be a type of the prayers of God's people in faith of the former. It was the custom, when the priest in the temple was burning incense, for the people to be praying without. Luke i. 10. "And the whole multitude of the people were praying without at the time of incense." And gracious prayer is compared to incense. Psal. cxli. 2. "Let my prayer be set forth before thee as incense; and the lifting up of my hands as the evening sacrifice." The prayer of faith is as a fragrant savour to God, through the merits of him towards whom that faith is exercised.

REFLECTIONS

1. Here are great motives for all earnestly to seek that they may become true Christians. It is a great honour to be priests of God. It was a great honour of old to be a priest under the law; it was a greater in some respects than to be a king; because they were nearer to God, and they in their work were more im-

mediately concerned with him; it was a more holy and divine office. But more honourable is it to be of the spiritual priesthood. The access to God is nearer, and an infinitely greater privilege. Especially is the access to God which they will have in another world, where they shall see God, and shall converse with Christ as a man with his friend. If ever a king was ambitious of the honour of the legal priesthood, surely you may well desire the spiritual, which is an eternal priesthood.

Consider that you are capable of receiving this priesthood. Of old, those who were not of the posterity of Aaron, were incapable of the priesthood; it was in vain for them to seek it; but it is not in vain for you to seek this spiritual priesthood. Consider also that you have a call to it, you have warrant sufficient. It would be a dreadful presumption for you to seek this honour if you had not a call to it. Heb. v. 4. "No man taketh this honour unto himself, but he that is called of God, as was Aaron." But you are called; and now it would be presumption and profane contempt in you to refuse it; to refuse such an honour as God offers you. Take heed, therefore, that there be not among you any profane person as Esau, who for a morsel of meat sold his birthright, and sold the priesthood that belonged to it. Take heed that you do not sell this spiritual priesthood for a morsel of meat, or for the trifles of this world, that you are not more concerned about a little worldly pelf or vain glory, than about that which is so sacred and honourable.

For direction, that you may be one of this spiritual priesthood, seek of God his holy anointing; that is, that God would pour out his Spirit in his sanctifying influences upon you. The priests of old were consecrated by the holy anointing oil. Exod. xxix. 7. "Then shalt thou take the anointing oil, and pour it upon his head, and anoint him." Exod. xxx. 30. "And thou shalt anoint Aaron and his sons, and consecrate them that they may minister unto me in the priest's office." If you are here separated for this holy station and service, you must have that holy anointing of the Spirit of God, typified by the oil that was poured upon Aaron's head; the holy anointing oil of God must be upon you.

2. Let all who profess themselves Christians take heed that they do not defile themselves and profane their sacred character. There was great strictness required of old of the priests, lest they

should defile themselves and profane their office, and it was regarded as a dreadful thing to profane it. So holy a God hath
threatened in the New Testament, that "if any man defile the
temple of God, him will God destroy." 1 Cor. iii. 17. As Christians are here called the *temple of God*, so it is said, in the fifth
verse, "Ye are a *spiritual house*, an holy priesthood." Avoid
the commission of all immoralities, or things that have a horrid
filthiness in them, things that will dreadfully profane the sacred
name by which you are called, and the sacred station wherein
you are set.

Take heed especially of lascivious impurities. Such things
were looked upon as defiling the holy office of the priesthood of
old, insomuch, that if but a daughter of a priest was guilty of
whoredom, she was to be burnt. Remember Hophni and
Phineas, how sorely God dealt with them for profaning their
office by their impurities; and with good Eli, that he was no more
thorough to restrain them. God brought a curse upon the
whole family which never was removed. God took away the
priesthood from him, and took away the ark of the covenant
from him and from Israel, and delivered it into captivity, and
fulfilled his threatening, that there should not be an old man of
his house for ever.

Take heed of every sin: an allowing any sin whatever is a
dreadful presumption of your holy character.

3. See that you well execute your office. Offer up your heart
in sacrifice. Get and keep a near access to God. Come with boldness; offer up a heart broken for sin; offer it up flaming with
love to God; offer praise to God; praise God for his glorious excellency; for his love and mercy. Consider what great things you
have to praise God for; the redemption of Jesus Christ, his sufferings, his obedience, and the gift of that holiness, which makes
you like unto God.

Be ready to distribute, willing to communicate, and do good;
consider it as part of your office thus to do, to which you are
called and anointed, and as a sacrifice well-pleasing to God; pity
others in distress; be ready to help one another; God will have
mercy and not sacrifice.

And be much in offering up your prayers to God; and see that
all your offerings are offered upon the right altar, otherwise they
will be abominable to God. Offer your hearts to God through

Jesus Christ. In his name present the sacrifice of praise, obedience, charity: of prayer on the golden altar perfumed with the incense of Christ's merits. Your reward will be to have this honour in heaven, to be exalted to that glorious priesthood, to be made a priest unto God for ever and ever.

III. True Christians are a holy nation. And here I shall briefly show,

1. How they are a distinct nation.
2. How they are holy.
1. Christians are a distinct nation.

First. The saints are all of the same native country. Heaven is the native country of the church. They are born from above; their Father, of whom they are begotten, is in heaven. The principles that govern their hearts are drawn from heaven, since the Holy Ghost, whose immediate fruits those principles are, is from heaven. The word of God, which is the seed by which they are begotten, is from heaven. The Bible is a book, as it were, sent down from heaven. The saints in this world are not in their native country, but are pilgrims and strangers on the earth, they are near akin to the inhabitants of the heavenly world, and are properly of that society. Heb. xii. 22, 23. "But ye are come unto mount Sion, and unto the city of the living God, the heavenly Jerusalem, and to an innumerable company of angels, to the general assembly and church of the first-born, which are written in heaven, and to God the Judge of all, and to the spirits of just men made perfect." Heaven is a country that much better suits their natures than this earth, because it is their native climate. When they are in heaven, they breathe their native air; in heaven is their inheritance. Heaven is the proper country of the church, where the greater part of the church is, and where they all will be, and where is their settled abode; from thence all that are now upon earth are derived, and thither they will return again. Though they are for a little while dwelling at a distance from their native country, yet they are of the same nation with those who now dwell there.

Secondly. All Christians speak the same language. They all profess the same fundamental doctrines; they hold fast the form of sound words that was once delivered to the saints. 2 Tim. i. 13. "Hold fast the form of sound words, which thou hast heard of me, in faith and love which is in Christ Jesus." They all use the same language to God in prayer and praise; they express the same humility and repentance in confessing their sins, the same adoration and admiring sense of God's glory and excellency, the same humble submission and resignation, and the same thankfulness. In like manner do they show forth God's praises, expressing the same faith and humble dependence in the mercy of God, and the same love and longing desires after God. The saints in all ages speak the same language with David and the saints of old. The Spirit of God teaches the saints the same language in their prayers; their prayers are the breathings of the same Spirit.

Indeed the saints while in this world are but learning the heavenly language, and therefore speak it but imperfectly, and with a stammering tongue, and with a pronunciation that in many things resembles their old language. The tongues of the saints are renewed in their conversion. Thus the conversion of the Gentiles is represented by their having a new language. Zeph. iii. 9. "For then will I turn to the people a pure language, that they may all call upon the name of the Lord, to serve him with one consent." And in this sense is that also to be understood. Isa. xix. 18. "In that day shall five cities in the land of Egypt speak the language of Canaan, and swear to the Lord of hosts: one shall be called, The city of destruction." As it is said of the new song which the saints sing, that no man could learn that song but those that are redeemed from the earth, so no man can learn that language but those who are of this holy nation.

Thirdly. They are under the same government. The Christians are one society, one body politic; and therefore, as here the church is represented by a nation, so oftentimes is it called a city. They are subject to the same King, Jesus Christ. He is the head of the church, he is the head of this body politic. Indeed all men are subject to the power and providence of this King; but those who are in his kingdom of grace, all acknowledge the same King, own his rightful sovereignty over them, are willing to be subject to him, to submit to his will, and yield obedience to his commands. Ps. cx. 3. "Thy people shall be willing in the day of thy power, in the beauties of holiness from the womb of the morning: thou hast the dew of thy youth."

They are all governed by the same laws, and all subject themselves to the same rules. The commands of God that are obeyed by the saints, are the same all over the world. There is the same method of government, there are the same means of government, the same outward and visible means, the same officers, gospel, and gospel ministers, in like manner appointed and sent forth by the head of the church, the same visible order and discipline appointed for all. And there are the same inward and special means of government. Christ governs his people in a peculiar manner. He immediately influences their will and inclinations, and powerfully brings them to a compliance with God's commands and rules. They are a society united in the same public interest and concerns. It is by the same covenant and promises that they have their inheritance, and that they hold their title to their enjoyments, as a people of the same nation hold their temporal rights by the same rule, and citizens hold their rights by the same municipal laws. The prosperity of this society tends to the advantage of the interests of the particular parts. A Christian has the same reason to be concerned for the flourishing of the church, and the advancement of religion, as a particular subject has for the flourishing of the nation or kingdom. When the church is in flourishing circumstances, the souls of particular saints are like to be flourishing; and when the church is in low languishing circumstances, particular souls are generally the same. When iniquity abounds, the love of many waxes cold. As it is the interest of every subject to have the nation flourish, so it is the interest of every Christian to have the church to flourish. So Christians have the same common enemies that seek their hurt and overthrow. He that is an enemy to one saint as a saint, is an enemy to all. They are jointly called to resist the same powers of darkness; the church here upon earth is as an army that goes forth under Jesus Christ, the Captain of their salvation, to resist the common adversary.

REFLECTIONS

Be exhorted to join yourself to this nation. As it was of old, those who were of other nations, if they were brought to the acknowledgment of the God of Israel, and to the true religion, and were circumcised, were received as being of the nation of Israel, and were accounted as those that were descended from

Abraham and Jacob; so now is there free liberty to any to come and join themselves to this nation, and they shall be received and admitted to the same rights and privileges, and be in all respects treated as the same people. And especially those now under the gospel are invited to come. Let them be who they will, they may come and join this people and be welcome. There is no wall of partition to separate this people from others, to exclude those of other nations. The gates of the new Jerusalem are always open to receive all whose hearts incline them to come. And here consider,

First. There is no nation under so happy a government as this. The Lord Jesus Christ is their King, and he is a most glorious King. He is the eternal and infinitely glorious Son of God. He is a most wise prince, he knows how to govern, he perfectly understands how best to promote the interest of his people. He is a most merciful and gracious King, who greatly loves his people, and most earnestly and faithfully seeks their interest. His people are redeemed with his own blood, and he will surely seek their welfare. And he is a most powerful prince. He is able to defend his people against all their enemies.

This nation is governed by most wise and righteous laws. As it was said of Israel of old, Deut. iv. 8. " What nation is there so great, that hath statutes and judgments so righteous as all this law which I set before you this day? " so and more eminent is it true of the spiritual Israel, since the law of God has been set forth to us in a far more clear and lovely light, by the rules and precepts of the gospel. The manner of Christ's government in the kingdom of his grace is most excellent, and different from that of all other kings; for he governs by the powerful influence of his Spirit upon the heart, whereby he sweetly inclines them to a willing and chosen subjection to him.

This nation is a free people. The happy government under which they live is most consistent with freedom; it does not in the least infringe upon the liberty of the subject, there is nothing like slavery in the kingdom of God. The law of this nation is a law of liberty. Those that are sinners, are slaves; they are slaves to their lusts, slaves to Satan, slaves to the cruellest of masters. But they whom the Son makes free, are free indeed. The subjects of the heavenly King are all as free under his government as a man's children are in their father's house. The government is a paternal government; the King looks upon all his subjects as children.

Under so happy a government are this nation. Be persuaded therefore to join yourself to them, and be of them. Ps. cxliv. 15. "Happy is that people that is in such a case. Yea, happy is that people whose God is the Lord." Ps. xxxiii. 12. "Blessed is the nation whose God is the Lord; and the people whom he hath chosen for his own inheritance."

Secondly. There is no nation that dwell in such love and peace as this holy nation enjoys. The happiness of a people very much consists in its peace: a nation is never more miserable than when it is rent by civil wars, or disturbed by intestine broils. Nothing tends more to the happiness of the people than when they are all united as brethren, and with one heart seek the good of one another, and the community.

But no nation enjoys so much happiness of this kind as this holy nation. The Lord Jesus Christ, who is the King of his people, is the Prince of peace; his kingdom is a kingdom of peace. Every member of this society has in his heart a principle of peace and love. Love is the bond of perfectness that unites the members of this society together. They all have a disposition heartily to seek and promote each other's good.

Thirdly. This nation have for their settled abode a most glorious land. The heavenly Canaan is *their* land, it is a land that God hath desired, and that he hath blessed above all lands. There is no land so fertile of excellent fruits, so full of delights. There grows the tree of life in plenty, there flows the river of the water of life. There is no curse, nothing that hurts or offends. This is a delightful garden, this is the paradise of God. Hearken, therefore, consider of the blessedness of this people; is it not well to be one of them? I would now invite you in the name of Christ, as Moses invited his father-in-law to join himself to that nation. Numb. x. 29. "And Moses said unto Hobab, the son of Raguel the Midianite, Moses' father-in-law, We are journeying unto the place of which the Lord said, I will give it you: come thou with us, and we will do thee good: for the Lord hath spoken good concerning Israel."

2. Christians, as a nation, are holy. Their holiness is relative, and it is also inherent.

First. Christians are a holy nation by a relative holiness, as they are set apart by God for a divine and holy use. So things are often called holy in Scripture. The utensils of the tabernacle and temple are in this sense called holy; the priests' garments are called holy, the places of worship appointed of God in the Old Testament are called holy, because they were set apart by him for a holy use and service.

Things thus set apart are said to be sanctified. Thus Jeremiah is said to have been sanctified, before he came forth out of the womb. Jer. i. 5. "Before I formed thee in the belly, I knew thee, and before thou camest forth out of the womb, I sanctified thee; and I ordained thee a prophet unto the nations." God sanctified, that is, God set him apart for this holy use and service, to be a prophet to the nations, as Paul says of himself, Gal. i. 15. "But when it pleased God, who separated me from my mother's womb, and called me by his grace." So the people of Israel of old seem to be called a holy nation. Deut. vii. 6. "For thou art an holy people unto the Lord thy God: the Lord thy God hath chosen thee to be a special people unto himself, above all people that are upon the face of the earth." Not that they were a holy people by inherent holiness, for God often tells them that they are a stiff-necked people. But God had called and separated them from other nations to be the keepers of the sacred oracles, and for other purposes.

So the saints are a nation that God has set apart for a sacred use. He hath set them apart to serve and glorify him, and to show forth his praise; to be vessels for their Master's use, to see the manifestations of God's glory, and eternally to ascribe the glory due to his name.

Secondly. They are holy by inherent holiness.

1. By holiness of heart.*
2. By holiness of life.*

IV. True Christians are God's peculiar people.

1. True Christians are God's peculiar people with respect to the value which he sets upon them. He values one true Christian more than all the wicked in the world. God puts a high value upon his saints; they are his jewels. God's high value of them appears in all the ways wherein persons are wont to show the great regard which they have for any possession. God keeps

---

* These two heads are not expanded.

them as the apple of his eye, he will by no means lose one of his saints, not one of all the number shall fail, he will suffer no one to do them harm, his almighty power is thoroughly engaged for them to defend them.

The life, the happiness, and the welfare of the saints are precious in God's sight. He shows the higher value that he sets upon the godly than others, by giving the wicked for them, making them subservient to them, and destroying them when they stand in the way of the welfare of the godly. Prov. xxi. 18. "The wicked shall be a ransom for the righteous, and the transgressor for the upright."

Whenever the life or welfare of the wicked stands in the way of the welfare of the righteous, God is wont to procure the welfare of his people, though it be at the expense of the lives and welfare of never so many. Prov. xi. 8. "The righteous is delivered out of trouble, and the wicked cometh in his stead." Thus God manifested how much he valued the patriarchs. Though there were but very few of them, yet even kings were rebuked for their sakes. Ps. cv. 12, 13, 14, 15. "When they were but a few men in number: yea, very few, and strangers in it. When they went from one nation to another, from one kingdom to another people. He suffered no man to do them wrong; yea, he reproved kings for their sakes; saying, Touch not mine anointed, and do my prophets no harm." So he showed how he valued the children of Israel, in that he gave nations for them. Isa xliii. 3, 4. "For I am the Lord thy God, the Holy One of Israel, thy Saviour; I gave Egypt for thy ransom, Ethiopia and Seba for thee. Since thou wast precious in my sight, thou hast been honourable, and I have loved thee: therefore will I give men for thee, and people for thy life."

When the Egyptians stood in the way of the welfare of the church, God brought plagues upon them one after another, wherein he sorely distressed them. When their lives stood in the way, God destroyed all the first-born of Egypt; and when Pharaoh and his host sought their destruction, he drowned them in the Red sea, and when the nations of Canaan stood in their way, God destroyed them; he destroyed many of them miraculously, by sending hail-stones from heaven upon them. God will sooner at one blow destroy all the wicked of the world than that one of his saints should be lost. There are many great men of the world, kings and princes, men of great power and policy, men of noble blood and honourable descent, men of great wealth, men of vast learning and knowledge in the world, that are honoured, and make a great figure, and great account is made of them in the world, who are wicked men and reprobates, and they all are not of so great value in God's sight as one true Christian, however humble his birth and low his standing; however poor, or ignorant, or unknown.

God has shown how highly he values his saints by several remarkable providences. He has often changed and intercepted the course of nature for their sakes. Nothing except God himself is more constant and unchangeable than the course and laws of nature; but yet so much doth God value his saints, that he did not think the procuring of their welfare too slight an occasion for stopping the sun in his course.

But above all hath God shown how great a value he sets upon his saints, by the great price which he has paid for them, the blood of his own Son. God values every saint so highly that he bought him with the blood of his own dear Son. There is no price of gold or silver that can be compared with the price of the blood of Christ.

2. They are his peculiar people with respect to the mercy that he bestows upon them. God bestows many mercies upon ungodly men; he is kind to the evil and the good, to the just and the unjust. He is good to wicked men in preserving their lives, in providing for their subsistence, and in giving them many comforts. Wicked men receive a great deal of goodness from God which they have cause to admire, and be thankful for every day, and but few live any considerable time who are not the subjects of special influences of God's goodness to them in deliverance from trouble and danger. He heaps temporal good things upon them, he gives them wealth, and ease, and honour, and great prosperity. He distributes the world among them, and they show their great ingratitude in that, notwithstanding all God's bounty to them, they will not learn righteousness. Isa. xxvi. 10. "Let favour be showed to the wicked, yet will he not learn righteousness: in the land of uprightness will he deal unjustly, and will not behold the majesty of the Lord." Thus Samuel reproves Saul for his great ingratitude, that he took no more notice of the great kindness of God to him. 1 Sam. xv. 17.

" And Samuel said, When thou wast little in thine own sight, wast not thou made the head of the tribes of Israel, and the Lord anointed thee king over Israel?" So there are many other wicked men that are advanced to the state of princes and nobles.

But God bestows more goodness upon one godly man than upon all the ungodly in the world. Put all their preservations, all their deliverances, all their wealth, all their comforts that have been heaped upon them by providence together, those things are but trifles that God bestows on ungodly men; but they are peculiar blessings which he bestows on the righteous, they are precious things that God has in reserve for his own favourites, in comparison of which all earthly treasure is but dirt and dross. As for the saints, Christ has died for them, they have all their sins pardoned, they are delivered from a hell of eternal misery, they have a title to eternal life bestowed upon them, they have God's own image conferred on them, they are received into favour, and will enjoy God's everlasting love.

3. They are God's peculiar people with respect to the interest which he has in them. God has a peculiar interest in godly men; they are his peculiar property, they are his as they are redeemed by him, and as they have given themselves to him. God has an interest in godly men's hearts, they have a true love and respect to him; they have true honour to him. God has a greater interest in their hearts than any thing else, greater than the dearest friend on earth, greater than the world or any earthly enjoyment. They prefer God before all other things, they preserve the throne of their hearts for God, they are of a spirit to exalt him as the greatest and highest, to love him as the most excellent, to praise him as the most gracious and merciful.

God has not interest in the hearts of natural men. Many of them seem to show respect to him outwardly. The Pharisees of old pretended to an extraordinary devotion, to a great love to God. And many hypocrites in these times come before God as his people come, they seem as though they delight to draw near to God, and make a high profession of religion; but God has indeed no interest in their hearts. They give him the outward appearance, they give him the words of their lips, but their hearts are far from him. It is from respect to something else, and not to him; they have not the least love to God.

But God has an interest in the hearts of true Christians: however small and inconsiderable it is in comparison of what it
ought to be, yet they are of a spirit to prefer God above all. He
has an interest in them, and they offer up their bodies a living
sacrifice to him; they serve and actively glorify him, with their
bodies and with their spirits. God is glorified in wicked men, as
they are occasions of the manifestations of his glory, or as he
glorifies himself in them; but Christians devote themselves to
serve and glorify God. Though it is but a small interest that
God has in the hearts of Christians in this world in comparison
of what ought to be, yet he hath a greater interest in one godly
man than in all the ungodly and hypocrites that are in the
world.

4. They are God's peculiar people, with respect to the complacence which he hath in them. God takes delight in his
saints. Psal. xi. 7. " For the righteous Lord loveth righteousness:
his countenance doth behold the upright." God doth as it were
rejoice over a convert, he delights in beholding that beauty and
those ornaments of mind which he hath given him; God takes
delight in the graces of a godly man's heart, and he delights in
the good works and religion of the Christian. Psal. xxxvii. 23.
" The steps of a good man are ordered by the Lord, and he delighteth in his way." God takes delight in the godly man's
prayers. Prov. xv. 8. " The sacrifice of the wicked is an abomination to the Lord: but the prayer of the upright is his delight."
He takes more delight in the sincere humble devotion of one
true saint, than in all the moral virtue and outward religion of
all the natural men in the world. If the wicked that are rich
should offer to God ten thousand sacrifices, or if they should
devote ever so much of their substance to religious uses, if they
should give all their goods to feed the poor; it would not be so
acceptable to God, as one cup of cold water given by a saint with
a spirit of true charity. Ungodly kings may do much in many
respects for religion; they may build stately churches for the
worship of God, they may encourage religion in their dominions
by their power and influence. Cyrus, a heathen prince, restored
the state of the Jews. But God has a greater delight in the
sincere worship and love of one poor, obscure Christian, than
in all that is done throughout the globe by irreligious kings and
princes.

REFLECTIONS

Hence it may well be expected of such as profess hopes of their being true Christians, that they should live after a peculiar manner, and be devoted to God for his use. There should be a great difference between their way of living and that of other men. Godly men should not be hurried away by the general example. If any evil practice is become a common custom, it may well be expected of those who profess themselves godly, that they should stem the stream of common custom and example, though they are despised for it.

Men are ready often to plead for their neglect of such and such duties, and the commission of such evils, that it is a *common custom.* "Who is there," say they, "but what does so? I should be singular if I did otherwise." But if evil things are common, God may well expect of them that their way should be singular and peculiar, for Christians are a peculiar people. There should be a difference, and a great difference, between them and the generality of the world; if their neighbours, and relations, and companions, fall in with the common custom, that is evil, yet they should be peculiar, and stand alone.

It may well be expected that they should go further than other men in doing their duty, and practising the christian religion. For instance, it is a common thing for men when they are affronted, or injured by their neighbours, to entertain a spirit of revenge, to drink in a spirit of ill will against their neighbour, and to wish him hurt. But Christians should be peculiar; they should forgive those that injure them, and not entertain any spirit of ill will to them upon that account.

It is common for men when injured, to endeavour to retaliate upon those that injure them in some way or other, either by acting or talking against them; but those who call themselves godly, should choose no kind of revenge, Matt. v. 38, 39. "Ye have heard that it hath been said, An eye for an eye, and a tooth for a tooth: but I say unto you, That ye resist not evil: but whosoever shall smite thee on thy right cheek, turn to him the other also." The generality of men will love their friends, and hate their enemies; it is very rare that it is otherwise. Men pretend that they do not hate their enemies, but they really do in their hearts. But Christians should be peculiar in this matter, their way should be different from the way of the world; for they are a peculiar people, and they should love their enemies from their hearts, and do good to them that hate them. However rare it is that there is any such thing, yet such a rare thing very well becomes God's peculiar people. Matt. v. 43, 44, 45. "Ye have heard that it hath been said, Thou shalt love thy neighbour, and hate thine enemy. But I say unto you, Love your enemies, bless them that curse you, do good to them that hate you, and pray for them which despitefully use you, and persecute you: that ye may be the children of your Father which is in heaven: for he maketh his sun to rise on the evil and on the good, and sendeth rain on the just and on the unjust."

It is a rare thing for persons to accustom themselves to great self-denial. Many will indeed deny themselves something for the sake of their duty, but if it very much crosses their interest, there are few that will be stedfast in their duty. But it may well be expected, that you should greatly deny yourself for the sake of God and Christ, and so be peculiar in this matter.

Self-interest governs the generality of men; they will mind their own interest rather than any thing else. But it may well be expected of those who profess godliness, that they should show themselves peculiar in this matter, and that they should sacrifice their private, separate interest to the glory and honour of God, and to the public good. Most men will content themselves and quiet their consciences by avoiding the more gross acts of sin, by avoiding an outward gratification of lusts; but it becomes Christians to distinguish themselves here, and avoid sinning so much as in their thoughts, not to indulge any lust so much as in their imagination.

It is a shame to professors of godliness that their light shines no brighter before men, that there is no more appearing in them of an amiable christian spirit, that they do not seem to shine any brighter in their outward conversation than many other men that do not make the profession that they do. Many such men seem to be as exact, and as careful to avoid sin, and to deny themselves, as they; yea, many, perhaps, that, for the outward practice of some particular virtues, shine brighter than they, are more liberal and kind, more courteous and obliging in their behaviour.

It is expected of those that are of this peculiar people that they should do more than others. Matt. v. 46, 47. "For if ye love them which love you, what reward have ye? Do not even the publicans the same? And if ye salute your brethren only, what do ye more than others? Do not even the publicans so?" Let me then apply this subject immediately to those who are present.

1. Here is a powerful argument to persuade those of you who are impenitent to become godly, that if you will forsake your sins, and with all your heart turn to God, you shall become of the number of God's peculiar people. You shall have the same privileges with those that have been mentioned, you will immediately upon your conversion become one of those that God sets such a high value upon. If you are assured of your conversion, you may withal be assured that God, the supreme Lord of heaven and earth, sets a higher value on you than upon all the reprobates in the world, that God has set so high a value upon you that he has given the blood of his own Son for your ransom.

If you do savingly turn to God, you will receive from God mercies and blessings greater in value than all the wealth and outward prosperity of all the ungodly men in the world. Put all the honour and all the wealth of the great men of the world together; put all that the kings of the earth possess, their treasures and revenues, their dominions and power, their stately seats and palaces, their costly robes and dainties, together, and they will not amount to so great things as God will bestow upon you.

If you will turn from your sins and come to Christ, the great God will accept of you, and delight in you: you then will have those spiritual ornaments that will be more amiable in the sight of God, than all the learning, and knowledge, and morality of all the ungodly men in the world.

If you continue in a natural condition, God will make no account of you; instead of being as his jewels, you will be esteemed as vile and refuse, and fit for nothing but to be trampled under-foot; instead of being gold, you will be esteemed as dross, Jer. vi. 30. "Reprobate silver shall men call them, because the Lord hath rejected them." Hereafter you will be thrown away as being good for nothing, you will be esteemed nothing worth, as is represented in that parable, Matt. xiii. 47, etc. "Again, the kingdom of heaven is like unto a net that was cast into the sea,

Q

and gathered of every kind: which, when it was full, they drew to shore, and sat down, and gathered the good into vessels, but cast the bad away. So shall it be at the end of the world: the angels shall come forth, and sever the wicked from among the just, and shall cast them into the furnace of fire; there shall be wailing and gnashing of teeth." Yea, you shall not only be cast away as good for nothing, but shall be cast out as filth into the great receptacle of the filth of the world; you will be cast into a furnace of fire, as barren branches are gathered up and burnt. John xv. 6. "If a man abide not in me, he is cast forth as a branch, and is withered; and men gather them, and cast them into the fire, and they are burned." Or as barren trees are cut down and cast into the fire. Matt. iii. 10. "And now also the axe is laid unto the root of the trees; therefore every tree which bringeth not forth good fruit is hewn down and cast into the fire." As the tares were gathered together in bundles and burnt, you will be looked upon as fit for nothing else but to be destroyed. 2 Peter ii. 12. "But these, as natural brute beasts, made to be taken and destroyed, speak evil of the things that they understand not, and shall utterly perish in their own corruption."

Instead of bestowing such peculiar mercies upon you, you in a little time will be stripped of all mercy. God will not have mercy on you, but your miseries will be as dreadful as those mercies that God bestows on his saints are valuable. They are but trifles that wicked men have bestowed upon them while in this world, in comparison of what the righteous shall have. The blessings of one righteous are more in value than the enjoyments of all the wicked. But hereafter wicked men will not have those; they will have nothing but the fiery wrath and indignation of God for their portion.

While you are in a natural condition, instead of your being God's peculiar ones with respect to the interest which God hath in your heart, the devil has the greatest interest in your heart. He has the government and possession there, and therefore you are, and will be, the devil's people, those that he claims, and those that will certainly fall to his share, at least if you continue in such a condition. Instead of being one in whom God has peculiar complacence, he has no pleasure in you; when you pretend to worship him, he has no delight in your hypocritical prayers and services, but they are an abomination to him.

II. If you are true Christians, then let God be peculiar with you.

1. Let God be your peculiar portion. If you are one of his peculiar people, he is so. All who are God's people have chosen him for their God and portion. Do this more, and more, and more. Let all other things be lightly set by, and treated by you with neglect, in comparison of God.

Let God be the object of your peculiar value and esteem. If God has made you one of those on whom he sets a peculiar value, you who are a poor worthless worm, if he has set such a value upon you, as to purchase you with the price of the blood of his Son, who are in yourself a filthy, despicable creature, how much more reason is there that you should peculiarly value God, who is so great and glorious! It is fitting that this value should be mutual; and it is fitting that it should be in an answerable degree.

It will be but a little thing for you to esteem God above all in comparison of what it is for God so to prize his saints. See to it therefore, that there be nothing that stands in any competition with God in your esteem; value him more than all riches; value his honour and glory more than all the world; be ready at all times to part with all things else, and cleave to God. Let God be your peculiar friend, and value his friendship more than the respect and love of all the world. When you lose other enjoyments, when you lose earthly friends, let this be a supporting, satisfying comfort to you, that you have not lost God.

2. Let God be your peculiar confidence. There is great encouragement in this doctrine for you to make him so, and reason to enforce it as your duty. God expects that those who are his peculiar people should put their trust in him, and well they may do so, for God has a peculiar favour for them, and is peculiarly careful and tender of them. Be sensible, therefore, that it is unbecoming any, but especially those who are so near to God, and so favoured by him, to trust in their own righteousness, or in any arm of flesh. The peculiar people of God should not trust in themselves, they should not trust in friends, they should not trust in great men, they should not trust in their estates, or in any worldly enjoyment as expecting happiness from it, but alone in the Lord God. He ought to be their refuge and hiding-place;

in time of trouble they should hide themselves under the shadow of his wings.

3. Make God the peculiar object of your praises. The doctrine shows what great reason you have so to do. If God so values you, sets so much by you, has bestowed greater mercies upon you than on all the ungodly in the world; is it too little a requital for you to make God the peculiar object of your praise and thankfulness? If God so distinguishes you with his mercy, you ought to distinguish yourself in his praises; you should make it your great care and study how to glorify that God who has been so peculiarly merciful to you. And the rather because there was nothing peculiar in you, distinguishing you from any other person, that moved God to deal thus peculiarly by you. You were as unworthy to be set by as thousands of others that are not regarded of God, and are cast away by him for ever.

Sermon IX

THE END OF THE WICKED CONTEMPLATED BY THE RIGHTEOUS

REV. XVIII. 20

*Rejoice over her, thou heaven, and ye holy apostles and prophets; for God hath avenged you on her.**

INTRODUCTION

IN this chapter we have a very particular account of the fall of Babylon, or the antichristian church, and of the vengeance of God executed upon her. Here it is proclaimed that Babylon the great is fallen, and become the habitation of devils, and the hold of every foul spirit, and a cage of every unclean and hateful bird; that her sins had reached unto heaven, and that God had remembered her iniquity; that God gave commandment to reward her, as she had rewarded others, to double unto her double according to her works; in the cup she had filled, to fill to her double, and how much she had glorified herself, and lived deliciously, so much torment and sorrow to give her. And it is declared, that these plagues are come upon her in one day, death, mourning, and famine; and that she should be utterly burnt with fire; *because strong is the Lord who judgeth her.*

These things have respect partly to the overthrow of the antichristian church in this world, and partly to the vengeance of God upon her in the world to come. There is no necessity to suppose, that such extreme torments as are here mentioned will ever be executed upon papists, or upon the antichristian church, in this world. There will indeed be a dreadful and visible overthrow of that idolatrous church in this world. But we are not to understand the plagues here mentioned as exclusive of the ven-

* The substance of two posthumous discourses, dated March, 1773.

245

which God will execute on the wicked upholders and
promoters of antichristianism, and on the cruel antichristian
persecutors, in another world.

This is evident by ver. 3. of the next chapter, where, with
reference to the same destruction of antichrist which is spoken
of in this chapter, it is said, "Her smoke rose up for ever and
ever;" in which words the eternal punishment of antichrist is
evidently spoken of. Antichrist is here represented as being cast
into hell, and there remaining for ever after; he hath no place
any where else but in hell. This is evident by ver. 20. of the
next chapter, where, concerning the destruction of antichrist, it is
said, "And the beast was taken, and with him the false prophet
that wrought miracles before him, with which he deceived them
that received the mark of the beast, and them that worshipped
his image. These both were cast alive into a lake of fire burning
with brimstone."

Not but that the wicked antichristians have in all ages gone to
hell as they died, and not merely at the fall of antichrist; but
then the wrath of God against antichrist, of which damnation is
the fruit, will be made eminently visible here on earth, by many
remarkable tokens. Then antichrist will be confined to hell, and
will have no more place here on earth; much after the same
manner as the devil is said at the beginning of Christ's thousand
years' reign on earth, to be cast into the bottomless pit, as you
may see in the beginning of the twentieth chapter. Not but that
he had his place in the bottomless pit before; he was cast down
to hell when he fell at first: 2 Pet. ii. 4. "Cast them down to hell,
and deliver them into chains of darkness." But now, when he
shall be suffered to deceive the nations no more, his kingdom
will be confined to hell.

In this text is contained part of what John heard uttered upon
this occasion; and in these words we may observe,

1. To whom this voice is directed, *viz.* to *the holy prophets and
apostles*, and the rest of the inhabitants of the heavenly world.
When God shall pour out his wrath upon the antichristian
church, it will be seen, and taken notice of, by all the inhabitants
of heaven, even by holy prophets and apostles. Neither will they
see as unconcerned spectators.

2. What they are called upon by the voice to do, *viz.* to *rejoice
over Babylon* now destroyed, and lying under the wrath of God.

They are not directed to rejoice over her in prosperity, but in flames, and beholding the smoke of her burning ascending up for ever and ever.

3. A reason given: for *God hath avenged* YOU ON HER; *i.e.* God hath executed just vengeance upon her, for shedding your blood, and cruelly persecuting you. For thus the matter is represented, that antichrist had been guilty of shedding the blood of the holy prophets and apostles, as in chap. xvi. 6. "For they have shed the blood of saints and of prophets." And in ver. 24. of this context, "In her was found the blood of prophets and of saints, and of all them that were slain on the earth." Not that antichrist had literally shed the blood of the prophets and apostles; but he had shed the blood of those who were their followers, who were of the same spirit, and of the same church, and same mystical body. The prophets and apostles in heaven are nearly related and united to the saints on earth; they live, as it were, in true christians in all ages. So that by slaying these, persecutors show that they would slay the prophets and apostles, if they could; and they indeed do it as much as in them lies.

On the same account, Christ says of the Jews in his time, Luke xi. 50. "That the blood of all the prophets, which was shed from the foundation of the world, may be required of this generation; from the blood of Abel, unto the blood of Zacharias, which perished between the altar and the temple: verily I say unto you, it shall be required of this generation." So Christ himself is said to have been crucified in the antichristian church, chap. xi. 8. "And their dead bodies shall lie in the street of the great city, which spiritually is called Sodom and Egypt, where also our Lord was crucified." So all the inhabitants of heaven, all the saints from the beginning of the world, and the angels also, are called upon to rejoice over Babylon, because of God's vengeance upon her, wherein he avenges them: they all of them had in effect been injured and persecuted by antichrist. Indeed they are not called upon to rejoice in having their revenge glutted, but in seeing justice executed, and in seeing the love and tenderness of God towards them, manifested in his severity towards their enemies.

SECT. I

When the saints in glory shall see the wrath of God executed on ungodly men, it will be no occasion of grief to them, but of rejoicing

IT is not only the sight of God's wrath executed on those wicked men who are of the antichristian church, which will be occasion of rejoicing to the saints in glory; but also the sight of the destruction of all God's enemies: whether they have been the followers of antichrist or not, that alters not the case, if they have been the enemies of God, and of Jesus Christ. All wicked men will at last be destroyed together, as being united in the same cause and interest, as being all of Satan's army. They will all stand together at the day of judgment, as being all of the same company.

And if we understand the text to have respect only to a temporal execution of God's wrath on his enemies, that will not alter the case. The thing they are called upon to rejoice at, is the execution of God's wrath upon his and their enemies. And if it be matter of rejoicing to them to see justice executed in part upon them, or to see the beginning of the execution of it in this world, for the same reason will they rejoice with greater joy, in beholding it fully executed. For the thing here mentioned as the foundation of their joy, is the execution of just vengeance: *Rejoice, for God hath avenged you on her.*

Prop. I. The glorified saints will see the wrath of God executed upon ungodly men. This the Scriptures plainly teach us, that the righteous and the wicked in the other world see each other's state. Thus the rich man in hell, and Lazarus and Abraham in heaven, are represented as seeing each other's opposite states, in the 16th chap. of Luke. The wicked in their misery will see the saints in the kingdom of heaven; Luke xiii. 28, 29. "There shall be weeping and gnashing of teeth, when ye shall see Abraham, and Isaac, and Jacob, and all the prophets, in the kingdom of God, and you yourselves thrust out."

So the saints in glory will see the misery of the wicked under the wrath of God. Isa. lxvi. 24. "And they shall go forth and look on the carcases of the men that have transgressed against me: for their worm shall not die, neither shall their fire be quenched." And Rev. xiv. 9, 10. " If any man worship the beast and his image, and receive his mark in his forehead, or in his hand, the same shall drink of the wine of the wrath of God, which is poured out without mixture into the cup of his indignation; and he shall be tormented with fire and brimstone, in the presence of the holy angels, and in the presence of the Lamb." The saints are not here mentioned, being included in Christ, as his members. The church is the fulness of Christ, and is called Christ, 1 Cor. xii. 12. So in the 19th chapter, ver. 2, 3. the smoke of Babylon's torment is represented as rising up for ever and ever, in the sight of the heavenly inhabitants.

At the day of judgment, the saints in glory at Christ's right hand will see the wicked at the left hand in their amazement and horror, will hear the judge pronounce sentence upon them, saying, "Depart, ye cursed, into everlasting fire, prepared for the devil and his angels;" and will see them go away into everlasting punishment. But the Scripture seems to hold forth to us, that the saints will not only see the misery of the wicked at the day of judgment, but the fore-mentioned texts imply, that the state of the damned in hell will be in the view of the heavenly inhabitants; that the two worlds of happiness and misery will be in view of each other. Though we know not by what means, nor after what manner, it will be; yet the Scriptures certainly lead us to think, that they will some way or other have a direct and immediate apprehension of each other's state. The saints in glory will see how the damned are tormented; they will see God's threatenings fulfilled, and his wrath executed upon them.

Prop. II. When they shall see it, it will be no occasion of *grief* to them. The miseries of the damned in hell will be inconceivably great. When they shall come to bear the wrath of the Almighty poured out upon them without mixture, and executed upon them without pity or restraint, or any mitigation, it will doubtless cause anguish, and horror, and amazement vastly beyond all the sufferings and torments that ever any man endured in this world; yea, beyond all extent of our words or thoughts. For God in executing wrath upon ungodly men will act like an Almighty God. The Scripture calls this wrath, God's *fury,* and the *fierceness of his wrath;* and we are told that this is to show God's wrath, and to make his power known; or to make known how dreadful his wrath is, and how great his power.

The saints in glory will see this, and be far more sensible of it than now we can possibly be. They will be far more sensible how dreadful the wrath of God is, and will better understand how terrible the sufferings of the damned are; yet this will be no occasion of grief to them. They will not be sorry for the damned; it will cause no uneasiness or dissatisfaction to them; but on the contrary, when they have this sight, it will excite them to joyful praises.—These two things are evidences of it:

1. That the seeing of the wrath of God executed upon the damned should cause grief in the saints in glory is inconsistent with that state of perfect happiness in which they are. There can no such thing as grief enter, to be an allay to the happiness and joy of that world of blessedness. Grief is an utter stranger in that world. God hath promised that he will wipe away all tears from their eyes, and there shall be no more sorrow. Rev. xxi. 4. and chap. vii. 17.

2. The saints in heaven possess all things as their own, and therefore all things contribute to their joy and happiness. The Scriptures teach that the saints in glory inherit all things. This God said in John's hearing, when he had the vision of the New Jerusalem; Rev. xxi. 7. And the Scriptures teach us to understand this absolutely of all the works of creation and providence. 1 Cor. iii. 21, 22. " All things are yours, whether Paul, or Apollos, or Cephas, or the world, or life, or death, or things present, or things to come; all are yours." Here the apostle teaches, that all things in the world to come, or in the future and eternal world, are the saints'; not only life but death; men, and angels, and devils, heaven and hell, are theirs, to contribute to their joy and happiness. Therefore the damned and their misery, their sufferings and the wrath of God poured out upon them, will be an occasion of joy to them. If there were any thing whatsoever that did not contribute to their joy, but caused grief, then there would be something which would not be theirs.

That the torments of the damned are no matter of grief, but of joy, to the inhabitants of heaven, is very clearly expressed in several passages of this book of Revelation; particularly by chap. xvi. 5-7. and chap xix. at the beginning.

SECT. II

*Why the sufferings of the wicked will not be cause of grief
to the righteous, but the contrary*

1. NEGATIVELY; it will not be because the saints in heaven are
the subjects of any ill disposition; but on the contrary, this rejoicing of theirs will be the fruit of an amiable and excellent
disposition: it will be the fruit of a perfect holiness and con-
formity to Christ, the holy Lamb of God. The devil delights in
the misery of men from cruelty, and from envy and revenge, and
because he delights in misery, for its own sake, from a malicious
disposition.

But it will be from exceedingly different principles, and for
quite other reasons, that the just damnation of the wicked will
be an occasion of rejoicing to the saints in glory. It will not be
because they delight in seeing the misery of others absolutely
considered. The damned suffering divine vengeance will be no
occasion of joy to the saints merely as it is the misery of others,
or because it is pleasant to them to behold the misery of others
merely for its own sake. The rejoicing of the saints on this occasion is no argument that they are not of a most amiable and
excellent spirit, or that there is any defect on that account, that
there is any thing wanting which would render them of a more
amiable disposition. It is no argument that they have not a spirit
of goodness and love reigning in them in absolute perfection, or
that herein they do not excel the greatest instances of it on earth,
as much as the stars are higher than the earth, or the sun brighter
than a glow-worm.

And whereas the heavenly inhabitants are in the text called
upon to rejoice over Babylon, because God had avenged them on
her, it is not to be understood that they are to rejoice in having
their revenge glutted, but to rejoice in seeing the justice of God
executed, and in seeing his love to them in executing it on his
enemies.

2. Positively; the sufferings of the damned will be no occasion
of grief to the heavenly inhabitants, as they will have *no love
nor pity* to the damned as such. It will be no argument of want
of a spirit of love in them, that they do not love the damned; for
the heavenly inhabitants will know that it is not fit that they

should love them, because they will know then, that God has no love to them, nor pity for them; but that they are the objects of God's eternal hatred. And they will then be perfectly conformed to God in their wills and affections. They will love what God loves, and that only. However the saints in heaven may have loved the damned while here, especially those of them who were near and dear to them in this world, they will have no love to them hereafter.

It will be an occasion of their rejoicing, as the *glory of God* will appear in it. The glory of God appears in all his works: and therefore there is no work of God which the saints in glory shall behold and contemplate, but what will be an occasion of rejoicing to them. God glorifies himself in the eternal damnation of the ungodly men. God glorifies himself in all that he doth; but he glorifies himself principally in his eternal disposal of his intelligent creatures, some are appointed to everlasting life, and others left to everlasting death.

The saints in heaven will be perfect in their love to God: their hearts will be all a flame of love to God, and therefore they will greatly value the glory of God, and will exceedingly delight in seeing him glorified. The saints highly value the glory of God here in this word, but how much more will they do so in the world to come. They will therefore greatly rejoice in all that contributes to that glory. The glory of God will in their esteem be of greater consequence than the welfare of thousands and millions of souls.—Particularly,

(1.) They will rejoice in seeing the *justice* of God glorified in the sufferings of the damned. The misery of the damned, dreadful as it is, is but what justice *requires*. They in heaven will see and know it much more clearly, than any of us do here. They will see how perfectly just and righteous their punishment is, and therefore how properly inflicted by the supreme Governor of the world. They will greatly rejoice to see justice take place, to see that all the sin and wickedness that have been committed in the world is remembered of God, and has its due punishment The sight of this strict and immutable justice of God will render him amiable and adorable in their eyes. They will rejoice when they see him who is their Father and eternal portion so glorious in his justice.

Then there will be no remaining difficulties about the justice of God, about the absolute decrees of God, or any thing pertaining to the dispensations of God towards men. But divine justice in the destruction of the wicked will then appear as light without darkness, and will shine as the sun without clouds, and on this account will they sing joyful songs of praise to God, as we see the saints and angels do, when God pours the vials of his wrath upon antichrist; Rev. xvi. 5-7. They sing joyfully to God on this account, that true and righteous are his judgments; Rev. xix. 1-6. Their seeing God so strictly just will make them value his love the more. Mercy and grace are more valuable on this account. The more they shall see of the justice of God, the more will they prize and rejoice in his love.

(2.) They will rejoice in it, as it will be a glorious manifestation of the *power* and *majesty* of God. God will show his own greatness in executing vengeance on ungodly men. This is mentioned as one end of the destruction of the ungodly; "What if God, willing to show his wrath, and make his power known, endured with much long-suffering the vessels of wrath fitted to destruction?" God will hereby show how much he is above his enemies. There are many now in the world, who proudly lift up themselves against God. There are many open opposers of the cause and interest of Christ. "They set their mouth against the heavens, and their tongue walketh through the earth." Then God will show his glorious power in destroying these enemies.

The power of God is sometimes spoken of as very glorious, as appearing in the temporal destruction of his enemies; Exod. xv. 6. "Thy right hand, O Lord, is become glorious in power; thy right hand, O Lord, hath dashed in pieces the enemy." But how much more glorious will it appear in his triumphing over, and dashing in pieces at once, all his enemies, wicked men and devils together, all his haughty foes! The power of God will gloriously appear in dashing to pieces his enemies as a potter's vessel. Moses rejoiced and sang when he saw God glorify his power in the destruction of Pharaoh and his host at the Red sea. But how much more will the saints in glory rejoice, when they shall see God gloriously triumphing over all his enemies in their eternal ruin! Then it will appear how dreadful God is, and how dreadful a thing it is to disobey and condemn him. It is often mentioned as a part of the glory of God, that he is a terrible God. To see the majesty, and greatness, and terribleness of God, appearing in the destruction of his enemies, will cause the saints to rejoice; and when they shall see how great and terrible a being God is, how will they prize his favour! how will they rejoice that they are the objects of his love! how will they praise him the more joyfully, that he should choose them to be his children, and to live in the enjoyment of him!

It will occasion rejoicing in them, as they will have the greater sense of *their own happiness*, by seeing the contrary misery. It is the nature of pleasure and pain, of happiness and misery, greatly to heighten the sense of each other. Thus the seeing of the happiness of others tends to make men more sensible of their own calamities; and the seeing of the calamities of others tends to heighten the sense of our own enjoyments.

When the saints in glory, therefore, shall see the doleful state of the damned, how will this heighten their sense of the blessedness of their own state, so exceedingly different from it! When they shall see how miserable others of their fellow-creatures are, who were naturally in the same circumstances with themselves; when they shall see the smoke of their torment, and the raging of the flames of their burning, and hear their dolorous shrieks and cries, and consider that they in the mean time are in the most blissful state, and shall surely be in it to all eternity; how will they rejoice!

This will give them a joyful sense of the *grace and love of God to them*, because hereby they will see how great a benefit they have by it. When they shall see the dreadful miseries of the damned, and consider that they deserved the same misery, and that it was *sovereign grace*, and nothing else, which made them so much to differ from the damned, that, if it had not been for that, they would have been in the same condition; but that God from all eternity was pleased to set his love upon them, that Christ hath laid down his life for them, and hath made them thus gloriously happy for ever, O how will they admire that dying love of Christ, which has redeemed them from so great a misery, and purchased for them so great happiness, and has so distinguished them from others of their fellow-creatures! How joyfully will they sing to God and the Lamb, when they behold this!

SECT. III

An objection answered

THE objection is, "If we are apprehensive of the damnation of others now, it in no wise becomes us to rejoice at it, but to lament it. If we see others in imminent danger of going to hell, it is accounted a very sorrowful thing, and it is looked upon as an argument of a senseless and wicked spirit to look upon it otherwise. When it is a very dead time with respect to religion, and a very degenerate and corrupt time among a people, it is accounted a thing greatly to be lamented; and on this account, that at such times there are but few converted and saved, and many perish. Paul tells us, that he had great heaviness and continual sorrow in his heart, because so many of the Jews were in a perishing state: Rom. ix. 1, 2, 3. "I say the truth in Christ, I lie not, my conscience also bearing me witness in the Holy Ghost, that I have great heaviness and continual sorrow in my heart. For I could wish that myself were accursed from Christ, for my brethren, my kinsmen according to the flesh." And if a neighbour die, and his death be attended with circumstances which look darkly as to the state of his soul, we account it a sorrowful thing, because he hath left us no more comfortable grounds to hope for his salvation. Why is it not then an unbecoming thing in the saints in glory to rejoice when they see the damnation of the ungodly?

Ans. 1. It is now our duty to love all men, though they are wicked; but it will not be a duty to love wicked men hereafter. Christ, by many precepts in his word, hath made it our duty to love all men. We are commanded to love wicked men, and our enemies and persecutors. But this command doth not extend to the saint in glory, with respect to the damned in hell. Nor is there the same reason that it should. We ought now to love all, and even wicked men; we know not but that God loves them. However wicked any man is, yet we know not but that he is one whom God loved from eternity; we know not but that Christ loved him with a dying love, had his name upon his heart before the world was, and had respect to him when he endured those bitter agonies on the cross. We know not but that he is to be our companion in glory to all eternity.

But this is not the case in another world. The saints in glory will know concerning the damned in hell, that God never loved them, but that he hates them, and that they will be for ever hated of God. This hatred of God will be fully declared to them; they will see it, and will see the fruits of it in their misery. Therefore, when God has thus declared his hatred of the damned, and the saints see it, it will be no way becoming in the saints to love them, nor to mourn over them. It becomes the saints fully and perfectly to consent to what God doth, without any reluctance or opposition of spirit; yea, it becomes them to rejoice in every thing that God sees meet to be done.

Ans. 2. We ought now to seek and be concerned for the salvation of wicked men, because now they are capable subjects of it. Wicked men, though they may be very wicked, yet are capable subjects of mercy. It is yet a day of grace with them, and they have the offers of salvation. Christ is as yet seeking their salvation; he is calling upon them, inviting and wooing them; he stands at the door and knocks. He is using many means with them, is calling them, saying, *Turn ye, turn ye, why will ye die?* The day of his patience is yet continued to them; and if Christ is seeking their salvation, surely we ought to seek it.

God is wont now to make men the means of one another's salvation; yea, it is his ordinary way so to do. He makes the concern and endeavours of his people the means of bringing home many to Christ. Therefore they ought to be concerned for and endeavour it. But it will not be so in another world: there, wicked men will be no longer capable subjects of mercy. The saints will know that it is the will of God the wicked should be miserable to all eternity. It will therefore cease to be their duty any more to seek their salvation, or to be concerned about their misery. On the other hand, it will be their duty to rejoice in the will and glory of God. It is not our duty to be sorry that God hath executed just vengeance on the devils, concerning whom the will of God in their eternal state is already known to us.

Ans. 3. Rejoicing at the calamities of others now, rests not on the same grounds as that of the saints in glory. The evil of rejoicing at others' calamities now, consists in our envy, or revenge, or some such disposition is gratified therein; and not that God is glorified, that the majesty and justice of God gloriously shine forth.

Ans. 4. The different circumstances of our nature now from what will be hereafter, make that a virtue now which will be no virtue then. For instance, if a man be of a virtuous disposition, the circumstances of our nature now are such, that it will necessarily show itself by natural affection, and to be without natural affection is a very vicious disposition; and is so mentioned in Rom. i. 31. But natural affection is no virtue in the saints in glory. Their virtue will exercise itself in a higher manner.

Ans. 5. The vengeance inflicted on many of the wicked will be a manifestation of God's love to the saints. One way whereby God shows his love to the saints is by destroying their enemies. God hath said, "He that toucheth you, toucheth the apple of mine eye." And it is often mentioned in Scripture, as an instance of the great love of God to his people, that his wrath is so awakened, when they are wronged and injured. Thus Christ hath promised that God will avenge his own elect, Luke xviii. 7, and hath said, that "if any man offend one of his little ones, it were better for him that a millstone were hanged about his neck, and that he were drowned in the depth of the sea." Matt. xviii. 6.

So the saints in glory will see the great love of God to them, in the dreadful vengeance which he shall inflict on those who have injured and persecuted them; and the view of this love of God to them will be just cause of their rejoicing. Thus, in the text, heaven and the holy apostles and prophets are called to rejoice over their enemies, because God hath avenged them of them.

SECT. IV

The ungodly warned

I SHALL apply this subject only in one use, *viz.* of *warning* to ungodly men. And in order to this, I desire such to consider,

1. How destitute of any comforting consideration your condition will be, if you perish at last. You will have none to pity you. Look which way you will, before or behind, on the right hand or left, look up to heaven, or look about you in hell, and you will see none to condole your case, or to exercise any pity towards you in your dreadful condition. You must bear these flames, you must bear that torment and amazement, day and night, for

R

ever, and never have the comfort of considering, that there is so much as one that pities your case; there never will one tear be dropped for you.

(1.) You have now been taught that you will have no pity from the *created inhabitants* of heaven. If you shall look to them, you will see them all rejoicing at the sight of the glory of God's justice, power, and terrible majesty, manifested in your torment. You will see them in a blissful and glorious state; you will see Abraham, Isaac, and Jacob, and all the prophets, in the kingdom of God; you will see many come from the east, and from the west, and from the north, and from the south, and sit down in that glorious kingdom; and will see them all with one voice, and with united joy, praising God for glorifying himself in your destruction. You will wail and gnash your teeth under your own torments, and with envy of their happiness; but they will rejoice and sing: Isa. lxv. 13, 14. " Therefore thus saith the Lord, Behold, my servants shall eat, but ye shall be hungry; behold, my servants shall drink, but ye shall be thirsty: behold, my servants shall rejoice, but ye shall be ashamed: behold, my servants shall sing for joy of heart, but ye shall cry for sorrow of heart, and shall howl for vexation of spirit."

(2.) God will exercise no pity towards you. If you might have his pity in any degree, that would be of more worth to you than thousands of worlds. That would make your case to be not without comfort and hope. But God will exercise no pity towards you. He hath often said concerning wicked men, that his eye shall not spare, neither will he have pity, (Ezek. v. 11, and vii. 4, 9. and viii. 18.) He will cast fury upon you, and not spare; you will see nothing in God, and receive nothing from him, but perfect hatred, and the fierceness of his wrath; nothing but the mighty falls or outpourings of wrath upon you every moment; and no cries will avail to move God to any pity, or in the least to move him to lighten his hand, or assuage the fierceness and abate the power of your torments.

Jesus Christ, the Redeemer, will have no pity on you. Though he had so much love to sinners, as to be willing to lay down his life for them, and offers you the benefits of his blood, while you are in this world, and often calls upon you to accept them; yet then he will have no pity upon you. You never will hear any more instructions from him; he will utterly refuse to be your instructor: on the contrary, he will be your judge, to pronounce sentence against you.

(3.) You will find none that will pity you in hell. The devils will not pity you, but will be your tormentors, as roaring lions or hell-hounds to tear you in pieces continually. And other wicked men who shall be there will be like devils; they will have no pity on you, but will hate, and curse, and torment you. And you yourselves will be like devils; you will be like devils to yourselves, and will be your own tormentors.

2. Consider what an aggravation what you have heard under this doctrine will be to your misery. Consider how it will be at the day of judgment, when you shall see Christ coming in the clouds of heaven, when you shall begin to wail and cry, as knowing that you are those who are to be condemned; and perhaps you will be ready to fly to some of your godly friends; but you will obtain no help from them: you will see them unconcerned for you, with joyful countenances ascending to meet the Lord, and not the less joyful for the horror in which they see you. And when you shall stand before the tribunal at the left hand, among devils, trembling and astonished, and shall have the dreadful sentence passed upon you, you will at the same time see the blessed company of saints and angels at the right hand rejoicing, and shall hear them shout forth the praises of God, while they hear your sentence pronounced. You will then see those godly people, with whom you shall have been acquainted, and who shall have been your neighbours, and with whom you now often converse, rejoicing at the pronunciation and execution of your sentence.

Perhaps there are now some godly people, to whom you are near and dear, who are tenderly concerned for you, who are ready to pity you under all calamities, and willing to help you, and particularly are tenderly concerned for your poor soul, and have put up many fervent prayers for you. How will you bear to hear these singing for joy of heart, while you are crying for sorrow of heart, and howling for vexation of spirit, and even singing the more joyful for the glorious justice of God which they behold in your eternal condemnation?

You that have godly parents, who in this world have tenderly loved you, who were wont to look upon your welfare as their own, and were wont to be grieved for you when any thing

R*

calamitous befell you in this world, and especially were greatly concerned for the good of your souls, and industriously sought, and earnestly prayed for their salvation; how will you bear to see them in the kingdom of God, crowned with glory? Or how will you bear to see them receiving the blessed sentence, and going up with shouts and songs, to enter with Christ into the kingdom prepared for them from the foundation of the world, while you are amongst a company of devils, and are turned away with the most bitter cries, to enter into everlasting burnings, prepared for the devil and his angels? How will you bear to see your parents, who in this life had so dear an affection for you, now without any love to you, approving the sentence of condemnation, when Christ shall with indignation bid you depart, wretched, cursed creatures, into eternal burnings? How will you bear to see and hear them praising the Judge, for his justice exercised in pronouncing this sentence, and hearing it with holy joy in their countenances, and shouting forth the praises and hallelujahs of God and Christ on that account?

When they shall see what manifestations of amazement there will be in you at the hearing of this dreadful sentence, and that every syllable of it pierces you like a thunderbolt, and sinks you into the lowest depths of horror and despair; when they shall behold you with a frighted, amazed countenance, trembling and astonished, and shall hear you groan and gnash your teeth; these things will not move them at all to pity you, but you will see them with a holy joyfulness in their countenances, and with songs in their mouths. When they shall see you turned away and beginning to enter into the great furnace, and shall see how you shrink at it, and hear how you shriek and cry out; yet they will not be at all grieved for you, but at the same time you will hear from them renewed praises and hallelujahs for the true and righteous judgments of God, in so dealing with you.

Then you will doubtless remember how those your glorified parents seemed to be concerned for your salvation, while you were here in this world; you will remember how they were wont to counsel and warn you, and how little you regarded their counsels, and how they seemed to be concerned and grieved, that there appeared no more effect of their endeavours for the good of your souls. You will then see them praising God for executing just vengeance on you, for setting so light by their counsels and reproofs. However here they loved you, and were concerned for you, now they will rise up in judgment against you, and will declare how your sins are aggravated by the endeavours which they to no purpose used with you, to bring you to forsake sin and practise virtue, and to seek and serve God; but you were obstinate under all, and would not hearken to them. They will declare how inexcusable you are upon this account. And when the Judge shall execute the more terrible wrath upon you on this account, that you have made no better improvement of your parents' instructions, they will joyfully praise God for it. After they shall have seen you lie in hell thousands of years, and your torment shall yet continue without any rest, day or night; they will not begin to pity you then; they will praise God, that his justice appears in the eternity of your misery.

You that have godly husbands, or wives, or brethren, or sisters, with whom you have been wont to dwell under the same roof, and to eat at the same table, consider how it will be with you, when you shall come to part with them; when they shall be taken and you left; Luke xvii. 34, 35, 36. "I tell you, in that night, there shall be two men in one bed; the one shall be taken and the other left. Two women shall be grinding together; the one shall be taken and the other left. Two men shall be in the field; the one shall be taken and the other left." However you may wail and lament, when you see them parted from you, they being taken and you left, you will see in them no signs of sorrow, that you are not taken with them; that you ascend not with them to meet the Lord in the air, but are left below to be consumed with the world, which is reserved unto fire, against the day of the perdition of ungodly men.

Those wicked men, who shall go to hell from under the labours of pious and faithful ministers, will see those ministers rejoicing and praising God upon the occasion of their destruction. Consider, ye that have long lived under Mr. Stoddard's ministry,* and are yet in a natural condition, how dreadful it will be with you, to see him who was so tenderly concerned for the good of your souls while he was here, and so earnestly sought your salvation, to see him rising up in judgment against you, declaring your inexcusableness, declaring how often he warned you; how plainly he set your danger before you, and told you of the oppor-

* The author's grandfather and predecessor.

tunity that you had; how fully he set forth the miserable condition in which you were, and the necessity there was that you
should obtain an interest in Christ; how movingly and earnestly
he exhorted you to get into a better state, and how regardless
you were; how little you minded all that he said to you; how
you went on still in your trespasses, hardened your necks, and
made your hearts as an adamant, and refused to return! How
dreadful will it be to you to hear him declaring how inexcusable
you are upon these accounts! How will you be cut to the heart,
when you shall see him approving the sentence of condemnation,
which the Judge shall pronounce against you, and judging and
sentencing you with Christ, as an assessor in judgment; for the
saints shall judge the world (1 Cor. vi. 2), and when you shall see
him rejoicing in the execution of justice upon you for all your
unprofitableness under his ministry!

3. Consider what a happy opportunity you have in your hands
now. Now your case is very different from the case of wicked
men in another world, of which you have now heard; and particularly in the following respects.

(1.) God makes it the duty of *all the godly* now to be concerned for your salvation. As to those who are damned in hell,
the saints in glory are not concerned for their welfare, and have
no love nor pity towards them; and if you perish hereafter, it will
be an occasion of joy to all the godly. But now God makes it the
duty of all the godly, to love you with a sincere good-will and
earnest affection. God doth not excuse men from loving you, for
your ill qualities: though you are wicked and undeserving, yet
God makes it the duty of all sincerely to wish well to you; and
it is a heinous sin in the sight of God for any to hate you. He
requires all to be concerned for your salvation, and by all means
to seek it. It is their duty now to lament your danger, and to
pray for mercy to you, that you may be converted and brought
home to Christ.

Now the godly who know you, desire your salvation, and are
ready to seek it, and pray for it. If you be now in distress about
the condition of your souls, you are not in such a forsaken, helpless condition, as those that are damned; but you may find many
to pray for you, many who are willing to assist you by their
advice and counsels, and all with a tender concern, and with
hearty wishes that your souls may prosper. Now some of you

have godly friends who are near and dear to you; you are beloved of those who have a great interest in heaven, and who have
power with God by their prayers: you have the blessing of living
under the same roof with them. Some of you have godly parents
to pray for you, and to counsel and instruct you, who you may
be sure will do it with sincere love and concern for you. And
there is not only the command of God; God hath not only made
it the duty of others to seek your salvation, but hath given encouragement to others to seek it. He gives encouragement that
they may obtain help for you by their prayers, and that they
may be instrumental of your spiritual good. God reveals it to be
his manner, to make our sincere endeavours a mean of each
other's good. How different is the case with you from what it is
with those that are already damned! And how happy an opportunity have you in your hands, if you would but improve it!

(2.) Now you live where there is *a certain order of men* appointed to make it the business of their lives to seek your salvation. Now you have ministers, not to rise up in judgment against
you; but in Christ's stead, to beseech you to be reconciled to God;
2 Cor. v. 20. God hath not only made it the duty of all to wish
well to your souls, and occasionally to endeavour to promote your
spiritual interests, but he hath set apart certain persons, to make
it their whole work, in which they should spend their days and
their strength.

(3.) *Christ himself* is now seeking your salvation. He seeks it
by the fore-mentioned means, by appointing men to make it their
business to seek it; he seeks it by them; they are his instruments,
and they beseech you in Christ's stead, to be reconciled to God.
He seeks it, in commanding your neighbours to seek it. Christ is
represented in Scripture, as wooing the souls of sinners. He uses
means to persuade them to choose and accept of their own salvation. He often invites them to come to him that they may have
life, that they may find rest to their souls; to come and take of the
water of life freely. He stands at the door and knocks; and ceases
not, though sinners for a long time refuse him. He bears repeated
repulses from them, and yet mercifully continues knocking, saying, "Open to me, that I may come in and sup with you, and you
with me." At the doors of many sinners he stands thus knocking
for many years together. Christ is become a most importunate
suitor to sinners, that he may become their sovereign. He is

often setting before them the need they have of him, the miserable condition in which they are, and the great provision that is made for the good of their souls; and he invites them to accept of this provision, and promises it shall be theirs upon their mere acceptance.

Thus how earnestly did Christ seek the salvation of Jerusalem, and he wept over it when they refused; Luke xix. 41, 42. "And when he was come near, he beheld the city, and wept over it, saying, If thou hadst known, even thou, at least in this thy day, the things which belong unto thy peace! but now they are hid from thine eyes." And Matt. xxiii. 37. " O Jerusalem, Jerusalem, thou that killest the prophets, and stonest them which are sent unto thee, how often would I have gathered thy children together, even as a hen gathereth her chickens under her wings, and ye would not!" Thus Christ is now seeking your salvation; such an opportunity have you now in your hands. Consider therefore how many means Christ is using with you, to bring you to salvation.

Besides those things which have been now mentioned, some of you have a degree of the inward strivings and influences of the Spirit, which makes your opportunity much greater. You have Christ's internal calls and knockings. All the persons of the Trinity are now seeking your salvation. God the Father hath sent his Son, who hath made way for your salvation, and removed all difficulties, except those which are with your own heart. And he is waiting to be gracious to you; the door of his mercy stands open to you; he hath set a fountain open for you to wash in from sin and uncleanness. Christ is calling, inviting, and wooing you; and the Holy Ghost is striving with you by his internal motions and influences.

4. If you now repent, before it be too late, the *saints and angels* in glory will rejoice at your repentance. If you repent not till it is too late, they will, as you have heard, rejoice in seeing justice executed upon you. But if you now repent, they will rejoice at your welfare, that you who were lost, are found; that you who were dead, are alive again. They will rejoice that you are come to so happy a state already, and that you are in due time to inherit eternal happiness. Luke xv. 3-10. So that if now you will improve your opportunity, there will be a very different occasion of joy in heaven concerning you, than that of which the doctrine

speaks; not a rejoicing on occasion of your misery, but on occasion of your unspeakable blessedness.

5. If you repent before it is too late, *you yourselves* shall be of that joyful company. They will be so far from rejoicing on occasion of your ruin, that you yourselves will be of that glorious company, who will rejoice in all the works of God, who will have all tears wiped away from their eyes, to whom there will be no more death, nor sorrow, nor crying, and from whom sorrow and sighing shall flee away. You yourselves will be of those who will rejoice at the glorious display of God's majesty and justice, in his wrath on his enemies. You will be of those that shall sing for joy of heart at the day of judgment, while others mourn for sorrow of heart, and howl for vexation of spirit; and you will enter into the joy of your Lord, and there shall *never be any end or abatement of your joy!*

Sermon X*

PARDON FOR THE GREATEST SINNERS

PSALM XXV. 11

For thy name's sake, O Lord, pardon my iniquity; for it is great.

IT is evident by some passages in this psalm, that when it was penned, it was a time of affliction and danger with David. This appears particularly by the 15th and following verses: "Mine eyes are ever towards the Lord; for he shall pluck my feet out of the net," etc. His distress makes him think of his sins, and leads him to confess them, and to cry to God for pardon, as is suitable in a time of affliction. See ver. 7. "Remember not the sins of my youth, nor my transgressions;" and verse 18. "Look upon mine affliction, and my pain, and forgive all my sins."

It is observable in the text, what arguments the psalmist makes use of in pleading for pardon.

1. He pleads for pardon *for God's name's sake.* He has no expectation of pardon for the sake of any righteousness or worthiness of his for any good deeds he had done, or any compensation he had made for his sins; though if man's righteousness could be a just plea, David would have had as much to plead as most. But he begs that God would do it for his own name's sake, for his own glory, for the glory of his own free grace, and for the honour of his own covenant-faithfulness.

2. The psalmist pleads *the greatness of his sins* as an argument for mercy. He not only doth not plead his own righteousness, or the smallness of his sins; he not only doth not say, Pardon mine iniquity, for I have done much good to counterbalance it; or, Pardon mine iniquity, for it is small, and thou hast no great reason to be angry with me; mine iniquity is not so great, that thou hast any just cause to remember it against me; mine offence

* It is believed that this sermon was delivered before the year 1733.

is not such but that thou mayest well enough overlook it: but on the contrary he says, *Pardon mine iniquity, for it is great:* he pleads the greatness of his sin, and not the smallness of it; he enforces his prayer with this consideration, that his sins are very heinous.

But how could he make this a plea for pardon? I answer, Because the greater his iniquity was, the more *need* he had of pardon. It is as much as if he had said, Pardon mine iniquity, for it is so great that I cannot bear the punishment; my sin is so great that I am in necessity of pardon; my case will be exceedingly miserable, unless thou be pleased to pardon me. He makes use of the greatness of his sin, to enforce his plea for pardon, as a man would make use of the greatness of calamity in begging for relief. When a beggar begs for bread, he will plead the greatness of his poverty and necessity. When a man in distress cries for pity, what more suitable plea can be urged than the extremity of his case?—And God allows such a plea as this: for he is moved to mercy towards us by nothing in us but the miserableness of our case. He doth not pity sinners because they are worthy, but because they need his pity.

DOCTRINE. *If we truly come to God for mercy, the greatness of our sin will be no impediment to pardon.*—If it were an impediment, David would never have used it as a plea for pardon, as we find he does in the text.—The following things are needful in order that we truly come to God for mercy:

I. That we should see *our misery,* and be *sensible* of our need of mercy. They who are not sensible of their misery cannot truly look to God for mercy; for it is the very notion of divine mercy, that it is the goodness and grace of God to the miserable. Without misery in the object, there can be no exercise of mercy. To suppose mercy without supposing misery, or pity without calamity, is a contradiction: therefore men cannot look upon themselves as proper objects of mercy, unless they first know themselves to be miserable; and so, unless this be the case, it is impossible that they should come to God for mercy. They must be sensible that they are the children of wrath; that the law is against them, and that they are exposed to the curse of it: that the wrath of God abideth on them; and that he is angry with them every day while they are under the guilt of sin.—They must be sensible that it is a very dreadful thing to be the object of the wrath of God; that it is a very awful thing to have him for their enemy; and that they cannot bear his wrath. They must be sensible that the guilt of sin makes them miserable creatures, whatever temporal enjoyments they have; that they can be no other than miserable, undone creatures, so long as God is angry with them; that they are without strength, and must perish, and that eternally, unless God help them. They must see that their case is utterly desperate, for any thing that any one else can do for them; that they hang over the pit of eternal misery; and that they must necessarily drop into it, if God have not mercy on them.

II. They must be sensible that they *are not worthy* that God should have mercy on them. They who truly come to God for mercy, come as beggars, and not as creditors: they come for mere mercy, for sovereign grace, and not for any thing that is due. Therefore, they must see that the misery under which they lie is justly brought upon them, and that the wrath to which they are exposed is *justly* threatened against them; and that they have *deserved* that God should *be* their enemy, and should *continue* to be their enemy. They must be sensible that it would be just with God to do as he hath threatened in his holy law, *viz*. make them the objects of his wrath and curse in hell to all eternity.— They who come to God for mercy in a right manner are not disposed to find fault with his severity; but they come in a sense of their own utter unworthiness, as with ropes about their necks, and lying in the dust at the foot of mercy.

III. They must come to God for mercy in and *through Jesus Christ* alone. All their hope of mercy must be from the consideration of what he is, what he hath done, and what he hath suffered; and that there is no other name given under heaven, among men, whereby we can be saved, but that of Christ; that he is the Son of God, and the Saviour of the world; that his blood cleanses from all sin, and that he is so worthy, that all sinners who are in him may well be pardoned and accepted.—It is impossible that any should *come* to God for mercy, and at the same time have no *hope* of mercy. Their coming to God for it, implies that they have some hope of obtaining, otherwise they would not think it worth the while to come. But they that come in a right manner have all their hope through Christ, or from the consideration of his redemption, and the sufficiency of it.—If persons thus come to God for mercy, the greatness of their sins will be no impediment to pardon. Let their sins be ever so many, and great, and aggravated, it will not make God in the least degree more backward to pardon them. This may be made evident by the following considerations:

1. *The mercy of God* is as sufficient for the pardon of the greatest sins, as for the least; and that because his mercy is infinite. That which is infinite, is as much above what is great, as it is above what is small. Thus God being infinitely great, he is ˙˙as much above kings as he is above beggars; he is as much above the highest angel, as he is above the meanest worm. One finite measure doth not come any nearer to the extent of what is infinite than another.—So the mercy of God being infinite, it must be as sufficient for the pardon of all sin, as of one. If one of the least sins be not beyond the mercy of God, so neither are the greatest, or ten thousand of them.—However, it must be acknowledged, that this alone doth not prove the doctrine. For though the mercy of God may be as sufficient for the pardon of great sins as others; yet there may be other obstacles, besides the want of mercy. The mercy of God may be sufficient, and yet the other attributes may oppose the dispensation of mercy in these cases.—Therefore I observe,

2. That the *satisfaction of Christ* is as sufficient for the removal of the greatest guilt, as the least: 1 John i. 7. "The blood of Christ cleanseth from all sin." Acts xiii. 39. "By him all that believe are justified from all things from which ye could not be justified by the law of Moses." All the sins of those who truly come to God for mercy, let them be what they will, are satisfied for, if God be true who tells us so; and if they be satisfied for, surely it is not incredible, that God should be ready to pardon them. So that Christ having fully satisfied for all sin, or having wrought out a satisfaction that is sufficient for all, it is now no way inconsistent with the glory of the divine attributes to pardon the greatest sins of those who in a right manner come unto him for it.—God may now pardon the greatest sinners without any prejudice to the honour of his holiness. The holiness of God will not suffer him to give the least countenance to sin, but inclines him to give proper testimonies of his hatred of it. But Christ having satisfied for sin, God can now love the sinner, and give no countenance at all to sin, however great a sinner he may have

been. It was a sufficient testimony of God's abhorrence of sin, that he poured out his wrath on his own dear Son, when he took the guilt of it upon himself. Nothing can more show God's abhorrence of sin than this. If all mankind had been eternally damned, it would not have been so great a testimony of it.

God may, through Christ, pardon the *greatest sinner* without any prejudice to the honour of his majesty. The honour of the divine majesty indeed requires satisfaction; but the sufferings of Christ fully repair the injury. Let the contempt be ever so great, yet if so honourable a person as Christ undertakes to be a Mediator for the offender, and suffers so much for him, it fully repairs the injury done to the Majesty of heaven and earth. The sufferings of Christ fully satisfy justice. The justice of God, as the supreme Governor and Judge of the world, requires the punishment of sin. The supreme Judge must judge the world according to a rule of justice. God doth not show mercy as a judge, but as a sovereign; therefore his exercise of mercy as a sovereign, and his justice as a judge, must be made consistent one with another; and this is done by the sufferings of Christ, in which sin is punished fully, and justice answered. Rom. iii. 25, 26. "Whom God hath set forth to be a propitiation through faith in his blood, to declare his righteousness for the remission of sins that are past, through the forbearance of God; to declare, I say, at this time, his righteousness; that he might be just, and the justifier of him which believeth in Jesus."—The law is no impediment in the way of the pardon of the greatest sin, if men do but truly come to God for mercy: for Christ hath fulfilled the law, he hath borne the curse of it, in his sufferings; Gal. iii. 13. " Christ hath redeemed us from the curse of the law, being made a curse for us; for it is written, Cursed is every one that hangeth on a tree."

3. Christ *will not refuse* to save the greatest sinners, who in a right manner come to God for mercy; for this is his work. It is his business to be a Saviour of sinners; it is the work upon which he came into the world; and therefore he will not object to it. He did not come to call the righteous, but sinners to re-pentance, Matt. ix. 13. Sin is the very evil which he came into the world to remedy: therefore he will not object to any man, that he is very sinful. The more sinful he is, the more need of Christ.—The sinfulness of man was the reason of Christ's coming

into the world; this is the very misery from which he came to deliver men. The more they have of it, the more need they have of being delivered; " They that are whole need not a physician, but they that are sick," Matt. ix. 12. The physician will not make it an objection against healing a man who applies to him, that he stands in great need of his help. If a physician of compassion comes among the sick and wounded, surely he will not refuse to heal those that stand in most need of healing, if he be able to heal them.

4. Herein doth the *glory of grace* by the redemption of Christ much consist, *viz.* in its sufficiency for the pardon of the greatest sinners. The whole contrivance of the way of salvation is for this end, to glorify the free grace of God. God had it on his heart from all eternity to glorify this attribute; and therefore it is, that the device of saving sinners by Christ was conceived. The greatness of divine grace appears very much in this, that God by Christ saves the greatest offenders. The greater the guilt of any sinner is, the more glorious and wonderful is the grace manifested in his pardon: Rom. v. 20. " Where sin abounded, grace did much more abound." The apostle, when telling how great a sinner he had been, takes notice of the abounding of grace in his pardon, of which his great guilt was the occasion: 1 Tim. i. 13. " Who was before a blasphemer, and a persecutor, and injurious. But I obtained mercy; and the grace of our Lord was exceeding abundant, with faith and love which is in Christ Jesus." The Redeemer is glorified, in that he proves sufficient to redeem those who are exceeding sinful, in that his blood proves sufficient to wash away the greatest guilt, in that he is able to save men to the uttermost, and in that he redeems even from the greatest misery. It is the honour of Christ to save the greatest sinners, when they come to him, as it is the honour of a physician that he cures the most desperate diseases or wounds. Therefore, no doubt, Christ will be willing to save the greatest sinners, if they come to him; for he will not be backward to glorify himself, and to commend the value and virtue of his own blood. Seeing he hath so laid out himself to redeem sinners, he will not be unwilling to show, that he is able to redeem to the uttermost.

5. Pardon is as much *offered and promised* to the greatest sinners as any, if they will come aright to God for mercy. The invitations of the gospel are always in universal terms: as, Ho,

every one that thirsteth; Come unto me, all ye that labour and are heavy laden; and, Whosoever will, let him come. And the voice of Wisdom is to men in general: Prov. viii. 4. "Unto you, O men, I call, and my voice is to the sons of men." Not to moral men, or religious men, but *to you, O men*. So Christ promises, John vi. 37. "Him that cometh to me, I will in no wise cast out." This is the direction of Christ to his apostles, after his resurrection, Mark xvi. 15, 16. "Go ye into all the world, and preach the gospel to every creature: he that believeth, and is baptized, shall be saved." Which is agreeable to what the apostle saith, that "the gospel was preached to every creature which is under heaven," Col. i. 23.

APPLICATION

The proper *use* of this subject is, to encourage sinners whose consciences are burdened with a sense of guilt, immediately to go to God through Christ for mercy. If you go in the manner we have described, the arms of mercy are open to embrace you. You need not be at all the more fearful of coming because of your sins, let them be ever so black. If you had as much guilt lying on each of your souls as all the wicked men in the world, and all the damned souls in hell; yet if you come to God for mercy, sensible of your own vileness, and seeking pardon only through the free mercy of God in Christ, you would not need to be afraid; the greatness of your sins would be no impediment to your pardon. Therefore, if your souls be burdened, and you are distressed for fear of hell, you need not bear that burden and distress any longer. If you are but *willing*, you may freely come and unload yourselves, and cast all your burdens on Christ, and rest in him.

But here I shall speak to some OBJECTIONS which some awakened sinners may be ready to make against what I now exhort them to.

I. Some may be ready to object, I have spent my youth and all the best of my life in sin, and I am afraid God will not accept of me, when I offer him only mine old age.—To this I would answer, —1. Hath God said any where, that he will not accept of *old sinners* who come to him? God hath often made offers and promises in universal terms; and is there any such exception put in? Doth Christ say, All that thirst, let them come to me and drink, *except* old sinners? Come to me, all ye that labour and are heavy laden, except old sinners, and I will give you rest? Him that cometh to me, I will in no wise cast out, if he be not an old sinner? Did you ever read any such exception any where in the Bible? and why should you give way to exceptions which you make out of your own heads, or rather which the devil puts into your heads, and which have no foundation in the word of God?—Indeed it is more rare that old sinners are willing to come, than others; but if they do come, they are as readily accepted as any whatever.

2. When God accepts of young persons, it is not for the sake of the service which they are like to do him afterwards, or because youth is better worth accepting than old age. You seem entirely to mistake the matter, in thinking that God will not accept of you because you are old; as though he readily accepted of persons in their youth, because their youth is better worth his acceptance; whereas it is only for the sake of Jesus Christ, that God is willing to accept of any.

You say, your life is almost spent, and you are afraid that the best time for serving God is past; and that therefore God will not now accept of you; as if it were for the sake of the service which persons are like to do him, after they are converted, that he accepts of them. But a self-righteous spirit is at the bottom of such objections. Men cannot get off from the notion, that it is for some goodness or service of their own, either done or expected to be done, that God accepts of persons, and receives them into favour.—Indeed they who deny God their youth, the best part of their lives, and spend it in the service of Satan, dreadfully sin and provoke God; and he very often leaves them to hardness of heart when they are grown old. But if they are willing to accept of Christ when old, he is as ready to receive them as any others; for in that matter God hath respect only to Christ and his worthiness.

II. But, says one, I fear I have committed sins that are peculiar to reprobates. I have sinned against light, and strong convictions of conscience; I have sinned presumptuously; and have so resisted the strivings of the Spirit of God, that I am afraid I have committed such sins as none of God's elect ever commit. I cannot think that God will ever leave one whom he intends to save, to go on and commit sins against so much light and conviction, and with such horrid presumption.—Others may say, I have had risings of heart against God; blasphemous thoughts, a spiteful and malicious spirit; and have abused mercy and the strivings of the Spirit, trampled upon the Saviour, and my sins are such as are peculiar to those who are reprobated to eternal damnation. To all this I would answer,

1. There is no sin peculiar to reprobates but the sin against the Holy Ghost. Do you read of any other in the word of God? And if you do not read of any there, what ground have you to think any such thing? What other rule have we, by which to judge of such matters, but the divine word? If we venture to go beyond that, we shall be miserably in the dark. When we pretend to go further in our determinations than the word of God, Satan takes us up, and leads us. It seems to you that such sins are peculiar to the reprobate, and such as God never forgives. But what reason can you give for it, if you have no word of God to reveal it? Is it because you cannot see how the mercy of God is sufficient to pardon, or the blood of Christ to cleanse from such presumptuous sins? If so, it is because you never yet saw how great the mercy of God is; you never saw the sufficiency of the blood of Christ, and you know not how far the virtue of it extends. Some elect persons have been guilty of all manner of sins, except the sin against the Holy Ghost; and unless you have been guilty of this, you have not been guilty of any that are peculiar to reprobates.

2. Men may be less likely to believe, for sins which they have committed, and not the less readily pardoned when they do believe. It must be acknowledged that some sinners are in more danger of hell than others. Though all are in great danger, some are less likely to be saved. Some are less likely ever to be converted and to come to Christ: but all who do come to him are alike readily accepted; and there is as much encouragement for one man to come to Christ as another.—Such sins as you mention are indeed exceeding heinous and provoking to God, and do in an especial manner bring the soul into danger of damnation, and into danger of being given to final hardness of heart; and God more commonly gives men up to the judgment of final hardness for such sins, than for others. Yet they are not peculiar to reprobates; there is but one sin that is so, *viz.* that against the Holy

Ghost. And notwithstanding the sins which you have committed, if you can find it in your hearts to come to Christ, and close with him, you will be accepted not at all the less readily because you have committed such sins.—Though God doth more rarely cause some sorts of sinners to come to Christ than others, it is not because his mercy or the redemption of Christ is not as sufficient for them as others, but because in wisdom he sees fit so to dispense his grace, for a restraint upon the wickedness of men; and because it is his will to give converting grace in the use of means, among which this is one, viz. to lead a moral and religious life, and agreeable to our light, and the convictions of our consciences. But when once any sinner is willing to come to Christ, mercy is as ready for him as for any. There is no consideration at all had of his sins; let him have been ever so sinful, his sins are not remembered; God doth not upbraid him with them.

III. But had I not better stay till I shall have made myself better, before I presume to come to Christ. I have been, and see myself to be very wicked now; but am in hopes of mending myself, and rendering myself at least not so wicked: then I shall have more courage to come to God for mercy.—In answer to this,

1. Consider how unreasonably you act. You are striving to set up yourselves for your own saviours; you are striving to get something of your own, on the account of which you may the more readily be accepted. So that by this it appears that you do not seek to be accepted only on Christ's account. And is not this to rob Christ of the glory of being your only Saviour? Yet this is the way in which you are hoping to make Christ willing to save you.

2. You can never come to Christ at all, unless you first see that he will not accept of you the more readily for any thing that you can do. You must first see, that it is utterly in vain for you to try to make yourselves better on any such account. You must see that you can never make yourselves any more worthy, or less unworthy, by any thing which you can perform.

3. If ever you truly come to Christ, you must see that there is enough in him for your pardon, though you be no better than you are. If you see not the sufficiency of Christ to pardon you, without any righteousness of your own to recommend you, you never will come so as to be accepted of him. The way to be accepted is to come—not on any such encouragement, that now

you have made yourselves better, and more worthy, or not so unworthy, but—on the mere encouragement of Christ's worthiness, and God's mercy.

4. If ever you truly come to Christ, you must come to him to make you better. You must come as a patient comes to his physician, with his diseases or wounds to be cured. Spread all your wickedness before him, and do not plead your goodness; but plead your badness, and your necessity on that account: and say, as the psalmist in the text, not Pardon mine iniquity, for it is not so great as it was, but, "Pardon mine iniquity, for it is great."